Daily Wisdom for Women

2017 Devotional
Collection

© 2016 by Barbour Publishing, Inc.

Print ISBN 978-1-63409-898-4
Special Edition ISBN: 978-1-68322-004-6

eBook Editions:
Adobe Digital Edition (.epub) 978-1-68322-038-1
Kindle and MobiPocket Edition (.prc) 978-1-68322-039-8

Scripture quotations marked KJV are taken from the King James Version of the Bible.

Scripture quotations marked NKJV are taken from the New King James Version®. Copyright © 1982 by Thomas Nelson, Inc. Used by permission. All rights reserved.

Scripture quotations marked NIV are taken from the HOLY BIBLE, NEW INTERNATIONAL VERSION®. NIV®. Copyright © 1973, 1978, 1984, 2011 by Biblica, Inc.™ Used by permission. All rights reserved worldwide.

Scripture quotations marked MSG are from *THE MESSAGE*. Copyright © by Eugene H. Peterson 1993, 1994, 1995, 1996, 2000, 2001, 2002. Used by permission of NavPress Publishing Group.

Scripture quotations marked NLT are taken from the *Holy Bible*. New Living Translation copyright© 1996, 2004, 2015 by Tyndale House Foundation. Used by permission of Tyndale House Publishers, Inc. Carol Stream, Illinois 60188. All rights reserved.

Scripture quotations marked NASB are taken from the New American Standard Bible, © 1960, 1962, 1963, 1968, 1971, 1972, 1973, 1975, 1977, 1995 by The Lockman Foundation. Used by permission.

Scripture quotations marked AMP are taken from the Amplified® Bible, © 1954, 1958, 1962, 1964, 1965, 1987 by The Lockman Foundation. Used by permission.

Published by Barbour Books, an imprint of Barbour Publishing, Inc., P.O. Box 719, Uhrichsville, Ohio 44683, www.barbourbooks.com

Our mission is to publish and distribute inspirational products offering exceptional value and biblical encouragement to the masses.

Member of the
Evangelical Christian
Publishers Association

Printed in China.

Daily Wisdom for Women

2017 Devotional Collection

BARBOUR BOOKS
An Imprint of Barbour Publishing, Inc.

Co-creators

In the beginning God created the heavens and the earth. The earth was formless and empty, and darkness covered the deep waters. And the Spirit of God was hovering over the surface of the waters.

GENESIS 1:1–2 NLT

Dear daughter of God, welcome to 2017! A new year stands before you. It is without shape, empty, and covered in deep darkness. But wait! You have been made in the image of a Master Creator. You bear His likeness. You, too, are a creator. So, you can make this year anything you want it to be! You are the one who will give your days shape, fill them with your presence, and illuminate them with your light. This may be the year you walk closer to God than ever before. And there is no need to be afraid. Because God is right by your side, hovering in your midst, moving in your life, drawing you deeper into a relationship with Him. And He has also gone before you, reaching out of the darkness of the unknown days ahead, ready to guard and keep you each moment. So rest in Him now in sweet communion as, together, you conspire to create this new year in your life.

Dear Lord, this year lies before me, a new beginning, another chance to do what You have created me to do. Walk closely by my side. Keep me in line with Your will. Fill me with Your love and light so that it pours out of me and drenches others. Thank You for this new year. In Jesus' name, amen.

Consider Forgiveness

*Rejoice the soul of Your servant, for to You, O Lord, I lift up
my soul. For You, Lord, are good, and ready to forgive, and
abundant in mercy to all those who call upon You.*
PSALM 86:4–5 NKJV

The beginning of a new year is a good time to consider those to whom
you have yet to extend forgiveness. Yes, there are people in our lives
who have an amazing capacity to push our buttons. And, yes, there
are people who have maimed us by their words and actions. But
because God is so willing to forgive those who push His buttons and
have harmed His good name, we should be willing to wipe the slate
clean of those who have frustrated and offended us. So before you
lift up Your soul to God, forgive and bless those who have hurt and
upset you. And while you're at it, forgive and bless yourself. Then go
to God, ready to have your missteps erased and to be renewed by
His amazing mercy and grace.

*Lord, I want to have a fresh start in this new year. So I am telling
You now that I have forgiven those who have hurt me in the past.
Please bless their lives this year. And now I lift up my soul to You,
asking for Your forgiveness and blessing. Fill me with Your mercy
and grace. Make me a better and more peaceful person
because I have been in Your presence. Amen.*

A Limitless God

Show me your ways, Lord, teach me your paths. Guide me in your truth and teach me, for you are God my Savior, and my hope is in you all day long. . . . My eyes are ever on the Lord.
PSALM 25:4–5, 15 NIV

God has plans for our lives. But oftentimes we find ourselves standing in His way. And in so doing, we limit His power and blind ourselves to what He is looking to create in our lives. The solution is to not be so determined with our own plans and schemes that we leave God out of the equation. Instead, look for His teaching. Make Him your number one adviser. Search out His word for your direction and path. Know that all is well. He is holding your hand as you walk, step by step. Amazing things are happening; the possibilities are limitless, and His blessings abundant. Just rest, knowing He has got you. He will never let you go. And everything is going according to His plan.

My hope is in You, dear Lord, for I know You have the best plan for my life. So my eyes are on You. Show me the way You want me to go. Lead me with Your wisdom. Shine Your light onto my path. I am getting out of Your way, trusting in Your plan, confident that You will provide all I need. In You my future is secure and my present is spilling over with blessings galore! What a marvelous God You are! Amen.

Our Strong Arm

But LORD, be merciful to us, for we have waited for you. Be our strong arm each day and our salvation in times of trouble.
ISAIAH 33:2 NLT

At times we may feel weak and discouraged. We don't even have the energy to lift our heads up and take on the next challenge. But God can turn us around. When we go to Him, when we seek His face, when we put all our cares on His shoulders, He comes to our rescue. He not only willingly takes our burdens away but also becomes our arm of strength. Through Him, we find more than enough energy to change the next diaper, tackle another project at work, seek a new path for our lives, deal with our teens and aging parents, cope with an illness, and find a way through a difficult relationship. Only God can turn our challenges into opportunities for Him to show His power. Just be patient. Wait on Him. And He will do more than see you through.

Lord, I am facing so many challenges, I don't even know where to start, what to do, how to approach them. And I feel so weak and powerless. My mind is confused, my emotions jumbled. So I am looking to You, am waiting on You in this very moment. Be my strong arm. Fill me with Your awesome, mountain-moving power. Rescue me from these troubles. Make a path through this debris. Be my defense so that I can catch my breath. I rest in You now, knowing in You I am as safe as a babe in arms. Amen.

Forget About It!

"Forget about what's happened; don't keep going over old history. Be alert, be present. I'm about to do something brand-new. It's bursting out! Don't you see it? There it is! I'm making a road through the desert, rivers in the badlands."
ISAIAH 43:16–21 MSG

Sometimes we get so stuck on something that happened in the past. We tell ourselves, *Get over it already*, but it still keeps coming up, filling us with anger, angst, and apprehension. Meanwhile, stuck in this proverbial rut, we miss the new things that God is doing. We don't hear Him say, *"Psst! Over here, woman! Forget about that. Look at this!"* To get unstuck, follow the example of the apostle Paul, who wrote, "But one thing I do: Forgetting what is behind and straining toward what is ahead, I press on" (Philippians 3:13–14 NIV). So forgive your husband for overlooking your anniversary. Forget about your child's ugly remark. Let go of the mistakes you have made. Get over the fact that gravity is taking over your body. Instead, get your focus back on God. Lift your feet out of the quicksand of old history and move forward to see what new thing He is doing for and revealing to you before you miss it!

I'm tired of the same old songs that have been replaying in my head, Lord. I'm ready for some new music. I'm going to get over the past so I can enjoy the present. Show me what You are doing in my life. I'm ready for something new. Speak to me, Lord! I'm listening! In Jesus' name I pray, amen.

Great Expectations

Trust in the LORD with all your heart; do not depend on
your own understanding. Seek his will in all you do,
and he will show you which path to take.
PROVERBS 3:5-6 NLT

Let's face it. Sometimes we have such grand plans. And the great day comes and our expectations are dashed against the wall. Nothing has turned out like we'd envisioned. And we find ourselves angry, frustrated, horribly disappointed, and feeling sorry for ourselves. Our thirtieth birthday came and went with no one batting an eye. On back-to-school night, teachers had nothing but discouraging things to say about our kid. Our grown-up daughter's visit was spent with her visiting her friends instead of one-on-one time with mom. The dream job we had sacrificed everything for turned out to be the worst career move ever.

Fortunately, there is an upside to all these scenarios. For we have a God who has a great plan for our lives. He's working things out so that these great disappointments will work for our good. We simply need to trust in Him. So don't try to figure it all out on your own. Just head back into His arms. Cry on His shoulder. And ask Him to show you the next step. Leave it to Him to straighten everything out. And He will transform your great expectations into something beyond your limited imagination!

Lord, I know You've got a grand plan for my life. So help me get over
my setbacks and trust that You have things all under control.
For I know all this will work to my good and Your praise! Amen.

Nothing Left Undone

"Know this with all your heart, with everything in you, that not one detail has failed of all the good things GOD, your God, promised you. It has all happened. Nothing's left undone—not so much as a word."
JOSHUA 23:14 MSG

In today's world it's difficult to find someone who actually does what he says he'll do. In fact, at times we may find ourselves making promises that, deep down, we know we may not be able to keep.

We tell our children we will keep them safe. And although we try our best, something may someday bring them harm. Our husbands promise to love and cherish us. But some days it seems as if they have fallen down on the job. When we are hired, our bosses promise us benefits, vacation, and more. Then a few years later, we find ourselves in the unemployment line. When we get married, our female friends tell us having a baby is the most wonderful experience imaginable. Then when we become pregnant, all the labor horror stories come out!

The point here is that there is only one Someone we can rely on, only one who keeps His promises: God. He will never leave us. He will protect and defend us. He will one day bring us home to live with Him forever. All we need to do is trust and believe. That's a promise!

Lord, thank You for giving me promises to hang on to, to rely on, to believe in. Leaning on Your promises, I not only survive but thrive! Amen.

Heart Strength

I would have lost heart, unless I had believed that I would see the goodness of the LORD in the land of the living. Wait on the LORD; be of good courage, and He shall strengthen your heart.
PSALM 27:13–14 NKJV

When things don't seem to be going our way, it's easy to lose heart. This is especially true when our difficulties revolve around life-changing losses. The sudden death of a loved one can be heartbreaking, leaving us gasping for breath, wondering how it happened and how we will ever find peace again. A devastating illness, a dashed dream, an ugly divorce, an alienation from a family member can leave us feeling untethered, without hope. When we're still reeling, having difficulty finding our feet, it's hard to stand up to even the littlest of daily challenges. Meanwhile, everyone else's life goes on as before and we feel as if we've been left behind in the dust of despair. But you *can* find a rainbow in the midst of these storms. It comes with the power of God and the belief that you will one day see His amazing goodness in your life. All you need to do is take courage and wait on Him. He will not only see you through but also give you whatever strength you need to find your feet and walk on stronger than ever before.

I've lost all hope that things will ever be normal again, Lord. So I'm hanging on to Your promise that I'll one day see Your goodness come streaming through. I'm waiting on You. Give me courage, hope, patience, and the strength I need to find my feet. Amen.

Change of Mind

Don't copy the behavior and customs of this world, but let
God transform you into a new person by changing the way
you think. Then you will learn to know God's will for you,
which is good and pleasing and perfect.
ROMANS 12:2 NLT

The world entices us with its fashion, beauty, and youthful preservation. But striving after and focusing on these things is not what God wants for us. He doesn't want us to become carbon copies of those who have face-lifts, breast enhancements, and the most up-to-date wardrobes. For when we become so conformed to this world, we lose out on the most important thing of life: God's transformational power! To keep us from becoming conformed to a society that is often self-serving, rude, egotistical, vain, and violent, God wants us to renew our minds each and every day. He wants us to have attitudes and ideals that reflect His goodness. He wants us to change ourselves and the world from the inside out. For when we have our heads on straight, God will work to bring the best out in ourselves to the good of all. So fix your face on God's, focus on His light and way, and see how brightly you begin to shine.

I'm being charmed by the world, Lord, and in the process I
am losing touch with Your will for my life. Help me get some
new thoughts and ideas, Lord, ones that would please You.
Give me a God-attitude so that I can grow into the woman
You created me to be. In Jesus' name, amen.

Unchanging Master

Jesus Christ is the same yesterday, today, and forever.
HEBREWS 13:8 NLT

It's said that the one thing we can count on is change—within and without. This is especially true for women because our bodies are constantly in flux, ruled by our hormones as they work to maintain a twenty-eight-day cycle. But that's just the beginning. A woman who experiences pregnancy embarks upon another process as a new life grows within. Then, once baby is born, mom's breasts begin producing nourishment for her offspring. When the child is weaned, her body goes back somewhat to its former self and the cycles begin all over again. After a handful of decades, her body takes on an entirely different pattern. Hot flashes and even more bizarre mood swings become the rule of the day as her estrogen decreases and testosterone increases. Needless to say, for a woman, it is sometimes difficult to determine from one day to the next who she'll wake up as or what will rule her day—her hormones or her heart? Amid these seemingly endless fluctuations, it's good to know there's one constant: Jesus Christ. No matter what cycle your body is in—or out of—you can count on the anchor of your faith in the never-changing Jesus. In Him you have a Master of waves and wind, one who can calm your storms within and without. Allowing Him to rule your day, heart, body, and mind is a sure course to a safe haven of peace.

Jesus, rule my day, my heart, my mind. Calm me within
so that I can serve You in the world without. Amen.

A Lonely Number

"This is my command—be strong and courageous! Do not be afraid or discouraged. For the LORD your God is with you wherever you go."
JOSHUA 1:9 NLT

One can be a lonely number. And sometimes that's how we feel. Totally abandoned. Lost. Alone. It comes on the heels of divorce, death, widowhood, or separation. Sometimes the feeling of loneliness can come upon us when we're surrounded by people, even friends and family members! Or it may strike in the midst of misfortune, when we imagine no one has ever gone through what we're going through. The point is that it's true! We're each unique, having different experiences in our upbringing, environment, relationships, desires, goals, and thoughts. But if you believe you are all alone in this world, you are believing in a lie. Because with God, you are never alone. He is with you no matter where you go. Although you may not be able to touch Him physically, you know deep down that He exists. You know that He is real—and that when you reach out for Him with your entire heart, mind, soul, and strength, your spirit will meld with His and you will experience an amazing joy, one that cannot be expressed with words. So take heart. Be strong and courageous. Leave fear and discouragement behind. God's with you. And He'll never let you go!

I'm feeling very alone today, Lord. Help me get out of this funk. Sweep me into Your presence. Fill me with Your strength. Sit beside me, hold me, love me. With You in my life, I need never be alone. Amen.

Queen of the Hill

Though the sheep pens are sheepless and the cattle barns empty,
I'm singing joyful praise to GOD. I'm turning cartwheels of joy to my
Savior God. Counting on GOD's Rule to prevail, I take heart and gain
strength. I run like a deer. I feel like I'm king of the mountain!
HABAKKUK 3:17–19 MSG

You haven't had a raise in five years. Your love life is dismal at best. Your kids aren't living up to your expectations. Your sister is ill. You've just totaled your brand-new car. Your mom recently passed away. And you don't have enough money for groceries this week. Your spirits are lower than low. What's a woman to do? It's simple. Change your lament of "Woe is me" to a song of joyful praise to God. Jump up and down, start skipping as you rejoice in your Lord. And before you know it, His strength will begin welling up within you. He'll make your heart truly sing. Instead of your being buried by your misfortunes, you'll be standing on top of them. Because of God and His amazing power, you are now Queen of the Hill. Your footing is sure. You have conquered your calamities! You are no longer a victim but a victor! Praise your Lord!

Whenever I am down, Lord, I know You'll raise me up in
Your power. So do so now, Lord, as I praise Your name.
I leap for joy at Your love for me. And I rise above it all,
Queen of the Hill standing beside my Lord of lords! Amen.

Strong Hands

"Do not fear. . .let not your hands be weak. The Lord your God in your midst, the Mighty One, will save; He will rejoice over you with gladness, He will quiet you with His love, He will rejoice over you with singing."
ZEPHANIAH 3:16–17 NKJV

Sometimes we may find ourselves heading in the wrong direction. This can happen because we've given in to a particular sin one time too many. Or we've stopped connecting with the Lord. Or we're listening to what He says but not obeying Him. Whatever the cause, the result is always the same. We become fearful, anxious, worried. And before we know it, our hands are lying listless in our laps. That's when we need to let God get ahold of us again. Remember, He is in our midst and doing amazing things. He is the one who will bring us back to Him, saving us from whatever is leading us away. And then He'll rejoice over our return! He'll calm our worries with His amazing love and light. And before we know it, we'll once again have the courage we so desperately need to live this life to which He has called us. Our hands will once again be strong, lifted up in prayer and praise. We'll be singing in harmony with our Lord.

I'm running back into Your open arms, Lord. I'm reveling in Your Son-shine, feeling Your breath upon my face. Only You can quiet my fears with Your love. Only You can strengthen my hands. In You, I find the song of my life. To You, I lift my hands and voice in praise! Amen!

Perfect Peace

You will keep in perfect peace all who trust in you,
all whose thoughts are fixed on you! Trust in the
Lord always, for the Lord God is the eternal Rock.
ISAIAH 26:3-4 NLT

Our lives are a series of moments. And that's what our minds get caught up in, the day-to-day minutiae, the little niggling worries, the what-ifs, the how-comes, and the why-fors. But God wants us to have a different perspective, not an in-the-moment viewpoint but an eternal one. Because when we look at the big picture, our day-to-day worries—the ones that get our hearts beating out of control and our thoughts ricocheting around in our heads—are really nothing to be upset about. That takes trust in a power so much higher than ourselves. But when we have that trust, that confidence in the eternal Rock who can never be moved, we are blessed with a peace that blesses us within, keeping us healthy in mind, body, spirit, soul, and heart. Such a calm also blesses those around us, for it's contagious.

So fix your mind on the one who sees and knows so much more than you ever will. Put your confidence in the one who has your name written on the palm of His hand. Practice being in His presence during quiet hours. And then, the moment stress and chaos begin creeping in, call God to mind, and He will surround you with that big-picture, perfect peace.

I need Your perfect peace, God. You are my eternal Rock.
Take me out of the present and into Your presence where
peace will reign and blessings abound. Amen.

Secret Desires

Trust in the LORD, and do good; dwell in the land, and feed on His faithfulness. Delight yourself also in the LORD, and He shall give you the desires of your heart. Commit your way to the LORD, trust also in Him, and He shall bring it to pass.
PSALM 37:3–5 NKJV

Some of us never pursue our deepest desires out of fear of what people will think or fear of failure. But such fears can keep us from living the life we long for. So how do we slay the dream killers? We lean on God and become confident in Him. We do things His way. It is then we find ourselves dwelling in His territory and being fed on His promises. Such faithfulness sustains us in a way worldly fears cannot. And when we take joy in God's presence, allowing Him to be our guide and giving all our secret plans and dreams over to Him, He will give us the desires of our hearts. So put all your faith in God, the dream maker. Bring your desires before Him. Listen for every whisper, every leading He sends your way. Then simply trust as you commit your way to Him, not forcing the issue but confident that in His will, His way, His timing, He'll bring all your dreams into being.

Lord, I sometimes hesitate to tell You what my soul really craves. But I know that You alone can satisfy my longings, can make my dreams come true. So, as I delight in You, lead me in the way You would have me go. I am putting all my hope in You. Amen.

A Man with a Dream

"Write the vision and make it plain on tablets, that he may
run who reads it. For the vision is yet for an appointed time;
but at the end it will speak, and it will not lie. Though it tarries,
wait for it; because it will surely come."
HABAKKUK 2:2–3 NKJV

Martin Luther King Jr. had a dream that people "will one day live in a nation where they will not be judged by the color of their skin but by the content of their character." And with this vision, he led nonviolent, peaceful marches based on his Christian beliefs. He made his vision plain so all could understand. And by following his dream, he advanced civil rights in the United States. Yet there is still much to be done to bring this dream to complete fruition. That's where you come in. For what does God ask of you? "He's already made it plain how to live, what to do, what GOD is looking for in men and women. It's quite simple: Do what is fair and just to your neighbor, be compassionate and loyal in your love, and don't take yourself too seriously—take God seriously" (Micah 6:8 MSG). Do so in all your dealings with all people, loving all as God loves you, regardless of skin color. Do it today and every day in memory of a man who had a dream that still begs to come true.

Lord, show me today what I can do, what I can say,
how I can love all people, regardless of race, creed, or color.
Help me help Your dream for us come true. Amen.

Heart Smart

Above all else, guard your heart,
for everything you do flows from it.
PROVERBS 4:23 NIV

Words have such power. In fact, God's words created the entire universe. And it's the words we hear, see, and plant within that create *our* universe. Unspiritual thoughts and words are to stay out of our hearts. God's thoughts and words are to stay in. For the entire course of our lives is determined by what flows out of our very core. As we keep our hearts guarded, making sure they neither are hurt nor hurt others, we will also be watching our mouths, making sure our words are good, encouraging, and positive (v. 24). Our guarded heart not only helps others but also aids us in retaining the wisdom needed to keep our eyes focused on God and His Word (v. 25) and our feet on His path (v. 26).

So be heart smart. Watch what you're putting in so that you'll only get the best out. For, as Jesus said, "A good man out of the good treasure of his heart brings forth good things, and an evil man out of the evil treasure brings forth evil things" (Matthew 12:35 NKJV). What's in your heart?

Help me, Lord, to be more aware of where I'm putting my attention
and, in turn, what I'm putting into my heart. Help me to stay
focused on You and Your Word so that I'm filled with Your light
and reflecting You to the world around me. In Jesus' name, amen.

A Touch of Faith

*"Courage, daughter. You took a
risk of faith, and now you're well."*
MATTHEW 9:20-22 MSG

There once was a woman who'd been hemorrhaging for twelve years. She sought help from a myriad of physicians and spent all that she had, but her issue of blood was worse than ever before. Then one day she heard a healer named Jesus was coming to town. Although she was considered the lowest of the low, someone who shouldn't even be out in public, she decided to make her way through the crowd and reach out to this Man. Risking all she had left, she came up behind Him and touched his garment, for she kept saying to herself, "If I can just touch his robe, I will be healed" (Mark 5:28 NLT). Instantly her bleeding stopped. But the story doesn't end there. Jesus immediately felt power flowing out of Him and demanded, "Who touched me?" (Mark 5:31 NLT). Shaking with fear, the woman confessed it had been her. Jesus responded with tenderness and encouragement, "Daughter, your faith has made you well. Go in peace. Your suffering is over" (Mark 5:34 NLT).

What issue have you needed Jesus' help with? What desperately bold exchange between your soul and Jesus have you kept secret? What story can you share with others to remind them of His power and tenderness, to give them a touch of faith?

*Give me the courage, Jesus, to not just come to You with
all my issues but to share my story with others, to touch
them with my faith in You and Your faithfulness to me. Amen.*

Make Praise

"Do not be afraid! Don't be discouraged by this mighty army,
for the battle is not yours, but God's. . . . But you will not
even need to fight. Take your positions; then stand still
and watch the LORD's victory. He is with you."
2 CHRONICLES 20:15, 17 NLT

When an army of troubles comes up against you, you have two choices. You can run and hide in fear or you can take courage, standing still and strong in your faith and God's power, and watch what He does.

That's what King Jehoshaphat did. When told that three mighty armies were coming to attack him, he, a king, got down on his knees and prayed to God. He recognized the weakness of himself and his kingdom, telling God, "We are powerless against this mighty army that is about to attack us. We do not know what to do, but we are looking to you for help" (v. 12). Knowing God would hear his prayer, he pleaded for guidance—and got it. Filled with faith and courage, he instructed his singers to "walk ahead of the army, singing to the LORD and praising him" (v. 21). The result? The armies attacked and killed each other. All that was left for Jehoshaphat's people was to pick up the plunder.

Got an army of troubles coming at you and your family (a.k.a. queendom)? Take heart, make praise, "and you will succeed" (v. 20)!

Lord, give me courage with this army of trouble
coming at me. Help me to praise You as I stand
strong in my faith and watch Your victory! Amen!

Just Be

God is our refuge and strength, a very present help in trouble.
Therefore we will not fear. . . . Be still, and know that I am God.
PSALM 46:1–2, 10 NKJV

Women, born nurturers, are constantly looking to fulfill the needs of others. We are usually the ones who not only plan the meals but also write up the grocery list, do the shopping, then cook them. We are usually the main caregivers, from children to aging parents. In our families, we are usually the go-to person—for missing socks, lost homework or car keys, a ride to soccer practice, etc. Then there are our coworkers who know we pride ourselves on multitasking, taking on big projects while also attending to the details no one else seems to be concerned about. In all these areas, we are running around *doing* and, as a result, can *do* ourselves right into the ground. But God wants us to first and foremost just *be*. He reminds us that because His presence and strength are all we need, fear has no place in our lives. When we believe in those facts, when we trust in Him with all we love, have, and are, we can relax. Be still. Rest in the silence of His presence. So forget about planning tomorrow. Instead, just *be* in today, knowing He's got it all under control.

I am here before You, Lord. Sitting in the stillness.
Being in Your presence. Taking in Your silence. Knowing You
are God. Fill me with Your love as I bask in Your light. Ah-men.

Back to the Beginning

*[Abram] went on his journey. . .to the place where his
tent had been at the beginning, between Bethel and Ai,
to the place of the altar which he had made there at first.
And there Abram called on the name of the LORD.*
GENESIS 13:3–4 NKJV

Before he was named Abraham, Abram obeyed God by going to a land God said He would show him, uprooting his family and relying on God to show him the way. That took a tremendous amount of faith. But once in Canaan, he discovered a severe famine. So, instead of trusting in God to provide, Abram went down to Egypt, where, fearing for his life, he encouraged his wife Sarai to lie and, in the process, almost lost her to the pharaoh. Afterward, he was sent out of town and ended up back where he started, to the place where the Lord had initially directed him.

We, too, can sometimes find ourselves walking out of the Lord's will only to suffer dire consequences. But thank God we have a Lord who is willing to give us a second chance, allowing us to come back, to call on Him once again.

Where have you wandered off to? Are you ready to go back to the beginning, to start again? To get back in God's will and way and see what blessings await?

*Lord, help me get off this side trip. I want to be where You called
me from the beginning, to trust You during feast and famine.
So I'm calling on Your name right now. Forgive me, Your daughter.
And bless me once again. Amen.*

The-God-Who-Sees

Now the Angel of the LORD found her. . . . [and] said to her,
"Return to your mistress, and submit yourself under her hand". . . .
Then she called the name of the LORD who spoke to her,
You-Are-the-God-Who-Sees.
GENESIS 16:7, 9, 13 NKJV

Hagar ran away from her circumstances: Sarai, an abusive mistress. Part of Hagar's trouble had been caused by her own actions. For having become pregnant by Abram, she had begun disrespecting the childless Sarai.

We, too, sometimes think we can run from our troubles. But when we come to the end of ourselves, God is there, ready to give us the wisdom we need but may not want. He may ask us to go back, telling us how to "be" in our circumstances: submissive, obedient, loving. He had a vision for Hagar that she would be the mother of a son and have many descendants.

Even today, this God-Who-Sees sees you and your situation. He is ready to reveal Himself to you and share His wisdom. He may not remove you from your circumstances, but He will give you the word you need to get through them. Afterward, you'll see your situation in a new light, with a new hope for your future, step by step.

Lord, You constantly reveal Yourself, manifest Yourself to me. In fact, You see me before I even come to You. So be with me now. Show me where You want me to submit. Remind me that You have a plan and vision for my life—and that it is all meant for my good. Amen.

Moving in God's Strength

I am full of power by the Spirit of the LORD. . . . In God I have put my
trust; I will not be afraid. . . . I am for peace. . . . My help comes from
the LORD, who made heaven and earth. . . . . Because You have been
my help, therefore in the shadow of Your wings I will rejoice. . . .
Now therefore, O God, strengthen my hands.
MICAH 3:8; PSALM 56:11; 120:7; 121:2; 63:7; NEHEMIAH 6:9 NKJV

At times, when a task lies before us, we begin to doubt our ability. Writers hesitate, their hands hovering above the keyboard. Mothers look at their to-do lists, the words blurring before them as overwhelmed feelings creep in. Businesswomen consider the meeting they will soon be leading, not sure of the words to say. Unfocused, unsure, untethered around the tasks before us, we flounder.

Let God take over. Tap into His power and claim it for yourself. Put all your trust in the God who vanquishes fear, who can help you do all He has called you to do. He's done so in the past, and He will definitely do so in the present. Rejoice in His presence, and allow Him to work through you as your hands begin moving in His strength.

Lord, truly I am full of power by Your Spirit. Trusting You,
I will not be afraid but be at peace because You are my help.
As I rejoice in You, I feel Your energy move through me,
Your strength moving my hands. And I begin. . . .

Become the Vision

Now may the God of peace. . .equip you with all you need
for doing his will. May he produce in you, through the power
of Jesus Christ, every good thing that is pleasing to him.
HEBREWS 13:20–21 NLT

God, who has known you *before* He formed you in your mother's womb (see Jeremiah 1:5), has a calling for you, a purpose for your life. In fact, God is already seeing you as who He created you to be. He has already equipped you and is with you to help you along the way. Remember when God visited Gideon, who considered himself the least of his family and clan? God saw Gideon for who he really was, as expressed in the first words He spoke to him: "The Lord is with you, you mighty man of valor!" (Judges 6:12 NKJV). In a poor shepherd boy, God saw the king David was to become. In Abram, who at ninety-nine had only one son, God saw a father of multiple children and changed his name to reflect that fact!

Take some time to look at yourself through God's eyes. Forget about your doubts, misgivings, and feelings of weakness. God has called you to a specific task and is just waiting for you to take on the mantle He has already fashioned—just for you! It's a perfect fit. All you need to do is believe and take that first step to become the vision God has of you.

Dear Lord, show me who I am in Your eyes. Then help me become
whom You have already made me to be. In Jesus' name, amen.

Open Up!

Who is the King of glory? The LORD, strong and mighty;
the LORD, invincible in battle. Open up, ancient gates!
Open up, ancient doors, and let the King of glory enter.
PSALM 24:8–9 NLT

It's so easy to get focused on the things of this world. But that's how we get dragged away from Jesus, forgetting His saving grace, strength, love, and presence.

Today's verses give us an Old Testament picture of the ark, which contained God's glory, being brought into the temple. These same verses can apply to us today if we consider how much Jesus longs to be in our hearts, His temple on earth.

Jesus pleads: "Look! I stand at the door and knock. If you hear my voice and open the door, I will come in, and we will share a meal together as friends" (Revelation 3:20 NLT).

Jesus is outside the gate of your heart, waiting for you to open up your total being—mind, emotions, and will—to His saving presence. He, strong and mighty, invincible, is knocking at the door of *your* heart. He wants you, His temple, to open up your gates so He can spend time with you. Do you hear His knock? Are you willing to let Him into not just a small corner of your life but your *entire* life? He will not force His way in, for it must be your decision. He will be gentle and loving, only wanting the best for you. Will you open up?

Jesus, my heart is open! Please come in! In Your sweet name I play,
pray, live, love, and breathe now and evermore! Amen.

A Happy Heart

For the despondent, every day brings trouble;
for the happy heart, life is a continual feast.
PROVERBS 15:15 NLT

British comedian, actress, and singer Joyce Grenfell once said, "Happiness is the sublime moment when you get out of your corsets at night." Of course, we no longer wear corsets, but what a wonderful feeling it is to take off those control-top panty hose and brassieres before getting into our pajamas. It's those modest moments of pleasure that make us smile. But they are so easy to overlook. The trick is to search for them each and every day.

Find some moments of pleasure in the smallest of things—the smile on your baby's face (regardless of whether or not it's from gas), the crazy antics of your cat or dog, the sparkle in your husband's eyes, the squirrels frolicking across your lawn. Instead of focusing on the troubles that lie before you, make sure you take time out for all the good things that are happening. And if good things seem far and few between, *make* them happen. Take a bubble bath while reading a good book. Paint your nails. Buy a coloring book and have at it! Play your ukulele. Do something that makes you laugh out loud or smile in utter contentment. Look to have a continual feast in the blessings of God as you serve Him and others with all the gladness in your heart.

Help me to find humor, joy, and contentment in the simple
things in life, Lord. Give me a happy heart that continues to
feast on Your goodness—and then passes that joy along! Amen.

Facts versus Faith

*GOD said to Abraham, "Why did Sarah laugh saying, 'Me?
Have a baby? An old woman like me?' Is anything too hard for GOD?
I'll be back about this time next year and Sarah will have a baby."*
GENESIS 18:13–14 MSG

God's promises can seem outlandish to us at times. Usually it's because we're looking at the facts, and when we take the facts of our circumstances and line them up next to God's promises, we begin to doubt the impossible.

Sarah faced the same quandary when God told her husband, Abraham, that he and she would have a son. Sarah, overhearing the conversation, began laughing because she was well past childbearing age. She couldn't even conceive of conceiving a child. It seemed physically impossible, especially because Abraham was an old man himself. And once past conception, she'd need strength for pregnancy and childbirth! Then there's the nursing, weaning, and rearing! On top of all this, she had been wishing for a baby her entire life—that's ninety years! How could this be? So, with all those facts stacked up against her faith, she laughed!

But there is nothing too hard or too wonderful for the Lord. He can do anything and everything if we have faith, believing God to keep His word, to do the impossible. What specific promise has God made to you? Do you have the faith, regardless of facts, to believe Him?

*Dear Lord, I'm taking Your promises as fact regardless of what
my situation looks like. There is nothing too hard for You.
Thank You for being Lord of the impossible! Amen!*

A Woman Reborn

"No one can enter the kingdom of God unless they are born of water and the Spirit. Flesh gives birth to flesh, but the Spirit gives birth to spirit. You should not be surprised at my saying, 'You must be born again.'"
JOHN 3:5-7 NIV

If you are a believer in Jesus Christ, the old excuses will no longer work. The idea that you can't lose weight, give up smoking, stop drinking, stop frowning, etc., because you were "born this way" no longer applies. When you accepted Jesus, He gave you a new life. A new Spirit that now resides within you has gifted you a divine and heavenly existence.

God once breathed life into you when you were born physically, but now you have been reborn spiritually, brought to life by the breath of the Holy Spirit. You are a new creation (see 2 Corinthians 5:17). Your aims and nature are different, your heart more tender. So erase the thought, *I was born that way*, that keeps playing in your mind. And replace it with God's truth: *I am a new creation in Christ, a daughter of God. With my Father, anything is possible because I can do all things through my Brother who strengthens me.* It's the new improved you, a woman reborn, now a sister of all, courtesy of heaven above.

God, thank You for this new life in Christ! Help me to let go of the old thoughts and embrace the truth. That I'm a new creation! I'm "a new person. The old life is gone; a new life has begun!" (2 Corinthians 5:17 NLT). In Jesus' name, amen!

Remember Lot's Wife

One of the angels ordered, "Run for your lives! And don't look
back or stop anywhere in the valley! Escape to the mountains,
or you will be swept away"... But Lot's wife looked back as she
was following behind him, and she turned into a pillar of salt.
GENESIS 19:17, 26 NLT

Betsy sat at her kitchen table, reminiscing about the past, wishing she could go back. For the future before her was unknown territory. And she wasn't sure she had the strength to deal with it.

We all think about the people, places, and things we have loved and left behind. But God doesn't want us to become like Lot's wife, so focused on the past that we miss what He's doing in the present. He wants our hearts fixed on His love and strength, our eyes focused on the road before us.

Jesus said, "Remember Lot's wife. Whoever seeks to save his life will lose it, and whoever loses his life will preserve it" (Luke 17:32–33 NKJV). Mrs. Lot is a blatant example of what happens when we try to save our lives. We're stopped in our spiritual tracks. But when we don't look back, when we stop clinging to what was, we end up saving our lives!

Where are your heart and eyes? Take stock now, find a way to let go, and grab hold of all God is doing on the road before you.

Lord, help me to let go of the things I love that I've left behind.
Help me to let go of my past so that I can live a new life in You! Amen.

Inside Out

Be energetic in your life of salvation, reverent and sensitive before God. That energy is God's energy, an energy deep within you, God himself willing and working at what will give him the most pleasure.
PHILIPPIANS 2:12–13 MSG

With the arrival of the new year comes a list of goals we're longing to achieve. The only problem is that we usually end up falling short of our greatest expectations.

So why not create a *theme* for the new year and choose to live it? This will help you shift things within, which will in turn bring you closer to the changes you desire without. Because that's how God works, from the inside out (see Romans 12:2). And the great thing about living a yearly theme is it's a way of being that has no success or failure attached to it.

Here are a few themes and their accompanying Bible verses you can choose. Or create one of your own that really speaks to your heart.

Enjoy and Allow Miracles (Hebrews 11:6)
Live in the Moment (Psalm 16:8–9)
Delight in the Lord (Psalm 37:3–4)
Simplify Your Life (Hebrews 13:5)
Take Risks for God (Matthew 25:14–30)
Look for God in Everything (Acts 17:27)
Celebrate the Little Things (James 1:17)

Remember, God's ready to help you change from the inside out!

Lord, I want to be sensitive to what You want me to change in my life. Now work within me to create in me not just a new heart but a new way of being—in You! Amen.

Triple Power

The Spirit of God, who raised Jesus from the dead, lives in you.
And just as God raised Christ Jesus from the dead, he will give life
to your mortal bodies by this same Spirit living within you. . . .
And because we are his children, God has sent the Spirit of his
Son into our hearts, prompting us to call out, "Abba, Father."
ROMANS 8:11; GALATIANS 4:6 NLT

Timid and shy? We needn't be.

God, the Giver of all things, sent us both His Son, Jesus, and the Holy Spirit. Meanwhile, Jesus, who paved the way for us to reach God, acts as our mediator. At the same time, the Holy Spirit helps us to pray, discern right from wrong, and understand God's Word.

This three-in-one power resides in each and every one of us, steering us to love God, ourselves, and others. When we live that life of love, we're surrounded by a screen of protection that shields us from evil.

So, daughter of God, what need do you have to be afraid? You've a mighty triple power within, enabling you to say, "Though a mighty army surrounds me, my heart will not be afraid. Even if I am attacked, I will remain confident" (Psalm 27:3 NLT).

So go now into the months ahead in love, knowing that with God, Jesus, and the Holy Spirit living and breathing within you, you have the courage to do all you have been called to do.

I am so blessed, Lord, to be guided, loved,
and empowered by You, Your Son, and Your Spirit.
I resolve to love and be strong in Your way. Amen.

The Strength of My Heart

Create in me a pure heart, O God,
and renew a steadfast spirit within me.
PSALM 51:10 NIV

Like most women, you probably pay close attention to your health. Perhaps you guard what you eat to keep your cholesterol down or you head to the gym to burn off excess calories. Maybe you hyperfocus on your clothing size or your BMI. Why? To ensure heart health, of course! Many women eat right, work out at the gym, count calories and carbs, and go for annual check-ups, all in the hope of staying on top of things. Kudos to these health-conscious women! How ironic, then, that so many fail to stay on top of their spiritual heart health. If twenty-first century women need anything at all, it's a healthy heart. Make a commitment today to keep your spiritual arteries open. No blockages! Let nothing hinder your time with God.

I want to have a strong heart, Father, not just physically but
spiritually as well. Help me keep those spiritual arteries open
so that You can freely flow in my life. When people look at me,
I pray they hear Your heartbeat, not mine. I choose this day to
honor You by keeping my spiritual arteries wide open. Amen.

Goals

Trust in the LORD with all your heart and lean not
on your own understanding; in all your ways submit
to him, and he will make your paths straight.
PROVERBS 3:5–6 NIV

Ah, goals. We have a love-hate relationship with them, don't we? They seem so doable. . .at first. In fact, we often get off on good footing, mentally, physically, and emotionally prepared. Then reality kicks in. Did you ever stop to think about why we so often don't meet our goals? Sometimes it comes down to momentum. We fly out of the gate, a hundred miles an hour. Nothing can defeat us. Then exhaustion hits. Maybe the goals were unrealistic. Maybe we used up too much energy with our first leg. Or maybe, just maybe, we didn't write our goals down. Did you know that writing down your goals (and giving them end dates) makes them more tangible? There's something about the process of writing things down that makes you take them more seriously. So grab that pen and paper, friend. Scribble down those doable goals and then watch them come to pass. And while you're at it, include your heavenly Father. God loves it when we set goals, and He's even more excited when we include Him in the process of reaching them. What we can't do on our own He can do through us!

Lord, thank You for making me a goal setter. I enjoy being motivated.
I want to accomplish great things this year and can't wait to see
my goals met. You're a good Father, and I love You! Amen.

Guilty!

If we confess our sins, he is faithful and just and will forgive
us our sins and purify us from all unrighteousness.
1 JOHN 1:9 NIV

Have you ever had a stain on a blouse that wouldn't come out? Maybe you massaged detergent into it and then washed it over and over again, all in hopes that you could make the errant spot go away. In the end, you tossed the blouse in the trash, unable to wear it because it made you look (or feel) less than perfect. Sin is the same way. It leaves a spot—an indelible mark—on us. We can't hide it. We can't scrub it away. We can't disguise it with a lovely scarf. It marks us for life. Until Jesus. When we encounter Jesus, when we take Him at His Word and ask for His forgiveness, He performs in an instant what we could not perform in years of trying. The sin—all that ugliness of the past—is gone. Poof. No guilt. No condemnation. No doubt. When we make Him Lord of our lives, we get the best "laundering" job of our lives. What a joy, to be spot free!

Father, I'm so grateful that I don't have to feel guilty or
condemned. Thank You for removing not only my sin but
the lingering guilt as well. I'm so grateful, Lord. Amen.

Time Steward

Teach us to number our days,
that we may gain a heart of wisdom.
PSALM 90:12 NIV

Some days the clock seems to run on warp speed. We glance up and an hour's gone by. Or two. Or three. Other days the hours tick by, seemingly endless. We wonder if the day will ever end. What we do with those hours really matters. While God calls us to rest, He's not keen on wasted time. We need to be good stewards (caregivers) of the twenty-four hours we're given in a day. Rest, yes. Play, yes. But at the expense of worship or time with the one who creates our days? Absolutely not. Today, give some precious time to the Lord and then watch Him magnify the remainder of the day. You might just be surprised at how beautifully the hours pass.

Lord, I want to be a good steward of the time You've given me. I
don't want to race the clock and feel worn out, but I don't want to
waste time, either. Help me to find a balance, Father, so that I can be
refreshed and effective. May all my hours be beautiful hours. Amen.

Leadership

*When he had finished washing their feet, he put on his clothes and
returned to his place. "Do you understand what I have done for you?"
he asked them. "You call me 'Teacher' and 'Lord,' and rightly so,
for that is what I am. Now that I, your Lord and Teacher,
have washed your feet, you also should wash one another's feet."*
JOHN 13:12–14 NIV

Oh, how we love leading others. . .mostly. There are days when we,
as women, lose our way. We push out ahead of others, insisting they
should follow us. We look at the end goal without paying much
attention to those we're dragging along behind us. We don't see
how weary or beaten down they are. We simply want to accomplish
what we set out to accomplish. . .at any cost. Today, take a close look
at those who are following you. Make sure they're in good shape,
spiritually and emotionally. If they're not, focus on their needs, their
health, their desires, their good will. You will reach your goals that
much sooner if everyone on the team is in tip-top shape!

*I haven't always been the best leader, Father. Sometimes I plow
people down or try to get my way. Sometimes I scoot to the back,
more willing to follow than lead. Thank You for the reminder
that my leadership skills can be honed by You. Give me a
servant's heart so that I can lead as You do. Amen.*

Trust

*"But blessed is the one who trusts in the Lord, whose confidence
is in him. They will be like a tree planted by the water that sends
out its roots by the stream. It does not fear when heat comes;
its leaves are always green. It has no worries in a year of
drought and never fails to bear fruit."*

JEREMIAH 17:7–8 NIV

Have you ever been asked to place your trust in the hands of a surgeon? That moment, just before the anesthesia kicks in, is one of complete surrender. What else can you do but trust that the doctor has things fully in hand and will perform his finest work as he operates on you? You drift off to sleep, anxieties lifted, cares behind you. He does his best work when you're completely submitted to the process. The same is true when it comes to trusting God. We have to relax. Submit. Lay ourselves at his feet, trusting that He will do His very best work. We can't look to ourselves or others for answers. They come from Him alone.

So many times I've put my trust in others, Lord, only to be let down. How grateful I am to know that You will remain faithful, no matter what. I can trust You, Father. . .and I choose to do so, no matter how difficult life's circumstances might get. Amen.

To Your Health!

*Dear friend, I hope all is well with you and that you
are as healthy in body as you are strong in spirit.*
3 JOHN 2 NLT

God cares about your health. He took the time to mention it in His
Word on multiple occasions. If you have any lingering doubts, just
look at the many, many times Jesus healed the sick. His heart always
went out to those who were struggling. With one touch, years of pain
and agony disappeared. Maybe you're like many women and struggle
with your health. Perhaps you're in chronic pain or live with an illness—
diagnosed or undiagnosed. Today, be reminded that God cares! He
longs to see you living life to your fullest potential. That same "touch"
that healed the leper in Bible times is still available today, and God
is no respecter of persons. What He's done for others He will do for
you. Instead of giving in to fear (or thoughts that you're alone), reach
out to Him. He loves you and longs to heal both your heart and body.

*Thank You, God, for caring about my health. It's such a relief to know
that You want me to be healthy, not just my heart and soul but my
body as well. I'm so grateful for Your healing, Father. Amen.*

Quiet Time

"But when you pray, go away by yourself, shut the door behind you,
and pray to your Father in private. Then your Father,
who sees everything, will reward you."
MATTHEW 6:6 NLT

Life is so noisy. Kids squabbling, televisions blaring, horns honking, people talking, coworkers arguing, phones ringing, computers dinging, text messages coming through. . .it can get crazy. Where can a woman go to find peace and quiet? Many have retreated to their bathrooms or even their closets for moments of alone time. Likely, you have your own special spot, meant for getaways. Of course, kiddos are probably beating on the door. In the middle of all the chaos, God longs for us to spend quiet time with Him. He doesn't care where this takes place, or even if it's completely silent in that place. All that matters is that you draw near to Him and tune in to hear His still, small voice. What's keeping you from doing that now? Take a few steps away from the noise and spend a little time with Him.

How wonderful to draw close to You, Lord. I love our times together.
Peaceful. Quiet. Sweet. Intimate. Okay, I can still hear the kids
beating on the bathroom door, but that doesn't bother me.
I love every precious moment I get to spend with You. I'm so
grateful that You woo me into a place with You. Amen.

A Great Reward

"But love your enemies, do good to them, and lend to them
without expecting to get anything back. Then your reward
will be great, and you will be children of the Most High,
because he is kind to the ungrateful and wicked."
LUKE 6:35 NIV

Loving your enemies. It's easier said than done, for sure. Perhaps you read this verse and think, *Me? I don't have any enemies.* Then you remember that friend at church who isn't speaking to you. Or the coworker who snubs you. Or the business partner who went her own way because she didn't want to link arms with you any longer. Truth is, all women have difficult people in their lives, folks who cause that pit-in-the-stomach feeling. Oh, how we wish all relationships could be easy! Women don't set out to make enemies, but it happens. God longs for relationships to be restored, for love to flow and for the reward to be great for all involved.

I want to be like You in all things, Lord, even when it comes to
loving my enemies. It's not easy. I've learned this firsthand.
But I see that the reward—both spiritual and emotional—
will be great. Show me day by day how to live this out, I pray. Amen.

Anger

Whoever is patient has great understanding,
but one who is quick-tempered displays folly.
PROVERBS 14:29 NIV

Cool down, sister! How many times have you wanted to use those words? Women can get so emotionally invested in a situation—or a conversation—that tempers flare without warning. And when an emotionally charged gal gets going. . .watch out! If you've ever opened a can of biscuits and watched how they exploded out of the container, you know the potential for pent-up anger. Things can blow up in a hurry, and there's often a mess after the fact that someone (likely you) will need to clean up. There's a reason people take deep breaths and count to ten when they're worked up. Those few seconds give you time to refocus your heart and to remind yourself that it's not worth it. But don't worry! If you do blow up, the Lord has a way of reminding you of that, all the same. How much better would it be to "temper" yourself ahead of time? What chaos you could avoid!

I'll admit it, Lord. . .I'm not always the first to control my
temper. Sometimes, when I least expect it, I blow a fuse.
Thank You for tempering me, Father. Help me keep my cool,
no matter what I'm facing. Amen.

Jealousy

For you are still controlled by your sinful nature.
You are jealous of one another and quarrel with each other.
Doesn't that prove you are controlled by your sinful nature?
Aren't you living like people of the world?
1 CORINTHIANS 3:3 NLT

Jealousy. The green-eyed monster. The great friend robber. The undeniable tool of the enemy, meant to bring division, dissatisfaction and other negative feelings. Why do women struggle so much with jealousy? Why do they long to have what others have? Whether it's looks, figure, money, husband, job, or position in ministry, each woman is entitled to what God gives her. It's hers and hers alone. God elevates and provides in His time and His way. It's not for us to decide or even comment on (though it's hard to keep our mouths shut when we're convinced God got it wrong). There's never a time when jealousy is okay. Never. No finger-pointing. No, "Why do good things always happen to her and not to me?" No, "I don't get it, Lord. Why did You make her so pretty and me so ugly?" Nope. None of that. Each to his—er, her—own. Now, while it's on your mind, speak to that green-eyed monster and watch him disappear!

Oh, how I need help with this one, Lord! I try so hard not to let
the green-eyed monster creep up on me, but sometimes I don't
win that battle. I can only overcome with Your help. I give my
insecurities and jealousies to You, Father, so that You can
cleanse my heart and make me new. Amen.

Grief

" 'He will wipe every tear from their eyes. There will
be no more death' or mourning or crying or pain,
for the old order of things has passed away."
REVELATION 21:4 NIV

How quick women are to skip past grief. The loss of a loved one. The loss of a relationship. The loss of a job. Women face these things far too often. And how do most respond? They stiffen the upper lip and plow forward, not always taking adequate time to truly mourn what they've lost. One of the hidden dangers of neglecting grief (and yes, you can neglect it) is illness. When women don't take the time to mourn their losses, the physical body pays a price. In fact, emotions pay a price, too. If you're not careful, your body will wear down and your emotions crater. And, if you let things go too long, your spiritual life will weaken, too. Today, many will need to hear these words: there's nothing wrong with grieving. God doesn't want you to park there too long, but do take the time to mourn. Then, once you're done, God will dry your eyes, lift your chin, and give you courage to face tomorrow.

I can't tell You how much it lifts my heart to know that grieving won't
last forever, Father. Sometimes it feels like it will. Your reassurance
gives me hope that tomorrow will be better. Thank You for that. Amen.

Movers and Shakers

*"But as for you, be strong and do not give up,
for your work will be rewarded."*
2 CHRONICLES 15:7 NIV

Women love to accomplish tasks. They work around the clock, taking on responsibilities that often test their strength and their health. Many times they say yes when they should say no. (Perhaps you can relate!) Today, take some time to assess your obligations. If there's too much "moving and shaking" going on in your life, maybe it's time to trim back and use that *no* word. Perhaps you're on the opposite end of the spectrum. You wish you could get the energy to set some goals, but you're too wiped out. Maybe it's time to check your diet and exercise plan to see if you can get some relief by eating better or getting the rest you need. One thing's for sure: God wants His daughters to accomplish great things for Him. When you're overworked or exhausted, that won't happen. Balance, my friend! It's what holds every schedule together!

Lord, I want to be a mover and shaker for You. I don't want my days to pass without being effective for the kingdom. Keep me motivated, Father, and help me to do my best, but show me when I've crossed over a line. All things in balance, Father. That's my prayer. Amen.

Be My Valentine

But because of his great love for us, God, who is rich in mercy, made us alive with Christ even when we were dead in transgressions—it is by grace you have been saved.
EPHESIANS 2:4–5 NIV

Every little girl loves Valentine's Day. She fixes her little box, knowing it will be filled with sweet notes from friends at school. She spends hours signing cards to be given away. All this to show affection for others. This Valentine's Day, God wants you to know that He spent a long time creating a special card just for you. It's all wrapped up in a special "box" called the Bible. Oh, the love letters you will find inside! They will satisfy every longing and fill your heart with peace and joy. They will bring fulfillment and quench doubt. They will make you as giddy as a schoolgirl on Valentine's Day. Today, spend some time reading God's special love letter. Then accept His free gift of a Savior, so that every day can be Valentine's Day.

Father, thank You for setting the best example of true love. Instead of Cupid's arrows, You chose death on a cross to demonstrate the kind of love that lays down its life for another. I cling to You and fully give You my heart afresh this Valentine's Day. Amen.

Rejoicing!

Always be full of joy in the Lord. I say it again—rejoice!
PHILIPPIANS 4:4 NLT

Have you ever watched a toddler laugh? It's amazing, isn't it? Those adorable giggles are contagious. Before long you can't help but join in, your laughter filling the room. After all, nothing compares to the sheer joy of an innocent child. It bubbles up from the deepest, God-given place, completely unhindered by concerns, worries, or distractions. How many times do we become so burdened by life's complexities that we forget to rejoice? What would it feel like to let those giggles rise to the surface, even on the worst days? What's that you say? You have nothing to feel joyful about? Look at those flowers blooming in the field! (Beauty!) Check out the food in your pantry. (Provision!) Glance into a grandchild's eyes or a coworker's heart. There's plenty of fodder for a joy-filled life. All we have to do is turn our focus from the pain to the glimpses of heaven right in front of us. Today, may your eyes be opened to many joy-filled moments.

I'm grateful for this reminder, Father, that I can be filled with joy, no matter the circumstances. They don't have to drive my emotions. Instead, my joy can drive my circumstances. Amen.

Using Your Gifts

*We have different gifts, according to the grace given to each
of us. If your gift is prophesying, then prophesy in accordance
with your faith; if it is serving, then serve; if it is teaching,
then teach; if it is to encourage, then give encouragement;
if it is giving, then give generously; if it is to lead,
do it diligently; if it is to show mercy, do it cheerfully.*
ROMANS 12:6–8 NIV

What's your gift? What's your overarching talent or ability? Are you using it to the fullest? Many women get so busy that they don't take advantage of the gifts God has given them. Then they wonder why they're ineffective or feel useless. When you're flowing in the stream of God's best (i.e., His perfect will), you'll find plenty of opportunities to use those gifts. In fact, He just might open doors in ways that surprise—and terrify—and delight—you! God is pretty amazing like that! So brace yourself. Polish those gifts and prepare to use them. The word is out. God's got big plans for you!

*Thank You for opening doors, Lord, so that I can use my gifts for You.
Lead me, step by step, in the right direction. I want to be useful to
Your kingdom. I'll trust the process, Father, and polish my
gifts so I'm ready when the time comes. Amen.*

Being, Not Doing

So there is a special rest still waiting for the people of God. For all who have entered into God's rest have rested from their labors, just as God did after creating the world. So let us do our best to enter that rest. But if we disobey God, as the people of Israel did, we will fall.
HEBREWS 4:9-11 NLT

Whew! We're very busy "doing," aren't we? Whenever we run short of things to do, we think up more things. Oftentimes women don't feel useful unless they're on the move 24-7. (That's how many modern women are wired, after all.) Maybe it's time to stop and ask the Lord, "What do You want, Father? Would You rather I 'do' or 'be'?" Likely, His answer would come in the form of two simple words: *just be*. The problem is, it's hard to "just be." We're wired by society to accomplish. We strive. We rush. We press. We are driven! As with all things, balance is key. Make a commitment today to spend some time "being." It will give you the energy you need to get out there and make a difference for the kingdom of God.

Oh, Father! I'm such a doer. Sometimes I forget to just "be." Thank You for reminding me that I don't need to impress You with my actions. You love me, just as I am. Show me how to "be" so that I'll be ready to "do" when the right moments come. Amen.

Generosity

"In everything I did, I showed you that by this kind of hard work we must help the weak, remembering the words the Lord Jesus himself said: 'It is more blessed to give than to receive.' "
ACTS 20:35 NIV

Society teaches us that getting is key. Consequently, we work hard to acquire clothing, homes, vehicles, and so on. Our lists are endless and grow even more as we watch what others have: vacations, RVs, jewelry. No matter how much we get, there's always more to want. We're like kids at Christmastime, making our lists and hoping Santa meets our expectations. The problem with that mentality is it's one-sided. If we would flip-flop our thinking and focus on what we can give, our entire focus will shift. A giving-minded woman has her antennae up. She's aware of the needs around her. And she is motivated by generosity. So ask God to balance your "need to have" with a need to give. You might just be surprised at how He does that.

I love the idea of blessing others, Lord. Oh, how fun to surprise them with little gifts when they least expect them. Point me toward those who need a blessing today, I pray. Amen.

Living in Harmony

Live in harmony with each other. Don't be too proud to enjoy the company of ordinary people. And don't think you know it all! Never pay back evil with more evil. Do things in such a way that everyone can see you are honorable. Do all that you can to live in peace with everyone.
ROMANS 12:16–18 NLT

Picture yourself at the symphony. The musicians file in, one by one, as the audience members take their seats. Before long a violinist begins to warm up. Then a clarinet player. Then another musician, followed by another. After a minute or so, you want to stick your fingers in your ears. There's no rhyme or reason to what they're playing. It's a cacophony, dissonant and painful to the ears. This is what life is like when you're out of harmony with those around you. You're like an individual instrument playing madly in a different key than the person next to you. God loves for you to live in harmony with those around you. Maybe it's time to step back, wait for the conductor's cue, then link arms with your family, friends, and coworkers to play the most beautiful tune of your life.

I'll admit, it's not always easy to live in harmony, Lord. Sometimes I get caught up in the bickering and complaining and don't see a way out. Thank You for teaching me the way out, Father. I want to live in harmony with others. Amen.

True Beauty

Charm is deceptive, and beauty does not last;
but a woman who fears the LORD will be greatly praised.
PROVERBS 31:30 NLT

Have you ever pondered the word *reflection*? When you stare at your reflection in the mirror, do you see your flaws or your beauty? Do you stare at your eyes or the wrinkles around them? Do you notice the intricacies of your mouth? Unless they're in putting-on-makeup mode, most women just take a quick glance in the looking glass before running out the door. Satisfied that the reflection meets expectation, a woman moves on. Oh, how God longs for His girls to see a different kind of beauty than the exterior. May your next glance in the mirror reveal a pure heart, generous hands, an uplifting mouth. When you fear/honor the Lord, your interior beauty will add all the sparkle and shine you need to an already lovely exterior.

Like most women, I focus too much on my looks, Lord. I see the good, the bad, and the ugly. Thank You for reminding me that true beauty isn't what I see in the mirror. It's what others see when they spend time with me. May I be a beautiful reflection of You. Amen.

Dreamer

"In the last days, God says, I will pour out my Spirit on all people. Your sons and daughters will prophesy, your young men will see visions, your old men will dream dreams."
ACTS 2:17 NIV

Ah, the dreamer! She sees all of life's possibilities and believes every dream can come true. And she has no shortage of dreams, either. Her creativity knows no bounds. She's got an idea a minute. Don't believe it? Just ask her! Perhaps you can relate to this fun woman of God. Maybe you're a dreamer, too. If so, you must surely enjoy seeing those once-upon-a-time ideas come to fruition. How excited the Lord must be when He peers inside the hearts of his dreamer-daughters. He placed that creative bent inside of them, after all. Today, spend some time glancing back at some of the dreams God placed in your heart. Have all of them come true? If not, maybe it's time to reawaken a few!

I don't mind admitting I've always been a dreamer, Lord. I have plans. Ideas. Creative streaks. I know You placed these dreams inside of me, and I can't wait to see which ones will come to fruition. Thanks for entrusting them to me! Amen.

Starting Over

Then Peter came to Jesus and asked, "Lord, how many times shall I forgive my brother or sister who sins against me? Up to seven times?" Jesus answered, "I tell you, not seven times, but seventy-seven times."
MATTHEW 18:21–22 NIV

Picture this: You're in the middle of a heated conversation with a friend. The two of you are at odds. You say something. She says something back. You respond, determined to make your point. She does the same, her jaw clenched. Things escalate, and before long you spout something mean-spirited and completely out of character for you. *Ack.* There's no taking that back, is there? Words stick. At times like this, you really wish you could have a do-over. If only you could hit the REWIND button! The good news is, you can. With God's help, you can have countless do-overs. Sure, there will still be a mess to clean up, but He's pretty good at that part, too! Why else do you think He told Peter there would be so many opportunities to forgive?

Ah, new beginnings! I'm so grateful for them, Lord! No matter how old I get, it seems I'm always needing a do-over. Thank You for being willing to give me a second chance. And a third. And so many more. Amen.

Loving Your Home

"But if you refuse to serve the Lord, then choose today whom you will serve. Would you prefer the gods your ancestors served beyond the Euphrates? Or will it be the gods of the Amorites in whose land you now live? But as for me and my family, we will serve the Lord."
JOSHUA 24:15 NLT

"As for me and my family." Think about the boldness of those words. When you say "me and my family," you're staking your claim. You're putting it out there. No one had better mess with your clan. You're sticking together. You're in this as a team. You won't be thwarted, in part because you're united, like-minded. God understands this power-in-numbers thing, and that's why He's so keen on families serving Him as one unit. Today, begin to pray for spiritual unity in your family. No weapon formed against your clan will stand as long as you're unified. Watch the enemy cower in fear as your family members step up to accept the spiritual authority they've been given!

You are the God of my home, Lord. You're the only one we will serve. We won't let addictions to electronics or our belongings become a problem. We'll keep our eyes on You. Amen.

Friendship

There are "friends" who destroy each other,
but a real friend sticks closer than a brother.
PROVERBS 18:24 NLT

Remember when you were a kid, how you put glue on your palms and let it dry? You waited until it hardened to peel it away, then grinned at the masterpiece it created. You could see every crease, every wrinkle, every joint. In some ways, a great friendship is like that. A friend who sticks closer than a great brother is, indeed, a masterpiece. She has your imprint on her heart, every tiny detail exposed. . .and yet she loves you anyway. She knows the good, the bad, and the ugly, and she chooses to adore you despite all that. She knows what makes you tick and understands your heart, your motivation. She's got your back when the enemy rears his head, but she's also the first to give godly guidance when you've lost your way. Want her to stick like glue for years to come? Just return the favor. Be the kind of friend you want to have.

I long to be the best sort of friend, Father. Show me how, I pray.
I want to be trustworthy, reliable, and truthful—always presenting
the truth in love. You're the very best example of friendship,
so I will continue to learn from You. Amen.

Think on These Things

*Finally, brothers and sisters, whatever is true,
whatever is noble, whatever is right, whatever is pure,
whatever is lovely, whatever is admirable—if anything is
excellent or praiseworthy—think about such things.*
PHILIPPIANS 4:8 NIV

Single-minded. Such an interesting word! When you're single-minded, you are hyperfocused on the goal in front of you. Your gaze doesn't shift to the right or left. Picture a target shooter, aiming at her mark. She's got the bow and arrow in hand, but she's not looking at them. No, her eyes are fixed on one thing. . .that center mark. She's determined to hit it. That's you, unwilling to deviate for a second, lest you miss your opportunity. One of God's greatest desires is for His daughters to hyperfocus on good things: things that are noble, right, pure, lovely, and admirable. No more doubts, fears, or insecurities. From now on, single-minded aiming at a lovely target. Think on such things.

*Sometimes I struggle to focus, Lord. I want to keep my mind walking
the straight and narrow, but my thoughts shift from one thing to
another. No longer will I focus on the bow and arrow, Father.
I will look only at the center mark. Thank You for showing me
how to think on You so that my focus is sure. Amen.*

Overcoming

"I have told you these things, so that in me you may
have peace. In this world you will have trouble.
But take heart! I have overcome the world."
JOHN 16:33 NIV

Remember, as a child, how you played red rover? What was the goal of the game? To try to break through the barrier on the other side, of course. In many ways life is like a game of red rover. You spend a lot of time running toward obstacles, hoping you can break through. God has promised you something pretty remarkable in His Word. You're not just "coming over," you're overcoming! You're leaping above walls that once held you bound. You're sailing above circumstances that threatened to destroy your psyche. You're celebrating victories over situations that once seemed impossible. Today, instead of seeing yourself as someone who's always running toward trouble, begin to see yourself as an overcomer in His name, then get ready to take flight!

I must confess, the word overcoming sounds like a lot of work. How
refreshing to realize that overcoming isn't something I have to do; it's
something You've already done on the cross. Thank You, God, for this
revelation. I'm so grateful to be an overcomer in Your name. Amen.

My Help Comes from Above

Commit everything you do to the LORD. Trust him, and he will help you. He will make your innocence radiate like the dawn, and the justice of your cause will shine like the noonday sun.
PSALM 37:5–6 NLT

Have you ever been on a quest to find the right doctor to cure a particular ill? Maybe you go to your primary care physician and he sends you to a specialist. Perhaps that specialist sends you to a subspecialist. At every step along the way you groan and say, "I just want someone who can help me!" Aren't you glad to hear that you have a straight shot to your heavenly Father? You don't need a referral. You don't need to wait in line. And He's got the solution to any problem you might be facing. You won't need a second opinion because He'll have things fixed up before you make it that far. Run to Him. Trust Him. He will give you all the help you need.

How wonderful to know that I don't have to go looking for help. You're standing nearby, ready to plead my case and to bring about justice when I face unjust situations. Have I mentioned how grateful I am, Lord? I am! Amen.

Victorious!

> *"For the LORD your God is going with you! He will fight for*
> *you against your enemies, and he will give you victory!"*
> DEUTERONOMY 20:4 NLT

Victory! It's a word we know well from our high school days when cheerleaders hollered, "V-I-C-T-O-R-Y!" in rousing chorus. Every team wants to win. Every business owner wants to succeed. Every married couple wants to thrive. We all want the same thing: victory. But victory over what? An invisible enemy? Financial woes? People who are out to get you? Drugs? Alcohol? Depression? What are you hoping to declare victory over today? Instead of looking at that thing, focus instead on the one who promises victory. If your eyes are on Him, not the problem, your chances of success are increased dramatically. Don't you love the promise in today's scripture, that He will go with you? Not only that, He will fight for you! You might be heading into some scary places, but He's right there, offering comfort and guidance and assuring your success. With your hand in His, victory is surely on its way!

Whew! I don't like to fight, Father. That's one reason I'm so grateful that You fight my battles for me. All I have to do is show up, face my enemies with my faith secure, then watch You move on my behalf. How can I ever thank You for all You've done? Amen.

Ash Wednesday

Where You Are, There I Am Free

I sought the LORD, and He heard me, and delivered
me from all my fears. They looked to Him and
were radiant, and their faces were not ashamed.
PSALM 34:4–5 NKJV

Ana could barely read when she came to faith, but her husband's passion for God and for His Word encouraged her to seek His presence. She struggled with each syllable as she studied her Bible between caring for her seven children. On the hills where she took Viorica, the milk cow, to graze she would often read and pray. The worries of being the wife to an itinerant preacher, who could be arrested at any time due to the political climate of the country, were many. She sought God and petitioned Him for peace. The Lord heard and brought deliverance countless times—from financial provision to physical protection.

Now an elderly woman in her late eighties, Ana has lost sight in one eye, making it even harder to read. She still seeks her Maker in daily conversation and in listening to Bible teachers expound the Word. Her face radiates peace when she hears the words of Jesus, holding nothing back as she retells it to her grandchildren. She sought and beautifully found Him. Through her diligence in faith, she broke from the fears and constraints of illiteracy, of poverty, of social marginalization, and of political repression. Adonai delivered her. Seeking Him requires persistence, but it leads to freedom.

Great Deliverer, give me diligence in seeking You. As You reveal more
of Yourself, let me radiate Your love in the likeness of the Son. Amen.

Being Sought

Thus says the LORD, who created you, O Jacob, and He
who formed you, O Israel: "Fear not, for I have redeemed you;
I have called you by your name; you are Mine."
ISAIAH 43:1 NKJV

It is a beautiful thing to know someone is seeking you out, taking the initiative and interest. Though we are called to search for God and to dive deep into who He is, we can only do this because He first called us. What encouragement to know that He asks the research and heart of humans only after He has done all He could to pursue us. Jesus is the One who does the knocking for us to open the door of our hearts. In C. S. Lewis's *The Silver Chair*, Aslan and Jill have a similar discussion: "'You would not have called to me unless I had been calling to you,' said the Lion."

There must be mutual concern and care, as in any relationship. We must seek Him, but knowing that He has done the hardest work for us and that, as we seek Him, He is still pursuing us. He gave the written word, the Word incarnate, and the Spirit to show how much He longs for us. God has provided rescue for humans while we were still sinners. He calls us by name to accept the sacrifice of Jesus and then to live in the light of His message. We seek because we are sought after; we must also, as in the likeness of Christ, seek out others.

Greatest of Seekers, thank You for such a persistent love. Amen.

Outcome of Heartfelt Supplication

"At the beginning of your supplications the command went out, and I have come to tell you, for you are greatly beloved."
DANIEL 9:23 NKJV

This prophet's prayer in a captive land is one of the most heart-stirring petitions to God in the Bible. The Holy Spirit revealed to Daniel that the seventy years of exile as prophesized by Jeremiah were about completed, and he begged God to remember His promises of old and bless Jerusalem and His people again—not because of their good deeds but because of His great mercy. Daniel confessed his sins and the brokenness of his people with such passion and sincerity that Abba did not refuse.

While Daniel prayed, God sent the angel Gabriel to "fly swiftly" (Daniel 9:21 NKJV) to Daniel and to encourage him with information and skill in understanding God's plan. The angel revealed to him that the command to help went out at the very beginning of his prayer of supplication. God knew the faithfulness of this man's heart and wanted him to know how greatly he is loved by his Father. Gabriel announced, "I have come to tell you, for you are greatly beloved." It may seem that the sorrow and pleas of our hearts go unnoticed, but we serve a God of mystery who sends His angels in times unexpected to remind us of His faithfulness and love.

"O Lord, hear! O Lord, forgive! O Lord, listen and act!" Let Your daughters pray with conviction and trust in Your mercy. Amen.

Seeking of the Foolish

"Then the kingdom of heaven shall be likened to ten virgins
who took their lamps and went out to meet the bridegroom.
Now five of them were wise, and five were foolish."
MATTHEW 25:1-2 NKJV

The Bridegroom is ready. He is adorned in all His wonder, traveling by cloud and to the sound of trumpets, anxiously awaiting union with the bride. But what of her? Christian poets Janette...ikz and Ezekiel Azonwu performed a dramatic reading of the poem "Ready or Not" in which the bride of Christ, representing the Church, is anything but ready.* She busied herself with superfluous actions and forgot the essentials.

Similarly, the women in Jesus' parable were waiting for the Bridegroom with lamps in hand. The foolish five readily took their lamps but no oil. They believed He was coming but did little in the way of serious preparation. It is frightening that though they also waited expectantly and claimed to know and love the groom, He did not recognize them. How must we live differently to ensure our seeking and waiting for the Lord is done in the wisdom of the five who entered the feast? Seeking God wisely means being fed with His Word and letting the Spirit work those truths in and through us—invoking His wisdom in all situations.

Greatly anticipated One, let me live with both lamp and oil
in hand. Help me fill my life with thoughts and actions rooted
in Your wisdom so that others now, and You on Your return,
will recognize me as Yours. Amen.

*You can find the performance online: https://www.youtube.com watch?v=T44LepcRUhk.

Do You Understand What You're Reading?

*Then the Spirit said to Philip, "Go near and overtake this chariot."
So Philip ran to him, and heard him reading the prophet Isaiah,
and said, "Do you understand what you are reading?"*
ACTS 8:29–30 NKJV

How often do believers read distractedly over Bible passages and miss the simple truths, let alone the more complex? God has something wonderful to reveal to readers in every page of the Bible. No matter how dull, there is always a "deeper magic." The Ethiopian eunuch that Philip met on the desert road was a believer in the God of Israel, since he was just coming back from worshipping in Jerusalem. He was reading the Tanakh (Old Testament) scrolls of the prophet Isaiah with interest, but not having the New Testament meant he needed a little extra help. Philip showed him that the suffering servant passage from Isaiah 53 was a prophecy made real by Jesus. The Ethiopian's understanding led to his baptism and to his continuing "on his way rejoicing" (Acts 8:39 NKJV).

If we look deeper, we see that just three chapters ahead of where he was reading, in Isaiah 56, God gives a beautiful promise to eunuchs, who were marginalized and without hope of having families and of passing on their names: "I will give them an everlasting name that shall not be cut off" (Isaiah 56:5 NKJV). What a joy the Ethiopian eunuch must have had on reading this! This is but a small example of the beautiful intricacies of God's story, revealing God's love through Jesus.

*Great Revealer, give me understanding of
Your Word and the joy that comes with it. Amen.*

Fault with Faith in Wisdom

...that your faith should not be in the
wisdom of men but in the power of God.
1 CORINTHIANS 2:5 NKJV

There is great danger in putting faith in wisdom—the wrong kind of wisdom, that is, or in worldly knowledge falsely claiming to be wisdom. The most damaging teachings of the modern era have reified skepticism and doubt. It is faith in intellectual doubt that has corrupted the definition of wisdom and lessened the power of God in the eyes of society. The teachers of such "wisdom" are the ones Paul warns Timothy about: they are always learning and never able to come to the knowledge of the truth (see 2 Timothy 3:17). Paul may have referred to the religious leaders of his day, an accusation often made by later Christians against the Jewish Talmudic or rabbinic tradition.

Joseph Rabinowitz, the father of the modern Messianic Jewish movement, initially embraced enlightenment rationalism against his Hassidic background but, by God's grace, came to know the truth and wisdom of God's plan in Jesus as Messiah for both Jews and Gentiles. He found the wisdom that is from above. This wisdom is pure, a source of peace, gentle, willing to yield, merciful, and produces good fruit, without partiality or hypocrisy (see James 3:17). Such wisdom can only be brought about by the power of God, and in this we can place our faith.

Adon ha-Gadol (our great Lord), give me such wisdom. Give me
understanding to discern it from that of the world's. Let me
put my faith in Your power and not in my wisdom. Amen.

Hope to the Full

Now may the God of hope fill you with all joy and peace in believing,
that you may abound in hope by the power of the Holy Spirit.
ROMANS 15:13 NKJV

Paul wrote this prayer in the context of explaining his ministry to non-Jewish Christians who could now believe that Jesus came for them as well. Throughout his letter to the Romans, Paul writes of the relationship between Jewish and Gentile Christians, encouraging them to work together since both groups clung to the hope that the Messiah brings. This is hope in a God who has a plan imbued with love for creation, hope that He will bring things together in blessing for His followers, and final hope in His return to bring His children in forever-union with their Maker.

Paul knew that at times belief in these truths could wane and they needed to hope. What is most beautiful about the prayer is that Paul did not ask his readers to try to foster and maintain hope on their own, but rather that they would look to God, the source of hope. In sticking to and living out our faith, God fills us with hope. (He helps us with the sticking and living out part also.) Joy and peace in what we believe allows us, with the help of the Spirit, to live hope filled no matter the circumstance. And we abound, living fully, in the faith that things will turn out all right in the end.

God of hope, fill me with joy and peace
to flourish in expectant faith. Amen.

Reasoning with God

"Come now, and let us reason together," says the LORD,
"Though your sins are like scarlet, they shall be as white as snow;
though they are red like crimson, they shall be as wool."
ISAIAH 1:18 NKJV

Rabbi Isaac Lichtenstein starts one of his defenses for Jesus as Messiah with these words: "Come let us reason together." He cleverly invokes the very reasoning of God to prove to his Jewish readers that Jesus of Nazareth is indeed the Savior promised since the beginning of sinful time. For the rabbi, as a man, to propose such a dialogue is not too unusual, but for the Maker of all to approach and beckon humans into a similar discussion is breathtaking.

In the previous verse God instructs the people to "learn to do good; seek justice, rebuke the oppressor; defend the fatherless, plead for the widow." Knowing that they failed and will continue to fail, He laid that all aside and asked His people what they think of this: He will wash and whiten them. They only need to live in willingness to be obedient. They must recognize the darkness of their brokenness and break from it. How humbling that the Almighty would stoop to speak with us below. His call to come and then His proposition to deliberate together with Him reveals how deeply He cares for us. So let us come and let us listen to what He proposes: life.

Adonai, Your reasoning is perfect, full of grace and love.
Let me come before Your altar ready to listen and
accept what You want of me. Amen.

Friends like Apples

A word fitly spoken is like apples of gold in settings of silver.
Like an earring of gold and an ornament of fine
gold is a wise rebuker to an obedient ear.
PROVERBS 25:11–12 NKJV

The apple tree in Jewish oral tradition symbolizes faith in God's commandments and His relationship to Israel. The medieval text called the Zohar also presents apples as the way God diffuses His beauty in the world. In this proverb, Solomon identifies apples with wise instruction and encourages his people to treasure words "fitly spoken."

Apples, silver, golden earrings, and ornaments. These similes clearly emphasize the value of speaking those much-needed words at the appropriate time. Being a true friend or really loving your neighbor requires this sacrifice of well-thought-out advice or correction. Sometimes we may be too willing to administer reproof, and that is why the writer stresses correct timing and wisdom when trying to help others.

Rebuking in good judgment is always difficult, but we must also be ready to act as the obedient ear when necessary. It may be that God is trying to mold us through the rebuke of another. Rather than letting it wound our pride and foster deprecating thoughts of the other or of ourselves, we must be keen to hear and to adorn that ornament of gold, not cast it to the rubbish bin. That is not the place for such costly advice, but our hearts are.

Lord, make my words apples in settings of silver. Let me
discern and put into practice the words of wise correction. Amen.

Excitement

Because Your lovingkindness is better than life, my lips shall praise You. Thus I will bless You while I live; I will lift up my hands in Your name. My soul shall be satisfied as with [fat and rich food], and my mouth shall praise You with joyful lips. When I remember You on my bed, I meditate on You in the night watches. Because You have been my help, therefore in the shadow of Your wings I will rejoice.
PSALM 63:3–7 NKJV

Sister Motea was a good example of what Jesus says to the church of Smyrna in the book of Revelation. She was poor by the world's standards—a village mother in southern Romania—but spiritually rich in her love of Christ. Loved ones fondly remember Sister Motea's joy in being together with the church family, not wanting to miss any occasion for fellowship. She joined along on youth trips, feeling just as young and desirous to be a part of the kingdom work. Her children grew up in this environment of excitement for the Lord. Of course, they didn't see mom tagging along all the time as much fun, so they would occasionally try to sneak off without her. For one particular church trip, Sister Motea slept in the car to make sure they took her along. Here was a woman whose age did not deter her. She yearned to share the joy that satisfied her soul.

Abba, give me such excitement for You. No matter my age, let me praise You with joyful lips and seek to always be in the shadow of Your wings, for You are faithful to help. Amen.

Lifting the Veil

And He will destroy on this mountain the surface of the covering cast over all people, and the veil that is spread over all nations.
ISAIAH 25:7 NKJV

When Moses came down from Mount Sinai, his face gleamed with having been in the presence of God. But this shining skin scared the people. So Moses wore a veil in public whenever he received God's commands and delivered them to Israel. Paul mentions how this veil remains over the hearts of the Jewish people who do not see Yeshua ben Yosef (Jesus son of Joseph) as Messiah. The nations outside of Israel also had a veil spread over their minds, but theirs was due to the election of the Jewish nation as the people of God. His covenant with the Jews started through faithful Abraham, and the rest of the world came to know Him through His relationship with the children of Israel. Ultimately, all creation is covered with the veil of sin and God had to come down Himself to bring us light.

God has lifted the veil. No, He has torn it, destroyed it. He offers a way back to the friendship humans had with Him before the fall into sin. Through Jesus the law was fulfilled and all nations given the truth. He swallowed up death that came with fear and ignorance.

HaShem, Name above all names, thank You for destroying the veil that kept Your creation in darkness. Let me not fear Your holiness such that I neglect Your presence. May I live in the joyous freedom of Your truth revealed. Amen.

Awaken the Dawn

*Awake, lute and harp! I will awaken the dawn. I will praise You,
O LORD, among the peoples, and I will sing praises to You
among the nations. For Your mercy is great above the heavens,
and your truth reaches to the clouds.*
PSALM 108:2–4 NKJV

A hiker preparing to climb Mount Rainier begins her journey in the wee small hours of the morning. She is awake before the dawn to see the majestic swirls of sky, earth, and rolling mountains. After the terrific toil of the morning, she reaches the top and declares along with His handiwork the awesomeness of the Creator. There she is, so close to the heavens and among the clouds spoken of in today's psalm.

David may not have done something as impressive as climbing Rainier when he penned this, but his poetic lines reveal intentionality in starting the day with an attitude of praise. He writes of waking up early to thank God for His mercy and of wanting to make everything around him sing because of God's goodness. Sometimes the heart may be too hurt for such feelings. The only balm is spending time with Him and remembering He is at work before the rising of each new day. Like the lute and harp that David summons, we are all part of God's orchestra—each with their unique sound, all created to be in a harmony of praise.

*Awake my soul, O God, to the song of creation, which was made
to dance in tune with You: Father, Word, and Spirit. Amen.*

Blessed Prison

The LORD also will be a refuge for the oppressed, a refuge in times of trouble. And those who know Your name will put their trust in You; for You, LORD, have not forsaken those who seek You.
PSALM 9:9–10 NKJV

Nicole Valery-Grossu was unlawfully detained for four years during the first Communist government of Romania, years in which she experienced the horrors of the socialist penal system. Nicole was arrested for her political activity in the National Peasantist Party (outlawed by the communists) and for being the niece of Iuliu Maniu, the famous leader of the Peasantists. Though she was imprisoned for purely political reasons, it was in prison that she came to know God in an intimate way. This resulted in added mockery from authorities who wanted her to be a communist and an atheist.

Her autobiography, *Binecuvântatâ fii, închisoare* (Bless You Prison), and Nicolae Mârgineanu's 2002 movie adaptation show how she grew to trust God as her refuge in times of great physical and spiritual oppression. Prison was the place where she experienced the truths of Psalm 9. God does not desert those who are in trouble and who call to Him. Nicole held her experiences in prison as a testament of how God works beautifully in the most horrific of places and situations. He is suffering alongside you because He identifies Himself as the God of the poor, the marginalized, the oppressed. He will not forsake those who seek Him.

You are my place of refuge, Lord. Let me truly know and trust Your name so that I can see You at work in the darkest of places. Amen.

Wisdom's Cry

Wisdom calls aloud outside; she raises her voice in the open
squares. . . . "How long, you simple ones, will you love simplicity?
For scorners delight in their scorning, and fools hate knowledge.
Turn at my rebuke; surely I will pour out my spirit on you;
I will make my words known to you."
PROVERBS 1:20, 22-23 NKJV

The first psalm in the Bible has the personification of wisdom, a woman, calling out in the streets in the style of the prophets (a type of pre-Jeremiah jeremiad). She chastises the people for being simple. Simplicity can be a virtue in this world filled with desire for material goods and always wanting to acquire more and more. Humbleness and beauty in simplicity are rare. However, Wisdom speaks here against complacency in regard to spiritual truths.

God has so much He wants to teach us—to make us understand why certain things are the way they are or even to help us understand why we cannot have complete knowledge at this time. Too often people are content to remain in their state of rebellion because they choose their own simple or narrow-minded arguments over the words and wisdom of God. Yet God offers us a chance to repent so that He can pour out His Spirit of comfort and understanding on us as He makes known to us His words.

Wise One, make me a woman of wisdom keen to obey the call and
not remain complacent in my sin. Give me strength to acknowledge
and repent of my faults and then rejoice in Your Spirit. Amen.

What Is Hard?

Good understanding gains favor,
but the way of the unfaithful is hard.
PROVERBS 13:15 NKJV

A heart open to understanding indeed gains favor; people will trust and seek her out for comfort and advice. Having an understanding heart is not easy. Why then does Solomon write that the way of the unfaithful is hard? It seems much easier to fall into unfaithfulness, to not bother with trying to understand the hurt or joy of others. On the outset it may seem like less work, but the outcome is bitter.

Faithful followers of God throughout the Bible, especially the psalmists and the prophets, reach a point where they see the wicked prosper while the faithful struggle. They question God's judgment, but they ultimately realize that the prosperity of the wicked is fleeting and that it often comes at the expense of others. While it is hard to remain faithful in this broken world—to read God's Word, to pray, to meet regularly with believers, and to love sacrificially—the path of the unfaithful offers no hope. It is hard: a brutal and self-inflicted separation from the One they were created to be with. We need spiritual eyes to see the consequences as deadly hard. For a growing spiritual awareness and for a heart good at understanding, we also need patience. "Patience, hard thing!" exclaims Gerard Manley Hopkins. But we have a patient Father, who in His "delicious kindness" gives us all we need.

Understanding One, let me choose the difficult life of faith now but which allows me to be with You here and in the hereafter. Amen.

Physical Pain and a Broken Spirit

The spirit of a man will sustain him in sickness,
but who can bear a broken spirit?
PROVERBS 18:14 NKJV

Dr. Kelly Kapic, in a talk on suffering, spoke of the danger that physical pain is to one's faith. A woman's spirit is dejected, discouraged, and doubts creep or flood in. Kapic gives the example of Martin Luther, the initiator of the Protestant Reformation, who went through great physical illness and in his letters reveals a deep struggle to maintain his faith. Even spiritual giants like Luther were brought low by poor health. Today's proverb mentions that a man or woman with a strong spirit will manage to remain at peace during their illness. But a broken spirit may fall to the despair and hopelessness of the disease or pain.

What is the spirit of a woman? It's her heart—all that makes her who she is, her hopes and joys. How can one make sure it isn't broken during the fragile stages of suffering? There is no formula except placing one's hope and trust in the goodness of God. Jesus said that the poor in spirit would inherit the kingdom of heaven. A broken spirit that struggles against the brokenness through the power and promises of Jesus has hope. The question from the proverb is answered. Jesus is the only One who can bear a broken spirit. We must lift our burdens, anger, and pain and the suffering of others to Him.

Jehovah Rapha (God our Healer), sustain my weary
heart and body. Strengthen my faith and the faith
of others who are going through pain. Amen.

Saving Ireland

And a vision appeared to Paul in the night.
A man of Macedonia stood and pleaded with him,
saying, "Come over to Macedonia and help us."
ACTS 16:9 NKJV

Few countries have such a well-known connection with their patron saint as does Ireland with Saint Patrick. Most accounts of Patrick's life say that he came from a Christian family (his father was a deacon and his grandfather a priest) in England but only came to faith after he was captured by Irish raiders. During his six years as a slave sheepherder, he came to know the true Shepherd and was adopted into His flock. God took care of this lamb-in-the-faith by rescuing Patrick from servitude and letting him see the work of salvation spread among the Irish people.

Legend has it that Patrick was called to go back to Ireland in a dream. He saw an Irishman pleading for him to return to teach them about Jesus. Centuries earlier the apostle Paul similarly saw a Macedonian pleading in a dream and obeyed the call, resulting in the formation of the church at Philippi. Paul's letter of encouragement to the Philippians, which we have in the Bible today, continues to edify believers. God used Patrick as He used Paul to bring His plan of redemption to the nations. Unlikely heroes: a slave shepherd and a Pharisee; both listened, heard, and obeyed God's voice.

Abba, thank You for how You used Patrick to spread Your Word.
Bless Ireland with a renewed love of You. May Your daughters
be ready to answer Your call in obedience. Amen.

Ready for Redemption

Then Paul answered, "What do you mean by weeping and breaking my heart? For I am ready not only to be bound, but also to die at Jerusalem for the name of the Lord Jesus."
ACTS 21:13 NKJV

Paul was in Caesarea at the home of Philip the evangelist when the prophet Agabus confronted him in a startling manner. He took off Paul's belt. Agabus bound his own hands and feet with the belt. He explained his surprising actions to be a message from the Holy Spirit, warning Paul that his return to Jerusalem would result in his arrest. Friends pleaded with the apostle in an attempt to change his resolve.

Earlier in chapter 21, Paul and his companions were prevented by the Spirit from going to Jerusalem. Those around Paul in Caesarea may have thought Agabus's actions to be yet another sign from God to protect Paul. It was God's provision but not in the way they imagined. God was preparing Paul for the difficult road ahead. He would be imprisoned, but the believers in Jerusalem needed to receive encouragement and sound teaching. Paul was ready to be bound and even to die if it meant that by it more people would know redemption. He would have loved to stay among friends in Philip's house, but Paul had given his heart to God and was ready to obey.

Omniscient Father, let me be ready to die to self or even physically in order to bring Your rescue message to others. Amen.

Truth, Obedience, and Heart

*I have chosen the way of truth; Your judgments I have laid before me.
I cling to Your testimonies; O Lord, do not put me to shame! I will run
the course of Your commandments, for You shall enlarge my heart.*

PSALM 119:30–32 NKJV

The psalmist saw the options available, analyzed the repercussions of different ways of life, and chose the way of truth. Pascal's famous wager that it is safer to believe in God than not is too simplistic, too lacking in heart, for the psalmist. He laid God's judgments as though on a table before him, read diligently through His promises, and probed the accounts of His provision for His people from times past. The psalmist learned that with God there is grace and that this compassion is truth—an absolute that cannot be shaken.

Having such surety is priceless in a doubt-filled society, and we, too, must cling to the testimonies of God's love. He will not put us to shame if we follow through with His words but will instead put the Holy Spirit—the Helper and Comforter—to work in us. He will enlarge the hearts of those who choose the way of truth, giving them the strength to overcome challenges. Though it takes effort to discover and pursue the way of truth—a path that requires obedience and faith—it is the stuff that our hearts long for.

*Heart of my own heart, let me choose, cling to,
and run in the light of Your truth so that my heart
may be ready for all that You have to pour into it. Amen.*

First Day of Spring

Springtime for Us

*My beloved spoke, and said to me: "Rise up, my love, my fair one,
and come away. For lo, the winter is past, the rain is over and gone.
The flowers appear on the earth; the time of singing has come."*
SONG OF SOLOMON 2:10–12 NKJV

None capture the essence of this season quite as aptly as poets. Emily Dickenson writes of wholesome madness; Gerard Manley Hopkins summons its "juice and joy" and sees it as a reminder of Eden. In King Solomon's song, considered a poetic interpretation of Jesus and the Church, the Beloved beckons His love to him with the coming of spring. Shoots of green color the sky, and flowers awake to share their fragrances and their petal splendor. The time proves to be a reminder that God has designed renewal into His creation on a cosmic scale.

There will not always be cold and darkness. The Light has come, and He calls out to those He loves to come with Him, to rise out of darkness at His voice. He entreats them to sing alongside Him with the birds that have returned from their winter homes and to dance with the trees and the hills. Sing, beloved daughter of God. Sing to Him even in your mourning. This is a time of rebirth, and we have been born again in Christ.

*Beloved, thank You for the newness of life this season brings.
I feel Your presence this first day of spring, but I await
Your final call to live in eternal spring with You. Amen.*

Uprooting Bitterness

*Pursue peace with all people, and holiness, without which no
one will see the Lord: looking carefully lest anyone fall short
of the grace of God; lest any root of bitterness springing
up cause trouble, and by this many become defiled.*
HEBREWS 12:14–15 NKJV

The character of Janie in Zora Neale Hurston's novel *Their Eyes Were Watching God* comes to a realization on the death of her second husband. If she had known some other way to speak to him and not let all the bitterness stored up for years burst out, his face may have been more peaceful. She thought she was pursuing peace by avoiding confrontation, but it was not a true peace. Janie kept building on her bitterness until it burst. Her tirade at her husband's deathbed held a good deal of truth, but it came too harshly and much too late.

The author of the book of Hebrews firmly warns readers to avoid letting even the smallest bit of bitterness take root because it has such a devastating effect. Pursuing godly peace—redemptive, reconciliatory peace, not just letting people take advantage—is part of the holiness the Spirit is working in our hearts. Many are defiled by or fall prey to the ravages of bitterness, preventing them from enjoying life as God intended. We are called to seek peace with all people because that is exactly what God is doing: bringing people into peace with Himself.

*God of Peace, pull out my roots of bitterness.
You died to bring me peace; let my selfishness die daily
to know this peace and to share it with others. Amen.*

To Make the Dry Flourish

"And all the trees of the field shall know that I, the LORD,
have brought down the high tree and exalted the low tree,
dried up the green tree and made the dry tree flourish;
I, the LORD, have spoken and have done it."
EZEKIEL 17:24 NKJV

In this season of nature's glory—the growing, the greening, the budding—God uses a nature metaphor to explain His judgments and His mercy. People, like trees, are a variety of shapes, sizes, colors, and temperaments. Some are proud and others humble. But unlike the course of nature, God promises to bring back to life what has dried up. He is, after all, the Author and has the power to change the nature of things.

He promises to humble the high, proud, and prosperous who boast in their own strength, who seek to make profit while others suffer. But those who are poor in spirit, who feel their strength withered and their hope gone, these He will exalt. He will encourage the poor and oppressed through His Spirit and will make them flourish.

It is spring and the time for grafting. God will cut what is exteriorly beautiful but not productive and add to His Church those who are willing to grow and produce fruit. The Lord spoke these promises to the prophet Ezekiel and has already accomplished them through Jesus. He continues to bring renewal to those who are dry and worn out.

Father, when I am proud, bring me to Yourself, and when I am dry,
pour Your living water over my parched soul. Amen.

Revealing and Healing

"Call to Me, and I will answer you, and show you great and
mighty things, which you do not know. . . . I will bring [them]
health and healing; I will heal them and reveal to them
the abundance of peace and truth."
JEREMIAH 33:3, 6 NKJV

God again beckons His people to put Him to the test. He wants His daughters to call to Him so that He can answer them. He longs to show them great and mighty things. One of these great and mighty things is healing—both physical and spiritual. Part of healing includes an abundant knowledge and experience of God's peace and truth.

In Jeremiah 33 God told the prophet His plans to restore Jerusalem, to bring the people back from captivity in Babylon and to forgive their rebelliousness. He promised mercy and the coming of a descendent of King David who would be called the Branch of Righteousness and who would rule in joy. Chapter 33 bursts with the beauty of God's grace as it points forward to the great plan of rescue, not just for the Jewish people captured by the Babylonian King Nebuchadnezzar during Jeremiah's time, but to the salvation of creation through Messiah Jesus. God accomplished in Jesus the mightiest of deeds, a plan for redemption which we could never imagine. Through Jesus, God revealed to us, daughters of Eve, peace and truth since He is the Prince of Peace and the Way of truth.

Lord of our righteousness, thank You for the
beautiful picture of healing in Jeremiah 33 and
for its fulfillment in Jesus. Keep healing! Amen.

Comfort of Darkness

For as many as are led by the Spirit of God, these are [daughters] of God. For you did not receive the spirit of bondage again to fear, but you received the Spirit of adoption by whom we cry out, "Abba, Father."
ROMANS 8:14–15 NKJV

John Bunyan describes a character in *Pilgrim's Progress* who is so preoccupied with his work of cleaning the rubbish that he does not see the angel trying to place a crown on his head. Christians often become so engrossed with the things around them that they forget God may have something better planned, or they are too comfortable where they are and they fear change even for the good.

Bulcsú, in Nimród Antal's 2003 film *Kontroll*, spends his whole existence underground as a ticket inspector of the Budapest metro stations. Although he does honest and noble work that is less than appreciated, he is possessed by a fear of leaving the metro. He would rather stay in the comfort of darkness and fight the evil he thinks he knows than to come into the unknown, all-exposing light. Someone eventually comes down to give him courage.

Paul also encourages believers that the Spirit of God has come from above to free them from fear. We are adopted by God, who as a loving Father wants to bring us out of darkness into His marvelous light. We must not cling to our comfort or our definition of good. The light may be blinding at times, but it is preferable to a spirit of fear that kills hope.

Abba, thank You for bringing me out of darkness.
Remove any fear and doubt. Amen.

Under Vine and Fig Tree

" 'And I will remove the iniquity of that land in one day.
In that day,' says the LORD of hosts, 'everyone will invite
his neighbor under his vine and under his fig tree.' "
ZECHARIAH 3:9–10 NKJV

The context of today's scripture is the prophet Zechariah's vision in which he saw Satan accusing Joshua, the high priest of Israel. Joshua was clothed in filthy garments, which represented his sin and thus revealed his inadequacy in serving as the spiritual leader of God's people. However, God rejected Satan's accusations and commanded that new clothes be given to Joshua. God took away his sins and gave him another chance to be the high priest. He promised to soon send His servant the Branch, at which time the sins of the people would be removed in a single day and there would be rejoicing.

About five hundred years later, Jesus came as the promised Branch of the family tree of King David. Through His sacrifice, our sins were removed and we were washed clean. In Hebrew the names Joshua and Jesus are the same: Yeshua, meaning "God who saves." Where earthly high priests, like Joshua of Zechariah's time, failed to bring redemption for people, Jesus, as the true High Priest (see Hebrews 7) and as the God who saves, offered Himself and made a way back to God. Now it is time to invite our neighbors to celebrate under our "vine and fig tree."

God of angel armies, thank You that where spiritual
leaders on earth fail, You sent Jesus to remind
us that You are the One who saves. Amen.

Immortal Diamond

Therefore we also, since we are surrounded by so great a cloud of witnesses, let us lay aside every weight, and the sin which so easily ensnares us, and let us run with endurance the race that is set before us, looking unto Jesus, the author and finisher of our faith, who for the joy that was set before Him endured the cross, despising the shame, and has sat down at the right hand of the throne of God. For consider Him who endured such hostility from sinners against Himself, lest you become weary and discouraged in your souls.
HEBREWS 12:1-3 NKJV

Sin easily ensnares. It is in the very fibers of fallen nature. Faithful daughters of God cannot help becoming tired in the battle of the race. They keep getting caught in the traps. Often their legs give out and the dust of the track covers them. Their hearts are not break proof. Yet they endure, not due to strength of their own but because they trust Jesus as Author and finisher of their story of faith. Jesus saw the joy at the end. He endured the pain and the shame so that we could become His and inherit His beauty. He sees the joy waiting for us not just at the end but even as we learn and grow closer to Him through the difficulties. We become more like Him: no longer "fading flesh, potsherd, matchwood, and ash," but in the words of Gerard Manley Hopkins, immortal diamond.

Great Author, help me not succumb to weariness and discouragement. Make me more like You, to endure for a hidden but lasting joy. Amen.

Surety in Spring

"Oh, that we might know the LORD! Let us press on
to know him. He will respond to us as surely as the
arrival of dawn or the coming of rains in early spring."
HOSEA 6:3 NLT

Here the prophet clearly identifies seeking God—pressing on to know Him—with the coming of spring. His response is just as certain as the coming of spring. The Old Testament book of Hosea focuses on the themes of God's judgment but ultimate plans for restoration. The people of God during Hosea's time allowed themselves to be influenced by the pagan practices around them, engaging in pleasure seeking activities and forgetting the goodness of God's provision for them up to the present time. God's love for them is revealed in His constant petitions for them to turn away from the things causing them pain. Whenever God allowed the winter of slavery on His people, He always brought spring. He tore but brought healing; broke the rebellious and then bound up the brokenhearted. The prophet laments the people's indifference and pleads with them to know their God again—to love Him as they did at first. God's response to those who press to know Him is as sure and as beautiful as the coming of early spring. His daughters have but to know Him and they will experience this surety.

My Surety, let me press on in knowing You. Hear the questions of
my heart and respond in the beauty and hope of renewal. Amen.

Stardust

"And take heed, lest you lift your eyes to heaven, and when you see the sun, the moon, and the stars, all the host of heaven, you feel driven to worship them and serve them, which the Lord your God has given to all the peoples under the whole heaven as a heritage."
DEUTERONOMY 4:19 NKJV

The Maker has given us beautiful things. Nature in all its spring glory is at its prime, while the creations of the created—the ever-progressing technology—continue to astound and captivate. Humans have a frightening tendency to turn these often beautiful things into idols.

In the Old Testament the physical worship of nature was prevalent among other nations, which is why God warns the Israelites through Moses not to "feel driven" to serve the sun, moon, and stars. They are nothing apart from God but were meant to bring Him honor and to bring us closer to Him as we see nature reflect His might and beauty. They are the heritage, God's gift, to the people on earth. There is, however, one star we are to worship: "A Star shall come out of Jacob; a Scepter shall rise out of Israel" (Numbers 24:17 NKJV). In the book of Revelation Jesus reveals that He is this Star and says, "I am the Root and the Offspring of David, the Bright and Morning Star" (Revelation 22:16 NKJV). He broke through the darkness, turning people to righteousness, and calls us to do the same (see Daniel 12:3). We are not only dust but stardust—exhibiting parts of our Creator.

Abba, may we share of the Star that is in us. Amen.

Le Concert

Indeed it came to pass, when the trumpeters and singers were as one, to make one sound to be heard in praising and thanking the LORD, and when they lifted up their voice with the trumpets and cymbals and instruments of music, and praised the LORD, saying: "For He is good, for His mercy endures forever," that the house, the house of the LORD, was filled with a cloud.
2 CHRONICLES 5:13 NKJV

Journalist and historian Ioana Haşu described the interactions of humans as being similar to instruments in an orchestra. Humanity was created to play in harmony with one another and with God. Each person, as each instrument, has the gift of a different sound, a unique contribution to the melody. The crucial part is their need to work hard, work together, and sacrifice their pride and selfishness. Humans are meant to be instruments of God's grace, but they unfortunately forget their part. In Genesis 49:5 (NKJV) the patriarch Jacob calls two of his sons, Simeon and Levi, instruments of cruelty for the way they deceived and slaughtered a neighboring tribe. By contrast, the daughters of God must seek to be instruments of joy and peace. Whether a percussion piece or a wind or string instrument, they should come together as one in praising God. When the Israelites were united in their thanks and honoring of God, He came among them in the cloud. His presence is powerfully felt when we are similarly united.

Greatest Conductor, help Your daughters follow the beat of Your heart and remain united in praising and thanking You. Amen.

Prayer as Seeking

So He said to them, "When you pray, say: Our Father in heaven,
hallowed be Your name. Your kingdom come. Your will be done
on earth as it is in heaven. . . . And forgive us our sins, for we
also forgive everyone who is indebted to us. And do not lead
us into temptation, but deliver us from the evil one."
LUKE 11:2, 4 NKJV

This month the devotions largely focused on seeking God and His wisdom. However, the intricacies of this seeking point to the centrality of prayer in the life of a Christian, since prayer was an essential part of Jesus' ministry on earth. His disciples recognized the importance and asked Jesus to teach them how to pray. The well-known "Lord's Prayer" was His answer.

Believers draw closer to God through prayer as they confess their brokenness. They accept His authority through initiating the act of conversation, and their love for and reverence of Him grow as the conversations become more frequent and sincere.

Prayer brings Christians into fellowship with God, but it also results in their being better neighbors as they learn to forgive, to petition for, and to love those around them. At the University of St Andrews in Scotland, the Christian Union organized morning prayer meetings twice a week where students were encouraged to pray for friends who didn't know Jesus and where they were able to share the fruit of those prayers at subsequent meetings. Being diligent in prayer is hard, but the results are beautiful.

We praise You, Abba, for Your mercy in Your holiness.
Teach Your children how to pray. Amen.

Alert Ears and Obedient Hearts

"He who has an ear, let him hear
what the Spirit says to the churches."
REVELATION 3:22 NKJV

Jesus addresses the seven churches of Ephesus, Smyrna, Pergamos, Thyatira, Sardis, Philadelphia, and Laodicea in chapters 2 and 3 of the book of Revelation. He reveals what is good and what is failing in each community, ending with a statement of hope for those who listen and endure in the faith. To each church He repeats today's scripture. Poetically, the repetition sounds good, but repeated phrases are never superfluous in the Bible. The Spirit is speaking these words of warning. As the promised Comforter and Helper, the Spirit was sent to make our hearts sensitive to sin and then seek repentance.

The admonitions toward these early churches are relevant throughout history. Christians must not leave our first love and passion for Jesus (Ephesus), and risk thinking we are okay when we are spiritually dead (Sardis). Churchgoers must avoid the lukewarmness of the Laodiceans who relied on their wealth but were in fact "wretched, miserable, poor, blind, and naked" (Revelation 3:17 NKJV). In poverty believers must be rich in faith (as the believers in Smyrna) and guard against false doctrines (what the churches in Pergamos and Thyatira failed to do). Though we may have little strength, we must remain faithful to Jesus' words and persevere like the Philadelphians. In the end, may Jesus recognize us for our "love, service, faith, and. . .patience" and say that our latter works are more than the first (Revelation 2:19 NKJV).

Head of the Church, let me hear with my heart and obey. Amen.

Return

*"So you, by the help of your God, return; observe mercy
and justice, and wait on your God continually."*
HOSEA 12:6 NKJV

Though the earth may be bursting forth with life, you may feel as distant and gray as the ocean's horizon on a January day. In our society where it's all about us, our happiness, and our well-being, we forget that a lasting relationship takes effort.

God has given us many analogies about our relationship with Him: Father and child, Shepherd and sheep, Master and servant. Children rebel, sheep wander, and servants run away. When we don't feel close to God, it's easy to think He has exited stage left, but this is a lie. We are the ones who move, leave, and stray from our relationship with Him. We skitter and play too close to the line of sin; and the more we hang out around that line, the more blurred it becomes. Rather than asking the Lord, "How far can I flee from this temptation?" we tend to ask, "How close can I get without technically sinning?"

We have a Savior who freed us from the chains and bondage of sin. Search your heart for areas that you have strayed, then repent and return to your God.

*Father, forgive me for straying. Place a thirst in my soul to
never stray again. I need You, though it is hard for
my prideful self to admit; I need You. Amen.*

Remembering Works

Sing to Him, sing psalms to Him; talk of all His wondrous works!
Glory in His holy name; let the hearts of those rejoice who seek
the Lord! Seek the Lord and His strength; seek His face evermore!
Remember His marvelous works which He has done,
His wonders, and the judgments of His mouth.
1 CHRONICLES 16:9–12 NKJV

We as selfish sinners really enjoy singing our own praises. It is fun, seemingly fulfilling, but is it healthy? When we don't see God's hand in small and significant events, we inevitably take credit or give credit to the wrong source. The kings prior to David took the credit and utterly disregarded God's hand in their lives and Israel's triumphs.

Our Lord is much too great, holy, righteous, and wise to not be recognized. Once we realize our complete dependence on God, this is when we truly seek Him. In today's passage David calls us to seek His presence continually. Why? Because there is nothing that exists outside of our Lord. If we are to find strength, purpose, and wonders, they are to be found in the Lord. We might find counterfeits in other areas, but they ultimately lead to a dead end and emptiness. At these hollow moments, we are like the prodigal son. We have the choice to run back to our Father, repent, and trust His sovereign character, or we search and find another false god. Satan is all too willing to give us another false god—a lifeless alternative. Will you abandon your pride, selfishness, and unbelief and run back to your Father, singing His praises?

Father, forgive me for disregarding Your glory and majesty.
I become wrapped up in my personal ambitions and shove You
to the side. Lord, I need You more than I need breath. Amen.

Holy Bowl

*In that day "HOLINESS TO THE LORD" shall be engraved on
the bells of the horses. The pots in the LORD's house shall be like
the bowls before the altar. Yes, every pot in Jerusalem and Judah
shall be holiness to the LORD of hosts. Everyone who sacrifices shall
come and take them and cook in them. In that day there shall no
longer be a Canaanite in the house of the LORD of hosts.*

ZECHARIAH 14:20–21 NKJV

If we are honest with ourselves, we don't think of things in terms of
"holy" and "unholy." Holiness is a concept that is uncomfortable for
most of us. What is holy? We know that God is "holy, holy, holy" and
He calls us to be holy. The prophet Zechariah sheds some light on
what is holy. Holy is anything consecrated or dedicated to the Lord
and for His glory. The high priest used to wear a plaque that had
"HOLINESS TO THE LORD" engraved on it.

Use what you have for God's glory. It doesn't matter if you are a
janitor, lawyer, mother, teacher, or brain surgeon. Your skills and gifts
are from the Lord and for the Lord.

*Lord, help me to live a life that is set apart for You. May my
focus be only on You. Help me to pause during the day
and reflect on Your goodness and steadfast love. Amen.*

Silent Fight

"The LORD will fight for you,
and you shall hold your peace."
EXODUS 14:14 NKJV

In this day and age when action is so heavily stressed, it is hard for us to wrap our heads around the thought of not acting. Is this truly what the Lord commands of us in times of struggle? Waiting on God's will and timing is one of the hardest acts.

We must remember God's might and power. He created the very atoms of the ground we tread, and if we are honest, there are many times we stomp around creating chaos in our lives when all we seek is order. The thought of ceasing from our plans and obeying God's will is frightening. We have an idea of the road God wishes us to walk and it's far outside our comfort zone. But then, think of the times we wrestled with His plan, gave in, and rejoiced in His work! When God calls us to reach outside of ourselves and forgive or trust, it tears us from our selfish pride, rids us of embittered desires, and cleanses the channels of our hearts. We must trust that the most strenuous and arduous tasks God gives us will bear the most fruit and draw us closer to Him. To know that the God of the universe fights for us, undeserving sinners, leaves us astounded.

Father, thank You for listening to my prayers!
Thank You for never forsaking me even in the fight.
You are a great and gracious Father! Amen.

Blinded Heart

*And David's heart condemned him after he had numbered
the people. So David said to the Lord, "I have sinned greatly
in what I have done; but now, I pray, O Lord, take away the
iniquity of Your servant, for I have done very foolishly."*
2 Samuel 24:10 nkjv

God knew David's heart. He knew David's prideful and selfish motives
in numbering the Israelites. We are fools to think that our motives go
unnoticed. Sin is alluring. Though from the outside we may be giving of
our time and resources, if we act out of false motives it is abominable
in the Lord's sight. We become the ultimate weasel.

David's response to his sin is utter humility and repentance. When
at the feet of the holy God, one who has granted mercy and grace, the
only thing we can do is stand in horror of our sin. David pleads with
the Lord, not as a groveling slave but as a convicted, sincere servant.
"Take away my iniquity" is David's cry, because if we truly know and
love the Lord, our sin will be odious to us.

Don't keep old and comfortable sins at arm's length. Plead for
the Lord to take them away and remove them as far as the east is
from the west. The Lord will not draw near to those whose hearts
are far from Him.

*Lord, please show me where I hold sin too close, and help me
to break the chains. Father, I wish to be closer with You than
any other person in my life. Help me to see the areas
of my heart where sin has blinded me. Amen.*

He Can Do All

*Then Job answered the L*ORD *and said: "I know that You can do everything, and that no purpose of Yours can be withheld from You."*
JOB 42:1–2 NKJV

Do we live in the knowledge that the Lord can do all things? Or do we walk each day hesitantly, as though He won't provide or will not answer our call? So very often we doubt, and our faith is small. How is it that we can worship such a great, vast God and have such a tiny belief?

Our unbelief robs God of His due glory and honor and it chains us to insecurity. There is nothing more powerful than the Lord; do we live as though this is truth? We store up so much knowledge of God's Word and promises in our heads, but we never let them settle and grow in our hearts. We keep them stashed away as nice facts that we can access when sorrow sets in, like aspirin for muscle pain, but we do not live by them. We need the Lord to help us place them in our hearts, as a seal. We need Him to help us bind them around our necks so that we are ever conscious of the Lord.

Father, there are many times that I act and believe that You are not in control of a situation. I run around trying to fix things and end up making it worse. Lord, forgive me, and help me to pause, pray, and listen for Your instruction. Amen.

Not Our Own

"Yet I am the Lord your God ever since the land of Egypt, and you shall know no God but Me; for there is no savior besides Me. I knew you in the wilderness, in the land of great drought."
HOSEA 13:4–5 NKJV

In our current culture, discrediting God is a popular pastime. We as sinners do not like to admit that we were created. The idea that we are not ruler of our lives makes us squirm. We want to rule our own destiny. This is an alluring temptation, and one that we all too often give in to.

There is no savior but God. So why do we turn to other things for help? If we are honest with ourselves, it is because we want to feel in control and reap the glory. The faster we realize our struggle with pride and unbelief, the closer we come to repentance and restoration.

We will only trust the Lord as much as we know Him. Strive to know Him more this year. When you examine the scriptures, search for God's character, not His actions. Attributes such as steadfast, unchangeable, wise, righteous, and untamed are only a few. God has known us "in the wilderness" and "in the land of great drought"; it is time to know Him.

Father, I admit that I do not know You as well as I think. Forgive me for making You second or third in my priorities. Amen.

Covenant

He has sent redemption to His people; He has commanded
His covenant forever: holy and awesome is His name.
PSALM 111:9 NKJV

Covenant is a word we stumble upon throughout scripture, but have we paused to examine its true meaning? We see God make covenants with Moses and Abraham in the Old Testament, and this same covenant is referenced as Israel strays from the Lord. *Covenant* is a bond beyond conditions and feelings; it is an unconditional reliance and relationship.

When we give our lives to Christ, we enter into a covenant with Him. Christ said that following Him would not be easy; there will be suffering and hardship. But we stand and rest in His unshakable character, power, and steadfast love. Our covenant with Him does not release us to chase after old sins. No, we must strive to know Him more each day. This is more than religion; it is a relationship with a holy and righteous God. We were created for this relationship. This does not mean we won't be tempted or we won't stumble, but we do have a Redeemer and lover of our souls. We are now free to follow Christ, to turn from sin, because He has conquered sin and death. Praise the Lord for a covenant relationship and covenant love.

Father, forgive me for breaking this covenant. Thank You that
You are unchangeable and faithful. Help me to seek You each day.
I wish to grow in my relationship and walk with You. Amen.

Light of the Morning

"The God of Israel said, the Rock of Israel spoke to me: 'He who rules over men must be just, ruling in the fear of God. And he shall be like the light of the morning when the sun rises, a morning without clouds, like the tender grass springing out of the earth, by clear shining after rain.' "
2 SAMUEL 23:3–4 NKJV

Spring moseys its way to our doors. Maybe it's a crocus on a morning walk or a waft of lilac in the breeze, but there are hopeful signs of spring. King David used creation for descriptors because creation simply magnifies the beauty and majesty of the Creator.

Our God is just. We as followers of Christ and children of God must know and pursue God as He is revealed in the scriptures. His justice is like the light of the morning. The rising sun is constant; our Savior is constant. The same justice He gave to the Israelites is the same justice He gives to us. Know that there will be darkness, there will be night, but morning comes.

Do not live this day as if it were your own; live it in the knowledge that your thoughts and actions are all performed before a holy and just God.

Lord, thank You for the beauty of Your creation. Thank You that it reminds me of Your promises that, though seemingly dormant, spring forth overnight. Lord, help me to live a daily life aware of You and dedicated to Your will. Amen.

Passover begins at sundown

Workmanship

For we are His workmanship, created in Christ Jesus for good works,
which God prepared beforehand that we should walk in them.
EPHESIANS 2:10 NKJV

Has anyone asked you, "What is your five-year or ten-year plan?" This is a popular interview question because it shows what goals you wish to achieve and how you are going to achieve them. The heart of this question touches on a person's purpose in life. Does she have drive and ambition? What is the point of existing?

As Paul writes to the Ephesians, he reveals what we are; we are God's "workmanship." He crafted us for His purpose to do "good works," works that He planned before time. Let's define "good works." A good work is simply responding and acting in the most Christlike manner. Christ embodies servanthood, and most of our prideful hearts and minds do not wish to be a servant, or if we do, it's on our own terms and within our comfort zone. But if we truly love and walk with the Father, we will desire to do the good works He sets before us.

Take time to meditate on services or good works that God has called you to, whether at home, in school, or in the workplace. How did you respond? Did you obey or disregard the call? Know that God has crafted you specifically for these tasks. How does this truth change your outlook and response to good works?

Lord, do I disregard Your call? Show me how to obey You.
Please change my heart to be Your servant. Amen.

Set Yourself Up

"Now set your heart and your soul to seek the LORD your God. Therefore arise and build the sanctuary of the LORD God, to bring the ark of the covenant of the LORD and the holy articles of God into the house that is to be built for the name of the LORD."
1 CHRONICLES 22:19 NKJV

So much of our work and service for the Lord is attitude. When it comes to money, the difference between saving and hoarding is attitude. Here in 1 Chronicles, David, a man after God's own heart, instructs Israel to "set" their hearts and minds to seek the Lord before preparing His temple. Do we take the same mind-set when going to church on Sunday or doing daily devotions? Or have these times with God become a check box on our schedules?

There is a fine line between worship and obligation. You know when someone is simply going through the motions; how much more does our Lord? Seeking God does not come naturally for us, and we must prepare ourselves. There will always be something seemingly urgent when you sit down to pray or read scripture. There will always be a distraction. These are Satan's tactics; he wants nothing more than to distract you from precious time with God. In those moments, cry out to your Father and ask for focus. This is not weakness; it is intimacy—intimacy that we desperately need.

Lord, I wish to know You more intimately. Show me and help me to set my heart to seek You throughout the day. Amen.

Upheld

*And so it was, when Moses held up his hand, that Israel prevailed;
and when he let down his hand, Amalek prevailed. But Moses'
hands became heavy; so they took a stone and put it under him,
and he sat on it. And Aaron and Hur supported his hands,
one on one side, and the other on the other side; and his hands
were steady until the going down of the sun. So Joshua defeated
Amalek and his people with the edge of the sword.*

EXODUS 17:11–13 NKJV

As God placed Aaron and Hur at Moses' side, so He places our friends and family to support us when we simply can't lift a hand. We were created to be a part of the body of Christ, whether that be a large church in Tennessee or an underground gathering in East Asia. There will be numerous times in our lives when the Lord doesn't stop our personal battles; instead, He gives us the resources to finish the fight.

Isolation is a dangerous way to live. We are most vulnerable when alone, and most susceptible to temptation. Satan wants you to think that no one else in the church can relate to your circumstances. He wants you to continue in silence; it's where he is most effective. But, if like Moses we allow our fellow brothers and sisters in Christ to support us and we lean on them for encouragement and wisdom, we can endure the suffering. Do not estrange yourself from the body of Christ; it is one way the Lord continually calls to us and provides for us.

*Lord, thank You for the body of Christ. Thank You for adopting
me into Your family. Father, forgive me when I have taken my
brothers and sisters in Christ for granted, and help me to
engage in the church, rather than estrange myself. Amen.*

Let All Things Be Silent

"And the Lord will take possession of Judah as His inheritance in the Holy Land, and will again choose Jerusalem. Be silent, all flesh, before the Lord, for He is aroused from His holy habitation!"
ZECHARIAH 2:12–13 NKJV

Throughout scripture we see the command to "be silent" or "be still." Have you ever taken a moment to meditate on and ponder this command? Why silence? In silence there is self-control, awareness, focus, wonder, awe, and deference. The God of the universe, all-powerful (omnipotent), all-knowing (omniscient), and all-being (omnipresent) deserves our thoughts and meditation. When we take the time to focus and listen, we glorify Him. No, there may not be a resounding voice that echoes in your soul, but when you dwell on God's character and His promises, you become more aware of and intimate with Him.

Intimacy with God is not easy. As women, we are highly relational, not in a groveling, clinging way, but we thrive on relationship. For some, intimacy with others has led to deep hurt. Intimacy involves vulnerability, and for some of us that is a tall order. We must be vulnerable with our Savior; it is the only way to grow closer to Him. Christianity is not a religion. It is a relationship with God that glorifies Him and fulfills our purpose.

Father, I pray that I can draw closer to You. I admit that I have shut myself off from Your presence and from my walk with You, and it has left me empty. Forgive me for leaving. Help me to seek You each day. I do not have the strength to, but I trust in You and cry out for help. Amen.

Good Friday

Three Days

In Him was life, and the life was the light of men. The light shines in the darkness, and the darkness did not comprehend it.
JOHN 1:4–5 NKJV

Jesus is hope, the hope for eternal life. Hope for redemption, that the lives we lead aren't worthless. God has set eternity in man's heart; that's why we all search for something more, something deeper than ourselves. It's not enough to be born, live a life, and die. We were never made to exist; we were created to live. The only hope of eternity rested with Jesus, and on Good Friday more than two thousand years ago, He died. The Man many had placed their hope and trust in was crucified by those He came to save. Like a candle, their hope was squelched. For three days they lived in the knowledge that there was no heaven, that what they faced at the end of their days was hell, no matter how hard they worked, how much they prayed, or how giving they were. Without Christ, there is no heaven. For three days the world was cloaked in darkness, both physical and spiritual. For three days there was no hope.

I have never lived without hope. I was born into sin, but I was also born into hope. I have never lived without hope, because on the third day Christ rose from the grave. Jesus faced death for me. I can write as many descriptions and metaphors about death. But here is the beauty in death; it is not the winner. Christ's death and resurrection turned death from a gaping mouth into an open door. A door that leads to eternity, to the life we were created to live.

Thank You, Lord, for hope in You. You are the greatest gift ever given to mankind. Thank You. Amen.

Most Satisfied

Oh, the depth of the riches both of the wisdom and knowledge
of God! How unsearchable are His judgments and His ways
past finding out! "For who has known the mind of the LORD?
Or who has become His counselor?" "Or who has first given to
Him and it shall be repaid to him?" For of Him and through
Him and to Him are all things, to whom be glory forever. Amen.
ROMANS 11:33–36 NKJV

We know that no one has lent God anything, nor has anyone given God advice. We were made in His image, but He is nothing like us and we are nothing like Him.

Everything, from the bright spring breeze to a newborn's laugh, was created by Him. God does not depend on anyone or anything. It is because He doesn't rely on anyone that He can love perfectly. How often do we seek man's acceptance over God's acceptance? If we are honest with ourselves, we do this daily. How often are our motives tainted with manipulation because we want to please or be pleased?

God is impervious to manipulation; it is not in His character. He will never tweak His ways to get us to like or accept Him. His complete independency means we can trust His love. He withholds things for our good; He grants things for our good. But don't miss the pinnacle part of Paul's message, "to whom be glory forever." Everything you do as a child of God is for His glory, and everything God does is for His glory. We are most satisfied when God is most glorified.

Thank You for withholding and giving me things that are only for
Your glory and my good. Help me to find peace in the trying times
and know that You are faithful, even in the midst of the storm. Amen.

Anchor

This hope we have as an anchor of the soul, both sure and steadfast, and which enters the Presence behind the veil, where the forerunner has entered for us, even Jesus, having become High Priest forever according to the order of Melchizedek.

HEBREWS 6:19-20 NKJV

We have this hope, not "we will" or "we had." As children of God we possess Christ as the anchor of our souls. The "veil" referred to was a physical, thick curtain that separated the holy of holies from the rest of the tabernacle. Only once a year could the high priest enter after being cleansed. Christ tore that veil in two with His sinless life, death, and resurrection. He opened the gates to a relationship with His Father. This is the good news that we now have a Redeemer who has brought us in relationship with the Father. Not a relationship that brings superhuman powers, but the defeat of sin. We can now enter the Lord's presence and, because of Christ, be seen as blameless. None of us has led a blameless life, which is why God sent His Son to do so for us. The debt that God demanded He also paid. What wondrous love is this that He would pay what we owe!

In Christ, we face each day redeemed. Have you taken the time to praise Him?

I praise You, Lord, that You and no one else is my anchor! Thank You for redeeming us, for coming to this earth and defeating sin! Amen.

Woe Be Gone

How long, O LORD? Will You forget me forever? How long will You hide Your face from me? . . . But I have trusted in Your mercy; my heart shall rejoice in Your salvation. I will sing to the LORD, because He has dealt bountifully with me.

PSALM 13:1, 5–6 NKJV

One misconception our society has about Christianity is that Christians have to be happy all the time, no matter the circumstances. Is it biblical to question God? Is it biblical to mourn?

We see throughout scripture mourning, frustration, righteous anger, and tears. The shortest verse in the Bible is "Jesus wept" (John 11:35). Our goal as a child of God is to glorify our Savior, not wear a plastered smile around town. Being sorrowful or frustrated is not sin, but how you handle these emotions can lead to sin.

In Psalms, David asks the Lord many times if He has forsaken him. We watch David question the Lord, then explain his troubles, pain, and circumstances. Always near the end of a psalm, David revisits God's great character and works. Loving-kindness, salvation, bountiful. . .he reflects, remembers, and trusts in God. We must do the same when God appears distant. Reflect on the God of the scriptures and the wonders He has done in your life.

Father, You never said it would be easy following You. Thank You for not lying, and thank You for life in Christ. I won't always understand, but help me to walk by faith and not by sight. Amen.

Behold Your God

He will swallow up death forever, and the Lord GOD will wipe away tears from all faces; the rebuke of His people He will take away from all the earth; for the LORD has spoken. And it will be said in that day: "Behold, this is our God; we have waited for Him, and He will save us. This is the LORD; we have waited for Him; we will be glad and rejoice in His salvation."

ISAIAH 25:8–9 NKJV

The Lord has written the earth's story and has given us, His children, the manuscript. We were not created for death; the Lord has set eternity in our hearts. These days the world seems to set a price on our souls. We feel as though there is a great debt measured up against our time and energy, and we simply cannot devote any more of ourselves. But our God doesn't rely on time; time relies on Him. And the same grace and mercy He showed the Israelites is the same grace and mercy He bestows on us.

We wait for Him in storms, calm, calamity, and confusion; we wait for His return. He is our God. He can't be shaken, and though people try and deny the Lord, they are wishful thinkers. No science can equate His power; we can only glimpse what He desires to demonstrate in creation. And yet, this mighty Lord is also the God who wipes away our tears and purges the world of suffering. He is our God.

Lord, help me to wait patiently. Help me to remain faithful in these trying times. Thank You that You are God, and no one can change that fact. Amen.

Servant Minded

Let this mind be in you which was also in Christ Jesus, who, being in the form of God, did not consider it robbery to be equal with God, but made Himself of no reputation, taking the form of a bondservant, and coming in the likeness of men.
PHILIPPIANS 2:5–7 NKJV

If someone were to ask you, "Do you consider yourself equal to God?" your answer would be an emphatic, "No!" But how often do our actions overwrite our answer? Where do you tend to worry, fret, take hold, and micromanage? We subconsciously think we know best or have the most knowledge of our finances, children, job, husband, or friend. But as scripture constantly reminds us, the Lord knows every aspect of our being.

In his letter to the Philippians, Paul is not merely suggesting that we have a Christlike attitude; he is adamantly instructing us to take this mind-set and make it our daily thought process. Notice, Paul doesn't say, "This mind is already in you." Humility is not natural for us; it is at times the hardest part of our walk with the Lord.

If Christ, fully God and fully man, did not consider equality with God a thing to be obtained, why do we? Christ's humility is astounding! He is God, but He became a servant. How effective is a servant who continually wishes to be the master? Until we realize that our sinful nature is what prevents us from entering into a relationship with the Lord and living for His glory, then walking with our Savior is not a thing to be grasped.

Father, forgive me for trying to be You. Though I don't want to admit it, my pride is a great and daily struggle. Lord, help me to wait, listen, and obey. Amen.

In the Wind

Then He said, "Go out, and stand on the mountain before the Lord."
And behold, the Lord passed by, and a great and strong wind tore
into the mountains and broke the rocks in pieces before the Lord,
but the Lord was not in the wind; and after the wind an earthquake,
but the Lord was not in the earthquake; and after the earthquake
a fire, but the Lord was not in the fire; and after the fire a still small
voice. So it was, when Elijah heard it, that he wrapped his face in his
mantle and went out and stood in the entrance of the cave. Suddenly
a voice came to him, and said, "What are you doing here, Elijah?"
1 Kings 19:11–13 nkjv

We serve a great and powerful God, yet He is also a Father. God shows such compassion to Elijah in today's passage. He doesn't come in the fire, wind, or earthquake; He approaches Elijah as a father would approach a scared child. God comes in a whisper and asks a simple question: "What are you doing here, Elijah?"

God knew full well why Elijah had fled, but He wanted Elijah to examine the situation. This compassion and pure fatherly love is how God directs us. Like a father comforting a child, the Lord asks us to step back and look at the situation with Him. Our trouble is not near as great as our Father's. Our circumstances cannot trump Him or thwart His plan. God said it Himself, "I am, who I am." There is no beginning or end to our God, and all these circumstances and troubles are a part of His plan.

Thank You, Lord, for speaking to me in a still, small voice. You are
kind and compassionate to hear my cry, listen, and answer. Amen.

Slow to Speak

So then, my beloved brethren, let every man be swift
to hear, slow to speak, slow to wrath; for the wrath
of man does not produce the righteousness of God.
JAMES 1:19-20 NKJV

How quick are we to give an opinion or proffer our observation? How eager are we to hold our tongues, listen, and discern, like a cautious child crosses the street? More times than we realize or care to admit, our tongues run away with our hearts, and we find ourselves saying dishonoring statements.

This need to be right and to be heard comes from a selfish and unbelieving heart. If we truly believed that God is all-powerful and all-knowing, then why do we jump in and verbally take the reins? Perhaps, though we confess it with our mouths, we do not believe the Lord is at work in the matter.

Ask the Lord to empty you of words and thoughts that do not glorify and honor Him. We need forgiveness when we have spoken harshly, acted foolishly, and disobeyed. Our disobedience is a great grievance and it does hurt our Father, like a disobedient child who strays from her parents. As scripture says, the wrath of man does not produce righteousness. We need help to resist the temptation of gossip and slander. Ask the Lord to teach you how to be slow to speak and quick to listen.

Lord, I admit I am quick to speak and slow to listen. Forgive me
for this, Lord. I have hurt many with my words. Father, help me
listen and learn, rather than jump to conclusions. Amen.

Who Is It For?

"Say to all the people of the land, and to the priests: 'When you fasted and mourned in the fifth and seventh months during those seventy years, did you really fast for Me—for Me? When you eat and when you drink, do you not eat and drink for yourselves?' "

ZECHARIAH 7:5–6 NKJV

We severely kid ourselves if we think and act as though God cannot see or know our motives. But don't we live most of our lives in a concealed manner? What areas of your life do you withhold from the Lord, either intentionally or subconsciously? For most of us it's "mundane" things, such as our job, weight/self-image, chores, getting the car fixed, the morning rush to school or church. There are so many small areas in our lives that we don't offer to Christ either because we don't want to or don't see the need to. This is where we sin.

When we see something as being too menial for the Lord to concern Himself with, we take ownership and add it to our domain—a domain that becomes the "kingdom of self." Whether it is a long process or quick transition, our selfish and prideful hearts begin to harden. We begin to see ourselves as the authority in these small areas.

Ask the Lord to reveal where you rely on yourself and hold your opinion higher than His command. It is in these small and mundane areas that we build a stronger relationship with the Lord.

Lord, where do I hold myself higher than You? I know there have been numerous times I take the reins and want to drive, and it hasn't ended well. Father, forgive my pride and reveal the areas of my heart that must be surrendered to You. Amen.

Wilderness Bloom

The wilderness and the wasteland shall be glad for them,
and the desert shall rejoice and blossom as the rose; it shall blossom
abundantly and rejoice, even with joy and singing. The glory of
Lebanon shall be given to it, the excellence of Carmel and Sharon.
They shall see the glory of the LORD, the excellency of our God.
ISAIAH 35:1–2 NKJV

After the bleakness of winter, a small crocus blossoms and gives hope. We revel in its color and fragrance. We itch to wear sundresses, shorts, and sandals. There are times when our spiritual walk feels like a desert. There are few signs of life or progress, things are dry and brown, and it's hard to stay hopeful. But as Isaiah points out, God is our restorer and rainfall in a dry land. His glory makes our desert souls rejoice and blossom like the crocus.

The excitement you feel for the coming spring—have you ever felt that excited about your time with the Lord? Have you ever anticipated your daily devotion? Many times we treat scripture as a Band-Aid or medicine; we only read and pray when we feel the need to. The Word of the Lord is vastly more powerful and abundant than a quick fix. You will never know the extent of scripture if you only read the red letters or psalms. Scripture can make a desert heart blossom. Take time to analyze how and when you call upon the Lord. The majesty of our God is all around this spring.

Father, thank You for the blessing of spring!
I pray these coming days reveal the areas of my
heart that need Your tender care and tilling. Amen.

Wise Woman

Then a wise woman cried out from the city, "Hear, hear!
Please say to Joab, 'Come nearby, that I may speak with
you'.... I am among the peaceable and faithful in Israel.
You seek to destroy a city and a mother in Israel."

2 SAMUEL 20:16, 19 NKJV

In the midst of a siege on a city, the Lord sent an unlikely messenger to the commander of King David's army. A wise and courageous woman speaks into the chaos and preserves the city. She is Christ's calm in the storm, bringing reason into a tumultuous time.

We are called to be the calm in a storm. The only reason this woman could possibly speak with Joab amid the battle is through God's wisdom, power, and protection. She lays out the matter at hand before Joab and shows him his folly. She speaks the truth with grace and humility.

The same wisdom, power, and protection the Lord gave this wise woman He offers to you. In times of crisis, speaking and thinking rationally are difficult feats, but anchor your trust in the one and only unchanging God.

This woman did not demand; she did not provoke or diminish. She questioned Joab and asked for understanding. Our God is a God of understanding and wisdom, and though there are times He will not reveal the reason or purpose of an event, we must trust and rest in His unshakable character.

Lord, may I stop and consider Your wisdom and Your
teachings when I face uncertainties. Forgive me
for trusting in myself and not in You. Amen.

Tempted without Sin

Then Jesus was led up by the Spirit into
the wilderness to be tempted by the devil.
MATTHEW 4:1 NKJV

Christ, being fully God and fully man, could (1) as a man be tempted and (2) as God resist all temptation. But Christ didn't merely refuse to act on Satan's terms and lures; He had no inward desire or inclination to sin, since these in themselves are sin (see Matthew 5:22, 28). We follow a Shepherd who went His entire life without sin. Just because He was fully God does not mean He did not struggle with hunger, pain, or sorrow. We serve a Lord who entered into our humanity and can empathize with us. When we wish to discuss a certain matter—health issues, parenting, relocating our lives—we don't seek sympathy; we wish to hear wisdom and encouragement from someone who has been there. We seek empathy. Our Savior has tread this earth, defeated death and sin. We don't serve an oblivious lord. Our Lord knows the intricacies of our hearts.

Lord, thank You for knowing temptation and not succumbing.
Thank You that You know what is occurring and have planned this
time. Help me to trust in Your promises and great name. Amen.

The God Who Fills

The LORD is near to all who call upon Him, to all who call upon Him in truth. He will fulfill the desire of those who fear Him; He also will hear their cry and save them. The LORD preserves all who love Him, but all the wicked He will destroy. My mouth shall speak the praise of the LORD, and all flesh shall bless His holy name forever and ever.

PSALM 145:18–21 NKJV

Be near to me, Father; let Your presence encompass my soul. The nearness of You is my good; apart from You I wither like late autumn vines. It is a comfort to know that You will draw near and You will fulfill not only my needs but also my desires. The promises You give are sometimes the only lifeline I have.

More times than I like to admit I do not praise You, and to be honest, there are only few times in my life I can recall praising You with my whole being. Lord, I do not live in the knowledge of You. I put a greater score on others' opinions of me than I do on Yours. You made me in Your image and I am constantly being shaped and molded by Your hands. Help me to be malleable in Your hands, for my heart hardens to anything that threatens my comfort zone and selfish desires.

Lord, You have blessed me beyond belief. You have granted me freedom through Your Son. May I never stop speaking of You in my life. May I never stop recollecting Your steadfast love and faithfulness. Amen.

Strong Shepherd

Behold, the Lord God shall come with a strong hand, and His
arm shall rule for Him; behold, His reward is with Him, and His
work before Him. He will feed His flock like a shepherd; He will
gather the lambs with His arm, and carry them in His bosom,
and gently lead those who are with young.
ISAIAH 40:10–11 NKJV

Have you ever watched lambs play? They skip and bounce with newfound joy. It is hard not to smile as you watch their little jig. Today's passage from Isaiah shows some of God's characteristics. He is mighty, and not the fake bodybuilding mighty but a power and strength that is timeless and has no limit. We have only glimpsed the Lord's power in rainstorms and wind. He uses this might and power to lead His flock. What an oxymoron. The God of the universe uses His infinite strength to care for His flock, to "carry them in His bosom, and gently lead those who are with young."

His is not a passive shepherd. Throughout the verses we see God come with might; we see Him rule, tend, gather, carry, and lead. He is our Protector. Why would we ever want to stray from this shepherd? Unlike man, God does not abuse His power. Throughout scripture and history we see dictators rise and fall, kings and queens take advantage of the poor; yet our God is just. He rules and leads His flock and nothing is outside of His control, not even the heart and soul of a dictator.

Father, thank You for being a diligent and mighty Shepherd.
Help me to take these truths to heart so that I may
trust You more each day. Amen.

Peace Placement

And He shall stand and feed His flock in the strength of the Lord,
in the majesty of the name of the Lord His God; and they shall
abide, for now He shall be great to the ends of the earth.
MICAH 5:4 NKJV

Shepherds were not society's most desired company. They tended to be rough, ragged, scrappy men who lived in the wilderness with the livestock. When the prophet Micah prophesized about the coming Messiah, he used language that the Israelites would not have guessed; Jesus will shepherd, be great, be their peace.

What is your peace? Do you place peace in your work, accomplishments, talents, or money? There are numerous things that offer peace, though they are not peace. Christ doesn't just bring peace; it's who He is. What a remarkable God we have who is the essence of peace and love—two things we strive to gain. When we strive, we feel compelled to work for peace, love, or righteousness, and all our works fall short. Christ did not come to earth and die and rise again so that we could meet Him halfway in a bargain. No, His incarnation, death, and resurrection were to pay the full price for our sins.

Praise the Lord for taking my sins away. The debt that You
demanded, You also paid. Lord, this fact is astounding.
Forgive me for placing my trust and hope in false gods.
Reveal the areas of my heart where I have strayed from You. Amen.

Unshakable Character

*The Lord is my shepherd; I shall not want. He makes me to lie
down in green pastures; He leads me beside the still waters.*
PSALM 23:1-2 NKJV

This celebrated psalm is one we probably learned in Sunday school or have seen painted on mugs or pictures, but have we ever taken time to actually look at the words and the progression? What we learn from the first two verses tells much about God and ourselves.

The Lord is our shepherd. He is our caretaker, master, guide, protector, provider, and deliverer. This is what He is; He cannot be anything else. Because of God's unshakable character, He will never change, and thus we will not want.

As our Shepherd, what is the first thing He makes us do? He makes us lie down. This means rest and contentment. How many times do we try to control things, running around like bleating sheep trying to handle the situation? Our small faith and lack of trust leaves us haggard and exhausted. Our Shepherd makes us lie down. Rest, trust in His provision and power.

When we follow our Shepherd, where does He lead us? He leads us beside still waters, a place where things are calm and in His control. This is not to say being one of the flock is an easy lifestyle. When we follow our Shepherd, it may be by quiet streams or tumultuous chasms, but with Him we walk *through*. We won't be trapped or lost, because we walk with Him.

*Father, thank You for rest in You. Thank You for
being my Shepherd, for pursuing me when I run away.
You alone are my provider and protector. Amen.*

Happy Are the Poor

"Blessed are the poor in spirit, for theirs is the kingdom of heaven. Blessed are those who mourn, for they shall be comforted. Blessed are the meek, for they shall inherit the earth. Blessed are those who hunger and thirst for righteousness, for they shall be filled."
MATTHEW 5:3–6 NKJV

Today's verses, heard numerous times from the pulpit, are not placed haphazardly; there is a progression. Jesus uses these verses to outline how we become filled with Christ and develop a deeper relationship with the Father. In order to be filled with Christ, we must first be emptied. "Poor in spirit," is a sinner's realization that she brings nothing to the table to pay the debt. We cannot save ourselves, so who can? "Those who mourn"—we mourn our sin, that we have fallen away from the Father and cannot reconcile ourselves. "The meek"—there is nothing left to boast of, for we owe an unquenchable debt. These three verses point us to the resounding fact that we need a Savior. "Hunger and thirst for righteousness"—once emptied, we desire the righteousness only Christ can provide. We cannot chip in for our salvation, and to think we can offer payment is a gross affront to Christ's dignity and sacrifice. His death and resurrection are thus all the more beautiful and astounding.

Lord, empty me of all that does not glorify You.
I want these distractions and false idols to fall away.
I want to follow and listen to You. Lord, help me find
the time and quiet to meditate on Your Word. Amen.

Watch What You Think

Let this mind be in you,
which was also in Christ Jesus.
PHILIPPIANS 2:5 KJV

As a young bride, Sue stayed at home while her husband went to work every day. With time on her hands after she finished the housework, Sue began watching soap operas. She enjoyed the stories even though some of the scenes were sexually suggestive and left little to the imagination. Like many other women, Sue didn't realize how addictive this form of entertainment could become, affecting her thoughts even when she wasn't watching the programs.

Women of all ages are faced with images and words on a daily basis that affect their thought processes. In an age saturated with electronic devices, it has become easy to receive and send messages, videos, and photos in mere seconds. It's all too easy to join in with whatever others may be reading, tweeting, or posting.

Paul cautioned his readers to have the mind of Christ—a pure mind that is pleasing to God. When we find ourselves deluged with carnal images, it's time to allow Christ to take control of our thoughts. Satan will steal our minds and hearts if we aren't careful. Ask God to give you the mind of Christ so you can stay pure in an impure world.

Father, let the mind of Your Son, Jesus, be in me. Let my mind
be a place of pure thoughts and images that glorify You. Amen.

Love God First

Take good heed therefore unto yourselves,
that ye love the LORD your God.
JOSHUA 23:11 KJV

"I love my home. It's everything I've always wanted."

"I love new clothes. They make me feel special."

"I love my new diamond earrings."

"I love being a part of this group. It makes me feel important."

The word *love* is overused in the twenty-first century. If something is pleasing to us, we describe it by saying we love it. And we seem to acquire a lot of material possessions that we "love." There's nothing wrong with having nice things, but if we're not careful, our focus will center on things and not on God.

One reason we love all these possessions is because they feed a need in our lives—to have what others have, to feel important, to experience pleasure. Unfortunately, the need is bottomless. If we're not careful, we want more and more material possessions which only satisfy on a temporary basis.

The scripture today cautions us to take heed that we love the Lord our God. Don't allow temporary pleasures to take the place of God in your life. He's the only One who can fill that bottomless hole and make you feel complete.

Father, give me a craving for more of You.
Fill that emptiness in my heart with Your love.
Help me keep my priorities in the proper order. Amen.

Don't Refuse Instruction

Hear instruction, and be wise, and refuse it not.
PROVERBS 8:33 KJV

Have you ever made the statement, "I wish I had listened to what they told me." Most people have either spoken or had that thought at some point in their lives. When we're young and naive, we think we know more than our elders. As we grow and mature, we realize just how smart and wise they were. By then, it's sometimes too late to sit at their feet and learn.

As a young girl, Vickie often heard her grandfather talk about how he rode in a covered wagon and the fact that his grandmother was part Cherokee. He experienced and endured many trials Vickie will never know about. When all that information was available to her, she thought it unnecessary. It was the past; it didn't apply to her life. Now she wishes she had learned more about the events that made her ancestors the hardworking individuals who loved their family and endured much hardship.

God has instruction for His people if they will listen and accept what He has to say. We're no longer children, but we still need instruction even as adults. We need the instruction of God's Word. The writer of today's proverb tells us to be wise and not refuse the instruction given to us. God's instruction means eternal life or eternal damnation. We would be wise to accept His words as our own.

God, give me instruction and the wisdom
to receive it and learn from it. Amen.

National Day of Prayer

Lord, Teach Us to Pray

And it came to pass, that, as he was praying in a certain place,
when he ceased, one of his disciples said unto him, Lord,
teach us to pray, as John also taught his disciples.

LUKE 11:1 KJV

The disciples of Jesus witnessed Him praying and realized they needed to be taught how to pray. What follows in the next three verses of Luke 11 is the Lord's Prayer.

As children, we may have been taught to pray by our parents. As adults our prayers may sound similar to those we worship with. The disciples were concerned about knowing the right way to pray. Are we as concerned as they were? Most of us can recite the Lord's Prayer from memory, but do we think about those words as we pray? Do we apply them to our own lives, or do we go through the motions of praying as we quote those familiar words?

Many times our prayers consist of "Lord, help me with this problem." There's nothing wrong with asking for His help, but on this National Day of Prayer, let's take a second look at how we pray and how effective our prayers are. Let's do more than just go through the motions. Let's pray for our nation and those around us instead of thinking only about ourselves. Before we begin, maybe we should say as the disciples did, "Lord, teach us to pray."

Lord, teach us to pray in a manner that pleases
You and will be effective for Your kingdom. Amen

God Gives a Sound Mind

For God hath not given us the spirit of fear;
but of power, and of love, and of a sound mind.
2 TIMOTHY 1:7 KJV

Turn on the evening news and be prepared to see tragedy and chaos. It seems most of the reports we receive are bad ones. Everywhere we turn, something horrific is happening to someone. Crime is rampant and affects all of us, either directly or indirectly. If we're not careful, fear will paralyze us and take over our lives. We must not lose sight of God's promises.

Timothy writes that this spirit of fear did not come from God. God has given us a spirit of power, love, and a sound mind. The mind is fertile ground for every evil thought the devil can bring to you. If we allow those thoughts to take root and grow, fear will overtake us. We must allow God's Spirit to rule our thinking process. We must accept the love He has shown to us and embrace the sound mind He has given us.

As we read God's Word and spend time in prayer with Him, He plants within our minds those things we need to have a sound mind. A sound mind is one the devil can try to attack, but his efforts will be futile. We must be on guard every day to preserve the mind God has given us. Fertilize it with good ideas that glorify God and His purpose.

Father, I accept the power, love, and sound mind You
have given me. Help me preserve it diligently. Amen.

Hold Me Up, Lord

Hold up my goings in thy paths,
that my footsteps slip not.
PSALM 17:5 KJV

It had been one of those weeks where it seemed everything Laura did was wrong. She had spoken critical words about someone without thinking, been involved in something she knew she shouldn't have, and felt resentment toward someone who had hurt her. By the end of the week, she felt like a total failure as a Christian. The same thought kept going through her mind, *How could I make such a mess of things? I'm a Christian who knows better.* Even more distressing was the thought that she had grieved God's Spirit by her actions.

Many of us have been in Laura's shoes at one time or another. We're only human, and we make mistakes no matter our age or how long we've been a Christian. But we can't dwell on past failures and allow them to drag us down. Satan would like nothing better than to discourage us and get us off track. The important thing is to correct those mistakes by admitting we were wrong and asking God to forgive us. He offers grace to those who want and need it.

The psalmist prayed that the Lord would hold him up as he walked so his feet wouldn't slip on the path, a good prayer for anyone who wants to follow Christ and please Him. We can't do it alone. We need His assistance.

Lord, You know I'm human. I need Your help. Hold me up.
Keep me going in the right direction. Amen.

A Soft Answer

A soft answer turneth away wrath:
but grievous words stir up anger.
PROVERBS 15:1 KJV

In the blink of an eye, a discussion can turn into a heated argument. This often happens with spouses if one blames the other for a problem or incident. Suddenly, the man you love is accusing you of something you didn't do or making an observation that puts you on the defensive. It's natural to want to defend yourself or get in the last word. Feeling hurt, you strike back in fiery indignation with harsh words. And just like that, you're in the middle of an argument that could have been avoided if you had simply refused to argue or given a soft reply to his accusation. Many broken relationships might have been saved if one of the participants had communicated their feelings in a quiet, gentle manner.

Do you often find yourself saying words you wish you could take back, words you would never have spoken under different circumstances? Do you hate the arguments that cut a rift in your relationships? Solomon in all his wisdom must have known about the old saying "It takes two to argue." He said a soft answer would turn away someone's anger, but harsh words would just stir it up. God is able to give us soft answers even in the middle of painful discussions. Ask Him to change your speech and your attitude.

Father, help me not to speak harsh words. Give me soft
answers that will turn away wrath and prevent pain. Amen.

Blessing Others

Therefore if thine enemy hunger, feed him; if he thirst, give him drink: for in so doing thou shalt heap coals of fire on his head. Be not overcome of evil, but overcome evil with good.
ROMANS 12:20–21 KJV

Susan glanced out the window to see her husband bending over a lawn mower in their driveway. The neighbor from across the street stood nearby. *He must be fixing something for her again*, Susan thought. She sighed, perplexed about this neighbor who asked for their help one day and yelled mean remarks at them the next. She treated everyone in the neighborhood the same way. One day she had scared a young boy who had dropped something in the street in front of her house and stopped to pick it up. His presence had aroused her dogs, who started barking furiously. She spoke harsh, unkind words to the boy who was innocent of any wrongdoing.

Regardless of the woman's actions and her attitude, Susan knew they had to be obedient to God's Word. They could not repay evil with evil. They shared vegetables out of their garden and helped her with problems such as the lawn mower repair. At Christmas, Susan had walked across the street with a gift basket. At times it all seemed in vain, but they could not allow themselves to be overcome of evil. The outcome lay in God's hands.

Do you have someone who treats you badly? Resolve in your heart not to let that person's evil overcome you. Turn it over to God and let Him handle the situation. His solution is always best.

Lord, help us to love our enemies and show them good even when they repay us with evil. Amen.

Be Filled with Joy

Now the God of hope fill you with all joy and peace in believing, that ye may abound in hope, through the power of the Holy Ghost.
ROMANS 15:13 KJV

Are you fighting a battle that seems futile? Have you lost hope of seeing a resolution? Take heart, you're not alone. Paul, the writer of today's verse, knew about battles, persecution, and rejection. He spent a lot of time writing his messages of hope while in jail. You may not be in a physical jail, but Satan may have you bound in a spiritual prison. It's time to break out of jail and be the victorious Christian you want to be. "How can I do that?" you ask. Look at what Paul wrote:

1. We serve a God of hope. Trust Him to supply you with hope to make it during dark days.
2. God is your source. Rely on Him to fill you with joy and give you peace in the time of trouble.
3. Believe that God is who He says He is, that He has made a way for you through His Son, Jesus.
4. Allow the Holy Ghost to empower you to abound in hope. We are often powerless to conquer our problems, but God's Spirit can arise within us to make us overcomers.
5. Push the darkness away. God is on your side. Allow Him to work for you.

Father, empower me by Your Spirit to abound in hope as You fill me with Your joy and peace through the Holy Ghost. Amen.

The Final Results

I have planted, Apollos watered;
but God gave the increase.
1 Corinthians 3:6 KJV

Sometimes, as women, we work until we're ready to drop and it seems as though it doesn't make a difference. We teach classes, sing on the praise team, and attend prayer services, but we don't see any results for all our hard work. We attend the women's group, visit the sick, and cook for all the church functions, but no one seems to notice how hard we work.

The problem is expecting something to happen immediately when the final result is in God's hands. We don't have the ability or power to save anyone or change lives. Relax. You're in good company. Paul said he had planted. He meant that he had done his part by planting the seed of the Gospel in people's hearts. Then Apollos came behind him preaching and teaching, watering the seed that Paul had planted. From that point on, they had to wait for God to do His part. He is the only one who can cause those seeds to take root and grow. Too often we try to do God's work for Him. We want to see results right away, but it could be months or even years before we see the result of the seed we've helped to plant. Our job is to continue planting or watering whether we see any results or not and allow God to bring forth the harvest.

Father, help me to do the work You've given me to
do and to leave the results in Your hands. Amen.

A Place for You

But now hath God set the members every one
of them in the body, as it hath pleased him.
1 CORINTHIANS 12:18 KJV

I'm not sure I fit in here. Everyone seems to have a place except me.

Have you ever had similar thoughts, feeling like you don't belong or feeling unimportant because you don't have a position? Don't allow that old lie from Satan to bring you down or discourage you. God has a place for everyone, and He has a place for you.

At a football game, the water boy hangs out at the sideline with a bottle of water and a towel, and hands these to the players when they need them. His job may seem insignificant, but without water during the game, a football player would not receive the cooling drink he needs to stay refreshed and hydrated. The water boy is part of the team even though he isn't on the field or prominent in the public eye.

When we accept Christ, we become a part of His Body. We are placed by Him into the position that pleases Him. It may not be a job where we get attention. We may be the one cleaning up the kitchen after a church dinner or addressing get-well cards to sick members. Whatever the task, it's important to the body of Christ. When everyone does their part, the church functions according to God's plan. Just knowing God has placed us where it pleases Him should be all the thanks we need.

Father, help me to find the spot where You have placed me,
and help me to serve there willingly. Amen.

Free through Christ

Stand fast therefore in the liberty wherewith Christ hath made us free, and be not entangled again with the yoke of bondage.
GALATIANS 5:1 KJV

At seventeen, Teresa ran away from home and became a topless dancer. Eventually, alcohol, drugs, and prostitution became the norm. She made lots of money, but she wasn't happy. She consumed alcohol and drugs to face the life she had chosen for herself. One day she overdosed and landed in the hospital. Afterward, she visited a church one night and there gave her heart to Christ. He set her free from the bondage of drugs and prostitution. Today, Teresa is a tireless witness for Christ. In her book, *Sold to the Highest Bidder*, she boldly shares her testimony of how Christ has set her free. She stands on God's Word and in the liberty Christ gave her. She works to help others find the same freedom she has found.

No matter what our past or present, Christ can set us free. There is no bondage that He cannot break, no power that can defeat Him. We become new creations in Christ when we surrender our lives to Him. The danger lies in our taking control and becoming entangled in the bondage of sin once again. We must allow Christ to be in complete control and then stand fast in the liberty through which He has set us free.

Jesus, I surrender my life to You. Take control of my heart and help me to stand fast in the liberty that has set me free. Amen.

A Good Work

*Being confident of this very thing, that he which hath begun
a good work in you will perform it until the day of Jesus Christ.*
PHILIPPIANS 1:6 KJV

Has anyone ever left you holding the bag? She promised to help you with something or be a part of a project or share a responsibility, and then she failed to do her part? It's not only frustrating and stressful because you have to do extra work, but also discouraging and painful because she let you down. You counted on her. You trusted her to keep her word.

One person you can always count on is Jesus Christ. He never fails to keep His word. Sometimes our confidence is placed in humans and they disappoint us, but Christ will never disappoint us. If He has started a work in you, rest assured that He will perform exactly what He said. God will finish what He starts.

Susan sensed the call to write as a young woman. She felt the leading of God's Spirit in her life, but not everyone agreed. Some tried to discourage her. Satan placed obstacles in her path to keep her from being confident of the work Christ had started in her life. But she knew God always keeps His promises, and He would perform the work He had started. It took a few years, but she's now a published writer.

*Jesus, help me to place my confidence in You
and Your promises, knowing that You are able to
perform the work You have begun in me. Amen.*

Mother's Day

A Mother's Faith

When I call to remembrance the unfeigned faith
that is in thee, which dwelt first in thy grandmother Lois,
and thy mother Eunice; and I am persuaded that in thee also.
2 TIMOTHY 1:5 KJV

Paul felt sure Timothy had the same kind of faith that his mother and grandmother had before him. These two women evidently had set a great example for him. Following their teachings and watching their lives had resulted in Timothy becoming a devout Christian.

Mothers and grandmothers play an important part in their children's lives. They influence them in ways no one else can. A mother is responsible for her child from the time it is conceived in the womb until that child leaves home as an adult. Even then, a mother never stops being a mother. She still feels the need to advise and counsel her children. And her children are encouraged not to forsake the law of their mother (see Proverbs 6:20).

If you had a godly mother, give her honor today. If she did her best to lead you in the right path, loved you, and always believed in you, show her your appreciation on this day set aside especially for her. If your mother set a good example for you, follow that example as you raise your own children, and like Paul, you may be able to say that your son or daughter has the unfeigned faith that Timothy possessed.

Father, help me to honor my mother all the days of my life, and help me to be the godly mother You would have me to be. Amen.

A Strong Tower

The name of the LORD is a strong tower:
the righteous runneth into it, and is safe.
PROVERBS 18:10 KJV

When a young man walked into a convenience store and pointed a gun at Dorothy, she managed to remain composed and do as he asked, but as soon as he left, she fell apart. The full implication of what had happened made her so afraid, she had to quit her job. When Anna's husband experienced a serious heart complication and had to be rushed into surgery, fear overwhelmed her and made it hard to pray. When a neighbor posed a threat to their security, David and Becky moved to a new neighborhood to feel safer.

Everyone has felt fear at one time or another. It may have been hearing a doctor's diagnosis of a terrible disease, being the victim of a crime, or being alone in a strange city, but everyone has been afraid at sometime in their life. Fear can paralyze us and keep us from feeling secure and confident. The name of the Lord is a place of safety for His people. We can't stop bad things from happening to us, but when they do, we can call on His name. He provides a haven of safety for us, both physically and mentally. The next time you feel afraid, run to Jesus. His name is the strong tower you need.

Lord, help me to remember that You are my strong tower.
I can run to You with every problem. Amen.

A Sanctified Vessel

*That every one of you should know how to possess
his vessel in sanctification and honour.*
1 THESSALONIANS 4:4 KJV

When a well-known celebrity posed nude for a magazine, she received lots of attention. She made the decision to expose her body to the world regardless of who saw it. She's not the first. Lots of people, both male and female, have participated in lewd acts for one reason or another.

Paul wrote to the people at Thessalonica about possessing their vessel (body) in sanctification and honor. They were not to participate in sexual or lustful acts. They were to keep themselves morally clean. He went on to write that God had not called them to uncleanness but to holiness (see 1 Thessalonians 4:7).

Living a holy life and possessing ourselves with honor includes watching our actions and thought processes. Do we dress in a provocative manner, or do we honor God in the way we look? Do our motives promote clean living, or are we careless in our actions around others? Do we watch movies or read books that invite unclean thoughts or habits? As Christians, we must be careful not to promote or follow this trend in our culture. God is pleased with those who strive to live a holy life before Him, a life that doesn't follow the trends of the world or the people who do.

*God, help me to live a clean life, one that honors You in every way.
Help me to cultivate thoughts and habits pleasing to You. Amen.*

Looking on the Heart

But the LORD said unto Samuel, Look not on his countenance,
or on the height of his stature; because I have refused him:
for the LORD seeth not as man seeth; for man looketh on the
outward appearance, but the LORD looketh on the heart.
1 SAMUEL 16:7 KJV

Everywhere you look, there are beauty products, weight loss programs, and procedures to make you look younger. It seems we never tire of trying to improve our appearance. There's nothing wrong with trying to look our best, but if we're not careful, we can become obsessed with our appearance. Many women worry about how they look to the world around them and whether they live up to the world's standards of beauty.

When God sent Samuel to anoint a new king for Israel, Samuel asked Jesse, the Bethlehemite, to bring out his sons. The sons of Jesse were evidently good-looking men, because Samuel thought that surely the Lord's anointed stood before Him. God said, *"No, I don't look on the outward appearance; I look on the heart."*

In our pursuit of improving our appearance, it's best if we first make sure our hearts are clean. We might look good on the outside, but if our hearts aren't pure before God, then we aren't pleasing to Him. Before we jump on the bandwagon and spend a lot of money on cosmetics, maybe we should ask God about our hearts and make sure He approves. It's far more important to please Him than to please the world.

Lord, give me a pure heart. Help me to desire
Your approval over man's approval. Amen.

A God of Comfort

*Yea, though I walk through the valley of the shadow of death, I will fear
no evil: for thou art with me; thy rod and thy staff they comfort me.*
PSALM 23:4 KJV

Loss of any kind is never an easy thing to go through, whether it's the death of a loved one, the loss of a relationship, or a financial mishap. When we lose someone or something, we lose a part of ourselves.

Bill and Sue were stunned when their friendship with another couple ended. The gap left by their friends wasn't easily filled, and they grieved the broken relationship. Victoria lost a good friend to a terrible accident and missed the talks they shared. Some grieve the loss of a job, a home, or a church. No matter what the loss, we can feel overwhelmed by the emptiness and the change it makes in our lives.

If you've been feeling the pain made by changes in your life, read Psalm 23. If anyone knew about loss or change, it was the psalmist David. King Saul wanted to kill him, forcing him to run for his life. He lived in caves, went hungry, and faced betrayal from his family, yet he knew God would restore him. He took comfort in God and His promises. We can do the same. No matter what we are facing, we can count on God to lead us beside still waters and walk with us through the valley of loss.

*Lord, give me comfort and peace. Help me to rest in
Your promises, knowing You will see me through
the shadows and dark times in my life. Amen.*

Hold On to Your Birthright

And Esau said, Behold, I am at the point to die: and what profit shall this birthright do to me?. . .and he sold his birthright unto Jacob.
GENESIS 25:32–33 KJV

Esau came home from hunting feeling so hungry he felt he might die. He begged his brother, Jacob, to give him a bowl of pottage. In return, Jacob asked him for his birthright. Esau agreed because at the moment his hunger was more important to him. He didn't realize that satisfying his physical desire for food would be costly in the future.

Our culture has much to offer and it looks good. We, like Esau, can allow our desires to overwhelm us to the point of deciding we have to meet that need regardless of the cost. The desires we must watch out for are those that come between us and God. Often those desires appear harmless, but sometimes they are like an iceberg. Underneath that small, harmless-looking tip is hidden danger. Esau's hunger was a natural, harmless desire, but he allowed that desire to rob him of his birthright as the oldest child. Later, he came face to face with the consequences of his choice and lost his standing in the family.

What desires are you facing that might strip you of your relationship with God? Be careful that you don't become so obsessed with them that you're willing to give up anything to get them. You might lose your spiritual birthright in the process.

*Lord, help me to cling to You regardless
of what the world has to offer. Amen.*

Only through God

For by thee I have run through a troop:
by my God have I leaped over a wall.
2 SAMUEL 22:30 KJV

We've all heard stories about people performing seemingly impossible acts of heroism in the face of danger—lifting a car off of someone, carrying an injured person for several miles to reach help. Other stories tell how people survive being stranded in a blizzard or walk away from a terrible accident uninjured. How did they do this? Common sense often plays a big part in survival, but today's scripture tells us where our strength comes from. God enabled the writer of this verse to survive the obstacles he faced.

We may never face the tragedies we read about or see on the news, but we deal with adversity every day. A job loss, a bad medical diagnosis, or a child being bullied at school are only a few of the problems faced by people like us every day. How do we handle it? We can deal with the trouble that comes our way through God and His powerful strength. We may not face a troop or have to jump over a wall, but by our God, we can face a financial crisis, divorce, or disease. Take courage today in knowing that God is here for you and you can leap over that wall of adversity.

Father, give me the strength to face life's
trouble and run the race until the finish. Amen.

Touching Jesus

*When she had heard of Jesus, [she] came in the
press behind, and touched his garment. For she said,
If I may touch but his clothes, I shall be whole.*

MARK 5:27–28 KJV

The woman with the issue of blood suffered for twelve years, and even though she had seen several physicians and spent all her money, she wasn't any better. She must have felt she was at the end of her rope. Then she heard about Jesus.

Sometimes we're at the end of our rope. We've done all we know to do and it hasn't solved a thing. We're so confident we can handle the situation, we have missed the secret this woman discovered. When she heard of Jesus, she made her way to Him. It wasn't easy. A crowd followed Jesus as He taught and healed people. She had to make her way through the throng of people who jostled and pushed against one another in their eagerness to be near Jesus. They may not have wanted to give way to her, but she pressed in, and when she reached Jesus, she touched His clothes and received healing.

The secret to solving any problem is to touch Jesus. We can't see Him in the flesh, but we can touch Him through prayer and His Word. Like the woman in this story, we must press through whatever may hinder us. Don't give up! Touching Jesus is all that matters.

*Jesus, give me the determination to press through the crowd
until I touch You and receive the answer I need. Amen.*

Stand Still

And Moses said unto the people, Fear ye not, stand still, and see
the salvation of the Lord, which he will shew to you to day. . . .
The Lord shall fight for you, and ye shall hold your peace.
EXODUS 14:13–14 KJV

The Children of Israel enjoyed a triumphant exodus from Egypt, but danger soon overtook them. They had only journeyed a short time when they looked up to see Pharaoh and his army marching toward them. They were afraid and immediately started making accusations against Moses, claiming he had brought them to the wilderness to die. They said they would have been better off staying in Egypt. But Moses encouraged them not to be afraid. They were to stand still. The Lord, their God, would fight for them. They were to hold their peace.

Are you facing an enemy? Do you feel afraid of impending danger? Moses told the people to do four things: fear not, stand still, see the salvation of the Lord, and hold your peace. The Children of Israel experienced a great victory that day. God parted the waters of the Red Sea so they could cross over on dry ground, then He allowed that same water to drown the Egyptian army. Moses' advice is good for us also. We can put our trust in God without fear and wait for God to do battle for us. Whatever is coming toward you, God can handle it.

Lord, help me to stand still and wait
for You to work on my behalf. Amen.

Lead a Quiet Life

*Make it your ambition to lead a quiet life: You should mind
your own business and work with your hands, just as we
told you, so that your daily life may win the respect of
outsiders and so that you will not be dependent on anybody.*
1 THESSALONIANS 4:11–12 NIV

Paul encouraged the church at Thessalonica to make it their ambition to live quietly, mind their own business, and work with their hands. In other words, stay busy and take care of your own life, not someone else's. By doing this, they might win the respect of others.

Minding their own business is difficult for some. Gossip is like the curiosity that killed the cat. Once we hear it, it nags at us to learn more until we end up seeing and knowing more than we should. And if we spread what we've learned, we're only promoting something that could hurt others. In the process of being curious, we may get involved in something we shouldn't have.

Paul's advice is good for us, too. In an age when you can learn just about anything through social media or the Internet, Christians must be careful not to cause harm to others by gossiping about something we see on Facebook or in a text. We will never be the witness or example for Christ that we need to be if we promote such actions. Leading a quiet life and minding our own business brings honor to God and shines His light on others.

*Father, teach me to be discreet and
wise about the things I say and do. Amen.*

Forgiveness

But Esau ran to meet Jacob and embraced him; he threw
his arms around his neck and kissed him. And they wept.
GENESIS 33:4 NIV

Jacob cheated Esau out of his birthright and the father's blessing reserved for the eldest son. Jacob's act changed both their lives forever. Esau hated Jacob for his deception and betrayal. His anger ran so deep that he planned to kill Jacob, and would have had Jacob not fled for his life. Jacob stayed away for twenty years and then started for home even though he feared Esau. What a surprise when Esau ran to meet him and threw his arms around Jacob. He had forgiven Jacob even though his betrayal had been a cruel one.

Forgiveness isn't always easy. Sometimes the hurt is deep and the pain lingers for a long time. The other person seems to get on with her life while you suffer. Esau could have hung on to his anger and killed Jacob when he saw him coming. Instead, he took the first step and ran to meet Jacob, forgiving him. We, too, can take the first step toward forgiveness. In doing so, we let go of the pain we've been carrying. We find freedom for ourselves and offer the same to the one who hurt us. Is there someone you need to forgive today? Take the first step toward reconciliation. God will give you the strength to go the full distance.

Lord, give me courage to take the first step toward
forgiveness even if it's the other person's fault. Amen.

Sing a Little Song

Is anyone among you in trouble? Let them pray.
Is anyone happy? Let them sing songs of praise.
JAMES 5:13 NIV

"Your face is giving you away."

"I know what you're thinking. I can see it in your expression."

Too many times, people allow their feelings to show on their faces. If we're mad, anger shows in the fiery darts coming from our eyes. Self-pity is portrayed by a turned-down mouth and an expression that says, "Poor me." When we disagree with someone, we often frown, wrinkle our forehead, or roll our eyes as a sign of disgust. We can't seem to keep from letting our thoughts show.

James teaches us how to respond to life's experiences. He says if you're in trouble, pray about it. We're much better off when we pray about what's bothering us, no matter what the problem, than to let it show for the world to see. Likewise, if we're happy, we can let those around us know it by singing. There's a gospel song that says, "I feel a little song coming on." When we pray about our troubles, we feel better and can then sing that song we feel in our hearts. Are you facing a problem today? Take it to God in prayer and let Him take care of it for you. Are you happy? Then sing that little song you feel coming on.

Lord, help me to rely on You in times of trouble and sing Your
praises when I'm happy. Let my expression shine for You. Amen.

Acceptable Words

Let the words of my mouth, and the meditation of my heart,
be acceptable in thy sight, O LORD, my strength, and my redeemer.
PSALM 19:14 KJV

When Jean wondered why Sally hadn't greeted some of the other members coming into the church. Sally jokingly said, "That's not my job." Later, during the service, her words came back to her and she felt ashamed that she had said it even in a humorous light. After the service, she went to Jean and asked if she had taken her seriously. Jean said no, but Sue felt that God hadn't been pleased with what she had said.

As Christians, we should be careful of the words we speak and what we meditate on. Matthew 12:34 (KJV) teaches us that "out of the abundance of the heart the mouth speaketh." If our hearts are clean, it helps keep our words acceptable. We never know when someone might take something we say the wrong way. There will always be those who take things wrong on purpose, but being aware of our words can keep us out of trouble. But even more importantly, our words should be pleasing to God. When our speech pleases Him, we won't be as likely to offend others. Proverbs teaches us that "the prudent hold their tongues" (10:19 NIV). If we ask Him, God will help us to hold our tongues and speak those words that please Him and are not offensive to others.

Lord, help me to speak words that are acceptable to
You and to meditate on things that please You. Amen.

Keeping Our Testimony

And the LORD was with Joseph, and he was a prosperous man;
and he was in the house of his master, the Egyptian.
And his master saw that the LORD was with him.
GENESIS 39:2–3 KJV

Joseph had been sold to some traveling merchants by his brothers. The travelers carried him to Egypt, where he was sold once again to Potiphar, an officer of Pharaoh. Joseph could have sat down in a corner and felt sorry for himself. He could have said, "I'm in a foreign country where no one knows me. I don't worship like these people. I can't live for God here." But Joseph didn't do any of those things. He proved himself a trustworthy servant, and his master took note of it, making Joseph his overseer. It made no difference that he had been brought to a different place; God was with him.

You may be living in a home or working at a job where you are the only Christian, but no matter where you are, God is able to bless you and direct your life if you allow Him to. No matter what environment you find yourself in, God will be there. Your situation may be painful, you may be fearful, the people around you may abuse you in some way, but like Joseph, God will be with you. Trust Him to take care of you.

Lord, help me to trust You in my situation. Give me the
strength to live a life pleasing to You so those around
me will take note that You are with me. Amen.

Serve the Lord with Gladness

Make a joyful noise unto the LORD, all ye lands. Serve the LORD with gladness: come before his presence with singing. . . . Enter into his gates with thanksgiving, and into his courts with praise: be thankful unto him, and bless his name.
PSALM 100:1–2, 4 KJV

Many people in our culture think of Sunday as a day to relax and watch football, go fishing, or fire up the grill and spend time with their family. A great number of people no longer think of Sunday as a day of worship. As of 2014, the Barna Group stated that "churchless people"—those who hadn't attended a service anytime during the past six months—stood at 114 million.

Some people may find that statistic astounding, but how faithful are we to attend our local house of worship? Has Sunday become just another day? Do we consider it "our time" to unwind and rest from the stress and pressures of the week? Do we go only when it's convenient or on a special occasion? Are we becoming a part of that alarming statistic?

Worship is a time of acknowledging God in our lives and showing Him we're grateful for all His blessings, a time to make a joyful noise and sing praises to Him. It's a matter of getting our priorities straight, deciding to give back to God a little of the time He's given us. Keeping God first in our lives means setting aside time to worship Him.

Father, help me to serve You by spending time in worship. Amen.

Set Up a Memorial

And Joshua set up at Gilgal the twelve stones they had taken out of the Jordan. He said to the Israelites, "In the future when your descendants ask their parents, 'What do these stones mean?' tell them, 'Israel crossed the Jordan on dry ground.' "

JOSHUA 4:20–22 NIV

God had given Joshua and the Israelites a great victory by allowing them to cross the Jordan River on dry ground. On the other side, Joshua built a memorial so that future generations would know what God had done for their ancestors.

In Washington, DC, several memorials have been erected in honor of the men and women who have served to protect and preserve our freedom. In Arlington Cemetery, the Tomb of the Unknown Soldier was built to honor an unidentified American killed in World War I. Inscribed on the tomb are the words "Here rests in honored glory an American soldier known but to God." Even though we don't know his name, the memorial stands as confirmation to all who see it and to future generations that he served our country. On this day, we honor all who have given their lives so that we might live free.

The cross stands as a memorial to what Christ did for the world. He paid a great price for our freedom from sin. Our lives should be a shining example to future generations who might ask what the cross means.

Father, enable me to live in such a way that my life will be a living memorial to You. Amen.

Christ Gives Strength

I can do all things through
Christ which strengtheneth me.
PHILIPPIANS 4:13 KJV

Shelly felt burned out and exhausted. Every day she faced a never-ending to-do list.

Between her job, family, housework, and church responsibilities, she didn't ever have time to relax and do things she enjoyed. She was becoming irritable with those around her. No one seemed to understand how much she had to do. It just wasn't fair.

Many women often feel like Shelly. We have many responsibilities, and often we take on more because we feel we should. It's possible for us to take on things we shouldn't. It's hard to be your best as a wife, mother, employee, or church member when you're exhausted and stressed. God doesn't want us to take on so many responsibilities that we can't be our best for Him and our families. We're all going to get tired sometimes, but when we do, Philippians 4:13 tells us that Christ gives us strength and we can do all things through Him. Maybe it's time we decided what is most important. Try making a list of priorities with Jesus at the top, then pray about what He would have you to do in order to please Him. Chances are, some things will be deleted from your life that you thought were necessary and you'll find yourself less stressed. Then rest in Christ and He will give you strength to do all you need to do.

Jesus, give me the strength to be what I need to be for You and others.
Give me wisdom as I make my choices in life. Amen.

A Virtuous Woman

Who can find a virtuous woman? for her price is far above rubies. The heart of her husband doth safely trust in her, so that he shall have no need of spoil. She will do him good and not evil all the days of her life.
PROVERBS 31:10-12 KJV

The women's movement has done a lot to see that women are treated equally in our culture. Years ago, women burned their bras in protest as a way of making a statement that they wanted things to be different for them. They wanted the right to be their own person in the world. Today, women have more privileges than ever before. They can be anything they choose to be, but without the proper choices, they lose everything they've worked for.

The virtuous woman described in Proverbs 31 is valuable. Her price is above rubies. A flawless ruby can cost as much as $2,500 per carat, more than a lot of us can afford. That makes it a precious treasure to those who own one. A man who has a virtuous wife has a priceless treasure. He knows he can trust her. Without trust, it's almost impossible to make a relationship of any kind work.

A trustworthy, virtuous woman makes her husband feel secure in the relationship. He doesn't worry that she will be disloyal or unfaithful to him. A virtuous woman is one who has made the right choice; she has decided to please God rather than herself.

*Lord, help me to make wise choices today
so that I will be pleasing to You. Amen.*

Live Out the Word

"Keep this Book of the Law always on your lips; meditate on it day and night, so that you may be careful to do everything written in it. Then you will be prosperous and successful."
JOSHUA 1:8 NIV

When Joshua becomes the leader of Israel, God gives him one thing to do: immerse himself in scripture and do everything written in it.

James gives a similar directive in the New Testament (James 1:22) when he tells us not to just listen to the Word but to be *doers* of it. In Acts, the Greek word for *doer* can be translated as "poet" or "performer." We can think of it as a command to act out the Bible, to live it on the stage of our lives.

What do our lives look like when we live out God's Word? We have examples in scripture. All scripture is God-breathed, not just the commands. So all of it is instruction for modeling our lives. We can read in the Bible about people like Stephen, David, Mary, Mary Magdalene, the Prodigal Son, the Good Samaritan, and many more. These are people who acted in godly ways as they worked to live out God's Word in their lives, and they serve as examples for us.

God promises to be with us and that obedience brings prosperity and success. We just need to take Him at His Word and obey.

Heavenly Father, thank You for always being with us. Thank You for giving us Your Word as instruction for our lives and examples of those who have lived it out. Amen.

Encouragement during Difficult Assignments

Then they answered Joshua, "Whatever you have commanded us we will do, and wherever you send us we will go. Just as we fully obeyed Moses, so we will obey you. Only may the LORD your God be with you as he was with Moses. Whoever rebels against your word and does not obey it, whatever you may command them, will be put to death. Only be strong and courageous!"

JOSHUA 1:16–18 NIV

God gives us difficult assignments just as He did with Joshua. We *know* God will bless us if we're faithful, but we don't always *feel* it. Often the job seems bigger than our capabilities, and we get discouraged. But God wants us to *know* and *feel* He is responsible for the outcome. We just need to be faithful to act.

As with Joshua, God brings people into our lives to encourage us. The men in today's verses encourage Joshua in four ways: they assure him of their allegiance and willingness to help, they pray for him, they take their own responsibilities seriously, and they offer Joshua words of encouragement he has heard before.

Our assignment is for our benefit and to benefit those around us. While we need to be obedient to do the next right step, we also need to encourage others around us. How can you use one of those four ways to encourage someone else?

Heavenly Father, thank You for loving us enough to include us in Your work. Bring people into our lives to encourage us on the journey, and open our eyes to see others who need encouragement. Amen.

The Courage to See God at Work

So the king of Jericho sent this message to Rahab:
"Bring out the men who came to you and entered your house,
because they have come to spy out the whole land."
JOSHUA 2:3 NIV

God had rescued the Israelites from Egypt by dividing the Red Sea. He led the way through the desert as a pillar of cloud by day and a pillar of fire by night. He provided food and water. For forty years, their clothes did not wear out.

The king of Jericho had heard of this big God and His people, who were camped outside his city ready to attack. Rahab, a prostitute, had heard of this God. But her decision was different from the king's. She looked at the same evidence as the king and made a different decision.

She heard that God was a punishing God and a rescuing God. Jericho had been a wicked city and was going to be punished. She hid the spies that came in to scout out the city. She told them she believed in their God and wanted to be rescued, along with her family. Her actions flowed from her realization of who God is. Her faith not only gets her mentioned in James and Hebrews, but she also becomes part of the lineage of Christ.

What does your knowledge of who God is lead you to do? How can you step out in faith?

Dear God, thank You for rescuing us. Reveal Your character to us in a new way, and show us how to act because of who You are. Amen.

Step Out in Faith

The priests who carried the ark of the covenant of the LORD
stopped in the middle of the Jordan and stood on dry ground,
while all Israel passed by until the whole nation had
completed the crossing on dry ground.
JOSHUA 3:17 NIV

Everyone needs to know they have a purpose in life. God's assignments to us give us purpose. But sometimes what God is asking us to do seems impossible. The Israelites felt that way. The Jordan was at flood stage. How could they cross it? They had to walk by faith and not by sight. We need to do the same thing.

There are three steps to walking by faith. One, follow God. The priests carrying the ark went into the Jordan first, and then the people were to follow. We can do this by being in God's Word and seeking godly advice.

Two, wait. Israel stopped at the edge of the river for three days. They knew they couldn't do this on their own. They spent the time consecrating themselves. When you are in a waiting period, is there sin you need to confess and remove? God will not work in all His fullness in the lives of people who are unwilling to open their hearts to Him.

Three, step out. The priests had to step into the raging river before God stopped the water. They had to show they believed Him.

Where do you need to step out in faith?

Lord God, open our eyes to see You working. Give us
the courage to trust You and step out in faith. Amen.

Friend or Foe?

Now when Joshua was near Jericho, he looked up and saw a
man standing in front of him with a drawn sword in his hand.
Joshua went up to him and asked, "Are you for us or for our enemies?"
JOSHUA 5:13 NIV

While Joshua was doing reconnaissance in anticipation of battling Jericho, he ran into the commander of the army of the Lord, who was actually Jesus in preincarnate form. He came to remind Joshua that it was God's battle Joshua was fighting, not the other way around. Joshua's question of "Are you for me or them?" is the wrong question, so God doesn't answer it. He changes the conversation to what really matters. He's not limited by our self-centered, nearsighted, either-or thinking.

Joshua understands immediately and asks what message God has for him. Joshua is receptive and eager to hear a word from God. Just like with Moses and the burning bush, the land Joshua is standing on becomes holy; he gets his anointing. And he submits by removing his sandals and bowing in worship. This is the beginning of his ministry and leadership.

Joshua's experience underlines what God wants us to know: He is in control and we just need to obey. He will be present and He will provide. How do our lives change when we recognize that God is always standing next to us?

Holy Father, thank You for never leaving us. Help us when we
don't take sin seriously enough, when we drift toward laziness.
Correct our steps. Make us eager for a word from You. Amen.

The Spoils of War

But the Israelites were unfaithful in regard to the devoted things. . . .
So the Lord's anger burned against Israel.

JOSHUA 7:1 NIV

When things don't go our way, sometimes it's because God's plan is different from ours. But sometimes it's our fault because of sin we have committed. In the book of Joshua, God shows us the results of obedience and disobedience.

When the Israelites obeyed God, they conquered the city of Jericho. This great, walled city was expecting the Israelite onslaught and was fortified against their attack. Joshua sought the Lord and received some odd advice, which he obeyed anyway. The Israelites were victorious because they obeyed God's instructions.

Their next battle was for the city of Ai. Spies reported this was a far easier city to conquer than fortified Jericho. But the Israelites were routed. Joshua was confused and went to God, who revealed Achan had sinned.

Achan coveted spoils of the war with Jericho that God had said belonged only to Him. Achan took what didn't belong to him. And because these things were obtained sinfully, he had to hide them and couldn't even enjoy them.

When Achan sinned, all Israel suffered. Thirty-six soldiers died. That is the way of sin. It promises many things, but it doesn't deliver anything but pain and suffering.

Lord God, please reveal to us things that should not be in our lives.
Open our eyes to the true nature of sinful things. Thank You for
sending Your Son to die for our sin and for forgiving us. Amen.

Obedience Triumphs over Disobedience

"I will not be with you anymore unless you destroy whatever among you is devoted to destruction."
JOSHUA 7:12 NIV

When Achan took spoils from the destruction of Jericho that belonged to God, he set in motion a series of events that affected everyone around him. Joshua, the leader of Israel, now had to deal with Achan's sin.

In the Bible, there are two kinds of things that are devoted to God. Leviticus 27:28 tells of things that are devoted to God by our own free will: children dedicated to the Lord, money pledged to God's work, a commitment to God regarding how we use our bodies, and so on.

But there is another kind of thing devoted to God—the detestable things that are devoted to destruction. Deuteronomy 7:26 talks about things that are evil and have no place in our lives: pornography, witchcraft, tarot cards, Ouija boards, drug and alcohol abuse, and other evil things.

When we possess devoted things, this makes us liable to destruction because God removes His protection from us. When Achan took the devoted things, all of Israel suffered. Joshua had to step in to make things right. Joshua's act of obedience overcomes Achan's act of disobedience. This is symbolic of what Jesus does for us (see Romans 5:18–19). Though Adam brought sin into the world, Jesus' death and resurrection saves us from the consequences of sin.

Lord God, please reveal any devoted things we might be hanging on to. We know You won't go with us until we remove the sin. Give us strength and wisdom to obey You. Amen.

Restored Relationships

Then the LORD said to Joshua, "Do not be afraid; do not be discouraged. Take the whole army with you, and go up and attack Ai. For I have delivered into your hands the king of Ai, his people, his city and his land."

JOSHUA 8:1 NIV

This is Joshua's second battle for Ai. The first ended in disaster because of Achan's sin. But it has been discovered, and the people have asked for forgiveness.

And God gives it freely. He shows Joshua He has restored their relationship and there is no lingering anger. While Joshua might be hesitant to return to the spot of his previous failure, God encourages him while giving battle orders.

God also displays His generosity. Unlike at Jericho, this time God allows the people to carry off the livestock and plunder after the battle to sustain themselves until they can make the land fruitful. At Jericho, Achan stole the plunder that was dedicated to God. His attitude was the same as Adam and Eve's in the Garden of Eden when they took fruit from the tree. They believed the lie that God was stingy and keeping good things from them. But what God withholds is often what He wants to give us later.

Our sin does not diminish God's faithfulness. In fact, His plan incorporates our failure and turns it into something good. Our sin can't overwhelm His promises. He is abundant with His love and grace.

Father God, thank You for Your generosity toward us. Remind us of sin we need to confess so we can maintain a right relationship with You and benefit from Your love and grace. Amen.

Ask God First

The Israelites sampled their provisions
but did not inquire of the Lord.
JOSHUA 9:14 NIV

The Gibeonites pretended to be from a distant land to make a treaty with Israel. The Israelites trusted in what they could see and made judgments based on appearances. They did not inquire of God.

Throughout scripture, God begs us to inquire of Him. Often we don't because we think we can handle it. We only go to Him for big things. But in the Gibeonites' case, the data was falsified; Israel was intentionally deceived. God knows all the information about a situation, far more than we ever could.

Asking for God's guidance doesn't mean everything will go the way we expect. But when we ask, the events of our lives do go according to God's plan. Jesus inquired of God before choosing the twelve disciples. Judas was among the twelve. God intentionally allowed Jesus to pick a man who would betray Him so God's plan for our redemption would be accomplished.

Asking God puts the burden on Him to reveal to us His will. In what area of your life have you been handling things on your own? Where do you need to seek God's will?

Heavenly Father, thank You for loving us enough to care
deeply about the details of our lives. Nothing is too small for You.
Show us Your will and give us the courage to step out in faith. Amen.

God Is in the Mess

"This is what we will do to them: We will let them live, so that God's wrath will not fall on us for breaking the oath we swore to them."
JOSHUA 9:20 NIV

The Gibeonites lived in the land the Israelites were to conquer, but they pretended to be from far away to make a treaty with Israel. This deception leads to an interesting history between the Gibeonites and the Israelites.

Joshua makes them woodcutters and water carriers for the tabernacle, and he goes to war to protect them because he swore an oath to do so. Later, Saul persecutes them and David makes reparations for that persecution. In Nehemiah, they work alongside the Israelites in rebuilding Jerusalem's walls.

Israel's own history is based on deception. Jacob lied to get Isaac's blessing, and his family eventually became the nation of Israel.

God can be glorified in the messiness of life. Paul tells us that the Gospel can be preached even if from wrong motives. The original sin isn't justified, but it doesn't hamper God's ability to work.

It can be hard to see God at work in the midst of difficult things, but He is there the whole time. Even when the sin is being committed, He is planting the seed of redemption. He does not abandon us to our sins or the sins of others.

God, thank You for never leaving us, for always being by our side no matter how messy our lives are. Remind us of sin we need to confess, and open our eyes to Your work. Amen.

The Price of Sin

The LORD said to Joshua, "Do not be afraid of them; I have given them into your hand. Not one of them will be able to withstand you."
JOSHUA 10:8 NIV

Joshua is following the book of the Law, just as God had instructed him, in taking the Promised Land. God is driving out Israel's enemies because of their wickedness, not because of Israel's righteousness. Israel is just the vehicle God uses to provide punishment to nations who refused to repent of their sin and turn to Him. Sin leads to death.

These nations were given a chance to make peace with God. Rahab did. The Gibeonites did, even though it was through deception. Anyone who wants peace with God gets it.

In the Garden of Eden, Adam and Eve were cursed because of their sin. But Christ's death—something that is normally considered failure—overturns Adam and Eve's rebellion and becomes the ultimate means of victory over death and sin. He paid the price for us, and we receive the blessing instead of the punishment.

Jesus' obedience and holiness were the only things that could take away the curse of our sin. God raised Him and made His enemies a footstool for His feet, just as He did for Joshua. Joshua's conquering of the Promised Land was a physical and temporary representation of what Christ does to sin on a universal and permanent basis. God did not abandon us to the brutality of our sin. Peace with God is possible because of Christ.

Lord God, thank You for rescuing us from our sin.
Show us how to live for You daily. Amen.

The Lord Will Fight for You

The LORD said to Joshua, "Do not be afraid of them; I have given them into your hand. Not one of them will be able to withstand you."
JOSHUA 10:8 NIV

Because Joshua was following God's instructions, God was not only giving the Israelites victory over the tribes in the Promised Land but also doing the fighting for them. And He will fight for us, too.

Psalms 15 and 24 both talk about who can dwell on God's holy mountain. Who can partner with God in His work? Those who keep an oath even when it hurts, such as Joshua did with the Gibeonites. Keep your promises, your commitments, your covenants and God will fight alongside you.

God partners with those who have clean hands and a pure heart, those who do not turn to idols or false gods. This means when adversity comes, we don't rely on our bank accounts, resources, or talents but instead look to God to deliver us. We have faith He will keep His promises.

When God fights for us, we have reassurance we are going to win. Often you can't tell your work from God's work, because He is working through you. And yet there are things only God can do. He wants us to boldly ask for what we need. He wants us to be in His work with Him.

Heavenly Father, thank You for allowing us to partner with You in Your work. Thank You that we can boldly go to the Creator of the universe and ask for what we need, knowing You care deeply for each of us. Amen.

Obedience Brings Peace

So Joshua took the entire land, just as the Lord had directed Moses,
and he gave it as an inheritance to Israel according to their
tribal divisions. Then the land had rest from war.
JOSHUA 11:23 NIV

Victory does not come without obedience. Joshua took the entire land because he followed God's instructions. Joshua battled enemies with greater numbers and better technology. In each battle, victory looked different, but in all of them God was faithful.

Our obedience will look different in each situation depending on what God wants us to do. We must ask for guidance. Obedience will keep us on the right track and away from contaminating influences. When we trust in our resources or the wisdom of the world, we will be led astray.

Additionally, obedience to those in authority over us is obedience to God. Joshua followed Moses' instructions. It can take more faith to see God speaking to us through other people.

Joshua battled for seven years. Obedience can take a long time. It's a daily choice, not a onetime act. Faithful obedience keeps our hearts soft before the Lord and keeps us out of a pattern of disobedience that leads to a hard heart that cannot hear God's voice.

Ultimately, obedience brings peace. We can't control our circumstances, but when we obey God, we will find peace in the midst of them. If you don't have peace, look for where you're not obeying. What are you trying to control that you should give to God?

Lord, open our eyes to the lie of control.
Show us that next step You want us to take. Amen.

The Lord Is Our Inheritance

*But to the tribe of Levi he gave no inheritance, since the
food offerings presented to the Lord, the God of Israel,
are their inheritance, as he promised them.*

JOSHUA 13:14 NIV

In the New Testament, Christians are called priests, like the tribe of Levi (see Revelation 1:6). Instead of inheriting land, Levi received the people's offerings to the Lord as their inheritance. Similarly, instead of a physical inheritance, we as Christians receive the Lord Himself as our inheritance. He is our portion, our share of the riches. Many verses in the Old Testament talk about what it means for the Lord to be our portion:

- Psalm 16:5 says He gives us provision, security, and His presence.
- Psalm 73:26 says God is our advocate and with us always.
- Psalm 142:5 says He is our refuge. He hears us. He protects us and gives us freedom. He is good to us.
- Lamentations 3:19–33 says His mercies are new every morning.

Today we celebrate the flag that represents our nation. We are blessed to live in a nation with religious freedom, one of God's blessings to us. Isn't it amazing to think that God belongs to us? He resides within us and is with us in everything we do. We can't lose Him. That's better than a plot of land any day.

*Heavenly Father, thank You for the gift of Your Son that allows
us to have You as our inheritance. Thank You that we don't
have to wait to receive it, that we have You with us every day.
Open our eyes to see Your presence. Amen.*

The Reward of Faith

"So on that day Moses swore to me, 'The land on which your feet have walked will be your inheritance and that of your children forever, because you have followed the Lord my God wholeheartedly.' "

JOSHUA 14:9 NIV

If we look back on the story of Caleb in Numbers 13 and 14, we see that his heart overflowed with confidence in God. If God said Israel was supposed to get the land, then it didn't matter who was living there; the Israelites would defeat them. Caleb believed that God would do what He said He would do. He was enthusiastically optimistic.

The Anakites, the giants Caleb and Joshua originally spied over forty years earlier, still controlled the land Caleb was to inherit. And he was eighty-five years old. But he was not ready for retirement. He had followed God wholeheartedly, the key to his effectiveness. He was filled with the presence and the power of God. He had pursued God, like a hunter closing the gap on his prey. Caleb still welcomed a challenge. Caleb believed God still had work for him to do and would give him the strength to remove the giants from his land.

Ultimately, this is God's story, not Caleb's. Caleb just applied the principle of sowing and reaping, and God showed up like He said He would. Like Caleb, we can rely on God's strength and power to work through us even if we have physical and mental limitations.

Heavenly Father, thank You for always showing up, bigger and better than we expect. Show us where we need to trust You. Amen.

A Glimpse of Heaven

" 'He will wipe every tear from their eyes. There will
be no more death' or mourning or crying or pain,
for the old order of things has passed away."
REVELATION 21:4 NIV

When the Israelites were preparing to cross into the Promised Land, they celebrated Passover. They had not been in the land long enough to cultivate it and create a rich harvest, but what they did eat they ate in anticipation of what God had promised them.

It is the same with heaven. Our time on earth is small and faded compared to the glory of heaven. While we are working through our difficulties here, we anticipate heaven, like the Israelites did the Promised Land.

Heaven will be a place of beauty. There will be no death, pain, fear, or impurity. God's creation will exist in the full glory He originally intended, not the wrecked-by-sin version we live in now. No sinfulness will mar it.

Relationships will deepen and expand and be deeply fulfilling without our sinfulness creating barriers between us and others. Rewards, restoration, and comfort are awaiting us. God will make it all up to us—all the loss, pain, and sorrow we experience in this world.

God gives us glimpses of heaven now to encourage us on our journey. He knows we can't see the whole picture, and He condescends to our frail humanity to give us what we need for the journey.

Heavenly Father, thank You for Your loving care of us.
Show us glimpses of heaven when the journey gets rough,
and encourage us with what awaits us. Amen.

The Definition of Faith

Now faith is confidence in what we hope for and assurance about what we do not see. . . . And without faith it is impossible to please God, because anyone who comes to him must believe that he exists and that he rewards those who earnestly seek him.
HEBREWS 11:1, 6 NIV

Eyes of faith help us see the spiritual gifts God gives us. Faith allows us to see things normally unseen. Throughout the Old Testament, there are stories of people whose faith in God demonstrates what faith in action looks like: Abel sacrificed to God with a heart of worship, Enoch started following God in his later years, Elisha saw angel armies, and Noah built an ark in a land without rain.

In whom or what do you place your faith? God's character and His promises are faithful. Faith is the pathway to our relationship with God. We have faith to please God, to earnestly seek Him and believe in His reward, even when we can't see it with earthly eyes. We need to cultivate our eyes of faith, knowing that most of our reward for a faithful life will not be found in this life but in the next.

How do you grow your faith? Start with obedience. Worship, walk by faith, and share your journey with others. Faith will follow your obedience. Ask God to help you exercise your eyes of faith so you can see Him working. If you can't see Him, ask Him to reveal Himself to you.

Heavenly Father, thank You for making a relationship with You possible. Help us to see You working in our lives. Amen.

How God Loves His Daughters

"Why should our father's name disappear from his clan because he had no son? Give us property among our father's relatives."
Numbers 27:4 NIV

The Promised Land of Israel was to be divided among the twelve tribes of Jacob. One of his descendants, Zelophehad, only had daughters, no sons. At that time, women were not allowed to inherit. But his five daughters went to Moses and asked for the land that would have belonged to their father.

Moses is so shocked by their request that, instead of making a ruling himself or consulting with his leaders, he takes their request to God to ask what to do. The culture perpetuated the lie that God didn't care about women. God acted in a countercultural manner and granted the women their request.

This story also shows that our spiritual inheritance is not determined by our earthly parents. The women admitted their father had died in his sin of unbelief, but God did not hold that sin against them. He provided the inheritance and blessings their earthly father could not.

These women demonstrated their faith in God's Word by asking for their share of the land *before* any of it had even been conquered. After God led Israel to conquer the land, they reminded Joshua of their inheritance.

God is passionately concerned about the unique challenges of being a woman in this world. He wants us to come to Him and ask Him for blessings. He is the perfect Father.

Heavenly Father, thank You for Your personal, individual love and care for us. Remind us that we can come to You for anything. Amen.

A Woman's Faith

Then Jesus said to her, "Woman, you have great faith! Your request is granted." And her daughter was healed at that moment.
MATTHEW 15:28 NIV

This Canaanite woman has a demon-possessed daughter. She and her daughter are descendants of the people Joshua and Israel drove out of the Promised Land due to their sin.

Jesus' treatment of this woman is puzzling at first. He begins by ignoring her pleas. But she keeps following Him and His disciples. Then when He does talk to her, He seems to imply that she is a dog and doesn't deserve His attention.

But Jesus is doing something much bigger here. In treating her the way that any Jewish man would, He is giving her an opportunity to express her faith in Him, something her heritage has denied her. Her determination proves the strength of her faith.

He is delighted to grant her request. He commends her faith, and He uses the same term of endearment, *woman*, that He used with His mother at the wedding where He turned water into wine. Jesus is proving to her that heritage doesn't determine her relationship with God; her faith does.

He invites you as His daughter to come to Him and relate to Him in a personal and loving way. Let Him show you how much He loves and values you.

Lord Jesus, thank You for providing the way for us to have a relationship with You. Thank You for loving us, for lifting us up beyond our earthly heritage and giving us immeasurable value in Your eyes. Remind us of how loved we are. Amen.

Follow Your Path

. . .fixing our eyes on Jesus, the pioneer and perfecter of faith.
For the joy set before him he endured the cross, scorning its shame,
and sat down at the right hand of the throne of God.
HEBREWS 12:2 NIV

Jesus endured the agony of the cross and considered it joy because His sacrifice made our relationship with God possible. Before Jesus' death, God's people had to make sacrifices often to cleanse themselves of their sins. But Jesus' sacrifice was perfect so no others needed to be made.

By His sacrifice we are cleansed. The only sacrifice God desires of us now is to do His will, to surrender. He wants us to follow, by faith, the journey He has set out for each of us. This is what pleases Him.

Some parts of the journey will be common to all believers. But there are things that will only be true on our own path. When we follow our path by faith, we please God, just as Jesus pleased Him with His sacrifice. And all those believers who have gone before us are cheering us on. The stories of their journeys are meant to encourage us, just as your journey can encourage others. So share with others what God is doing on your path.

We need to accept the path God has given to each of us—not with reluctance or annoyance but with faith and grace and trust, acknowledging that He knows best.

Father God, thank You for never leaving us.
Help us to take that next step, even when it's hard. Amen.

First Day of Summer

Expect the Unexpected

Then, leaving her water jar, the woman went back to the town and said to the people, "Come, see a man who told me everything I ever did. Could this be the Messiah?"
JOHN 4:28-29 NIV

In this story of the woman at the well, Jesus did the unthinkable by talking to a woman, which was not something men did in that time if they were not related to the woman. And He wasn't talking to just any woman but to a woman of ill repute—a fact the woman herself pointed out.

When she took up her jar to get water at the town well, timed to avoid the respectable women who drew water earlier, she had no idea how one conversation would change her life. It is easy to get comfortable in our routines and not look for the unexpected in our walk with Jesus. Like the woman at the well, we come to Him for one thing and get so much more.

Just as Jesus told the woman to leave her past behind and move forward, He wants us to move into the future He has for us, to move beyond just asking for one thing, and to change our thinking into serving Him and telling others about Him.

Lord Jesus, open our eyes to see Your hand working in unexpected ways. Give us courage to step out into the plans You have for us, to see how You would have us serve, and to tell others about the amazing things You have done for us. Amen.

Take Him at His Word

The royal official said,
"Sir, come down before my child dies."
JOHN 4:49 NIV

While people from Jesus' hometown were reluctant to believe Him, elsewhere people who had heard He performed miracles were desperate to have Him meet their needs.

One such desperate man was a royal official who asked Jesus to heal his sick son. But the way he did it reveals how often we limit our view of Jesus. The man told Jesus, "Go heal my sick son," because in his mind the only way his son could be healed was if Jesus went there to heal him.

Are we like that? We are limited in what we think God can do. Or we think He can only act in a certain way or only within the realm of our imagination. The official thought Jesus had to lay His hands on the boy to heal him. But Jesus only had to speak a word.

The man does show a capacity for growing his faith. When Jesus tells him to go home, that his son is healed, the man takes Jesus at His word and goes home. There is a lesson in that act of faith for us. When Jesus tells us something, we need to do it without arguing, complaining, or asking for an explanation. We need to trust that He works beyond our expectations.

Lord Jesus, we ask for forgiveness for the times we don't obey immediately or take You at Your word. Help us to have the courage to step out in faith and to trust You to work in unexpected ways. Amen.

Do You Want to Be Healed?

When Jesus saw him lying there and learned that he had been in this condition for a long time, he asked him, "Do you want to get well?"
JOHN 5:6 NIV

The pool of Bethesda was where disabled people would go, waiting for an angel to stir the waters. The legend went that if someone made it into the water when the angel troubled the waters, that person would be healed. So Jesus' question doesn't seem to make sense. *Of course* the man wants to be healed. He's at a place where people go when they want to be healed.

When Jesus asks a question, it's not because He doesn't know the answer. He asks because He's all-knowing. He's asking it for our benefit.

The man's response to Jesus' question is also interesting. Instead of saying, "Yes, of course! Heal me!" he makes excuses as to why he hasn't been healed.

Isn't that like us? We want to be healed, but we make excuses why we aren't. Jesus is right there waiting to heal us of our wounds, our addictions, our bitterness—anything that keeps us from the best life He has for us. But He doesn't force Himself on us. He asks us, "Do you want to be healed?" We must reach out to Him. We must exercise our faith in Him.

Lord Jesus, thank You for Your great love for us. Give us the courage to reach out to You for our healing. Help us move past our excuses and reach for that best life You have for us. Amen.

God's Got a Plan

"Here is a boy with five small barley loaves and two small fish,
but how far will they go among so many?"
JOHN 6:9 NIV

So often in life we want to know the whole plan up front. And if God doesn't give us the plan, we start making it up on our own. We get ten steps down the road and decide what can and can't be done. We think we are limited by our resources of time, talent, and finances.

But as today's verse shows, Jesus simply needs us to trust Him with a little and then let Him work. He doesn't need us to do His work, but He allows us to be part of His process. In the story, not only was there plenty to eat, but there were leftovers besides. These people had a physical need for food, and He gave them spiritual food as well.

Spiritually, Jesus gives us everything we need to be satisfied and then even more, so it spills over onto others. When we seek God and put His kingdom first, He provides for our physical and spiritual needs. He is our satisfaction. He is the ultimate answer.

Surrender to Him and see how He works beyond your limited thinking. He always exceeds our expectations.

Dear Jesus, thank You that You are not limited by what we can
see or do. Thank You for inviting us into Your work and allowing
us to see glimpses of heaven through it. Help us to see beyond
this world and to trust You with the outcomes. Amen.

God Isn't Surprised

A strong wind was blowing and the waters grew rough. When they had rowed about three or four miles, they saw Jesus approaching the boat, walking on the water; and they were frightened.
JOHN 6:18-19 NIV

The disciples are rowing for home without Jesus when a storm comes up. They're rowing through the storm, powering through with brute force. Jesus, not surprised by the storm, walks on water, at least three or four miles on it.

We are often surprised by the storms of life. Sometimes these storms come from sin. Sometimes storms arise because we did something right. Jesus tells us that we will have trouble in this world but that He has overcome it.

When we pray during life's storms, we tend to think God is going to make things the way we want, with ease, comfort, lack of conflict, and prosperity. But those things are not the things that draw us closer to Him and grow our faith. He promises to never leave us and to give us His peace, not the world's peace. His ways are different from ours, and we can't see the whole plan.

It can be hard to see God in the struggles of life. Often we are like the disciples, trying to power through on our own. We aren't looking for Jesus and may even be frightened when He shows up. But we should be expecting Him.

Lord Jesus, thank You for never leaving us to handle the storms of life by ourselves. Remind us to look for You and feel Your presence. Amen.

You Are What You Eat

Then Jesus declared, "I am the bread of life.
Whoever comes to me will never go hungry,
and whoever believes in me will never be thirsty."
JOHN 6:35 NIV

Jesus was talking to the disciples after the miracle of using five loaves and two fishes to feed five thousand people. Their focus continued to remain on the physical and natural world, while He was talking about spiritual needs. He wanted them to know that He would provide for them not just physically but spiritually as well.

This was a new idea for them to grasp. They knew that God had provided manna and water in the desert for the Israelites. But they couldn't understand that through providing for a temporary, physical need, God was foreshadowing His coming ability to give us the bread of life, which would satisfy all our spiritual longings.

What we feed on is what nourishes us and determines how we grow. It becomes a part of us. Later, when Jesus is talking about how the branches must remain connected to the vine in order to live, He is talking about this same principle. If we are not connected to the one who gives us life, we cannot stay alive, let alone grow and flourish.

Are you staying connected to the one who gives you life? What are you feeding your soul? Does your life reflect a spiritually healthy diet?

Dear Jesus, thank You for giving Your life so we could
live eternally with You. Remind us of the joy and
necessity of communing with You. Amen.

Worship with Abandon

*Mary then took a pound of very costly perfume of pure nard,
and anointed the feet of Jesus and wiped His feet with her hair;
and the house was filled with the fragrance of the perfume.*

JOHN 12:3 NASB

We can learn three things from Mary's gift to Jesus. First, it was costly. Not only was the perfume expensive, but Mary did something vulnerable and intimate, too. She humbled herself before her Savior in a way many would view as unseemly. It was costly to her pride and possibly to her standing in her community.

Second, her gift affected those around her. It wasn't just between her and Jesus. The fragrance of her gift filled the house. Everyone knew what she had done, and everyone was blessed in some small way by being near her as she gave that gift.

Third, it represented her trusting Jesus for her future. In ancient cultures, women were often given costly perfume as part of their dowry. If she didn't find a husband or he died, the perfume could be sold to support her. By giving what could have been her dowry to Jesus, she was putting her faith in His plans for her future.

Mary worshipped Jesus with abandon. She gave Him the most valuable thing she owned without condition or regard to those around her. She was fully sold out to Him.

*Lord Jesus, help us to worship You with the same kind of abandon that
Mary showed. What could be more precious than the gift of eternal
life You've already given us? Help us to bless others nearby with our
worship and to trust You for our present and our future. Amen.*

God's Upside-Down Kingdom

"Then, Lord," Simon Peter replied, "not just my feet but my hands and my head as well!"
JOHN 13:9 NIV

This is the well-known scene where Jesus is washing the disciples' feet before His death. Peter, the disciple known for his enthusiastic jump-first-then-look attitude, is having none of it. He is not letting Jesus wash his feet because he doesn't understand the purpose behind what Jesus is doing.

Jesus' reaction here is so different from what we might say. Instead of saying to Peter, "Stop telling me what to do! You have no idea what's going on here," He gently explains the lesson and purpose.

God loves our enthusiasm even if it's misdirected. Often we think we know what God is doing or would want done and so we jump ahead of Him. He calmly pulls us back and reminds us that our thoughts and plans are not His.

His plans can seem counterintuitive to us. They are opposite of the world's definition of success. Jesus was God, and He descended to earth to become man. And not a powerful man, but a poor man. And to His disciples, He became a servant. Our society tells us to push up, to rise to the top. But He descended, came down to save us by dying a criminal's death.

Dear Jesus, help us to emulate You and how You serve. Make us sensitive to the gentle nudge You give us to sacrifice, give, downscale, or decrease in some way to serve You and advance Your kingdom. Open our eyes to the blessings You have given us in ways we weren't expecting. Amen.

Our True Enemies

"I am not referring to all of you; I know those I have chosen.
But this is to fulfill this passage of Scripture: 'He who
shared my bread has turned against me.' "
JOHN 13:18 NIV

Jesus knows when He chooses His disciples that Judas would betray Him. That was the way God's plan of salvation would come about. And yet, until this point, Jesus never treats Judas in any way that would indicate He knew of Judas's impending betrayal. In fact, Jesus sharing His bread with Judas in this way shows honor. Jesus treats Judas with much more grace and love than we could imagine. For over three years, Jesus treats Judas like the other disciples.

But what Judas meant for evil was part of God's plan. Is it possible Christ loved Judas because He knew Judas was crucial to the redemption plan?

Ultimately, only God knows our true enemies. He reveals them to us when we need to know. Everything God does has a purpose, usually a far bigger one than we can see. Even when we are determined to do wrong, God loves us with an unfathomable love.

Is there something in your life you need to look at with new eyes, with the perspective that somehow God can use it for good and for His glory?

Lord Jesus, thank You for Your amazing sacrifice and for Your
unfathomable love for us. Help us to view people and situations
with Your eyes and to remember Your love for them. Amen.

God Is in the Details

Nevertheless, each person should live as a believer in whatever situation the Lord has assigned to them, just as God has called them. This is the rule I lay down in all the churches.
1 CORINTHIANS 7:17 NIV

Sometimes we wonder why God puts particular information in the Bible—like the parts of the Old Testament with numbers and dates that don't seem relevant to our lives. But its presence in God's inspired Word shows God is in the details and He loves us in a personal and intimate way. He has called us to the situations we are in, with the people who are around us, for a particular reason.

Other verses expand on this concept:

- Matthew 10:29–31 tells us God has His eye on us individually. He's focused on our needs. He sees us.
- Matthew 6:28–32 says God is well aware of our financial needs. He knows our specific needs and has plans beyond what we can see.
- Romans 14:2–4 tells us God sees our individual weaknesses and struggles. He provides specific ways to help us grow our faith and provides people and situations to help us stand.
- Romans 12:3–6 says we each have different gifts to serve, bless, and help others.

Think about a friend God brought into your life at a particular time when you needed that person, or when God provided for your needs in an unexpected way. Focus on how God loves you individually.

Dear Jesus, thank You for loving us in such a personal way and for having unique plans for each of us. Amen.

The One Choice That Brings Peace

You will keep in perfect peace those whose
minds are steadfast, because they trust in you.
Isaiah 26:3 niv

For the woman who wants to experience the peace God promises, there are only two choices: trust or torment. We must ask ourselves, "Will I rely on God, choosing to believe He can be trusted with all I don't understand and the concerns that consume my thoughts, or will I choose not to believe and trust Him?" The first choice brings rest and peace. The latter only brings torment.

Isaiah 30:15 (nlt) says, "In quietness and confidence is your strength." The one who chooses belief and trust experiences a confidence and quietness of spirit. The one who chooses not to believe and not to trust her Lord experiences a lack of confidence, and chaos overtakes her spirit. "What will happen now?" "Oh no! Awful things are going to happen; I just know it!" In this there is torment.

Belief and trust are chosen because life will always give you many reasons not to trust. It seems that every difficult experience invites us to unbelief, to focus on all that is going wrong and to look to the future in fear. It's not easy to make the choice to believe and trust because it's willful. It's deliberate. And sometimes it's moment by moment.

Lord, please help me to choose trust each moment today
so I can live in the abundance of Your peace. Amen.

Finding Joy in What You Do

So whether you eat or drink or whatever you do,
do it all for the glory of God.
1 CORINTHIANS 10:31 NIV

Maybe you wonder why you are here. One way you can discover why is to take a look at your deepest desires. You were made to love; you desire love. You were made for health; you desire health. And you were made to achieve, so you desire to achieve.

But here is something important to remember: When the reason we want to achieve is to serve ourselves, then we'll end up feeling very empty even if we achieve what we want. But when our desire to achieve points us toward Christ, when it points us toward our greatest purpose to love and glorify God (see Matthew 22:37), then we'll experience joy.

Some people believe they will be fulfilled if only they could discover some solitary purpose, but lasting and deep fulfillment doesn't come from just fulfilling a purpose or even using one's greatest gifts and talents. It comes from using your gifts and talents *and* knowing whom you are using them for. It comes from serving God through what you do.

The artist who paints a picture simply to paint or just to make money will never experience the same joy as the artist who paints to glorify her Creator. Glorifying and loving God gives meaning and deeper joy to everything we do.

Lord, please help me to love You so much that
everything I do flows from that love. Amen.

The Reason Many Relationships Fail

"There is no one righteous, not even one."
ROMANS 3:10 NIV

When someone fails to love the way God desires, they may not have recognized this great flaw in their character because it was hidden behind blame as they made copious mental notes about the shortcomings of their beloved. And these shortcomings have led the lover to believe they cannot love their beloved because it's impossible. *If only she wasn't so insensitive. . . If only he was more complimentary. . . If only she took better care of herself. . . If only he was more supportive. . .then I could love.*

This way of thinking is unwise. Another's flaws—and even sin—may stretch or test our love and even make us feel like it's impossible to love. But another's imperfections are never justification for why we can't love, because love is a choice when the emotions of love fail us. Anything less is not genuine love but only self-service. Certainly, in extenuating circumstances we may not be able to maintain a relationship with someone, but we can always love them with the agape love of Christ, which has their best interest in mind.

When the imperfections of those closest to us do their good work to make us more like Jesus, they will drive us to our knees in supplication: *Lord, please help me to be less selfish! Teach me how to love!* But when we don't allow others' imperfections to illuminate our selfishness, inflexibility, and pride, their flaws can even become the reason we justify our ungodly actions, and this is a great tragedy.

Lord, please help me to love with Your love by examining my heart to see if I am selfish or prideful in any way. Amen.

Freedom Isn't Free

Not only so, but we also glory in our sufferings,
because we know that suffering produces perseverance;
perseverance, character; and character, hope.
ROMANS 5:3–4 NIV

Have you seen a bumper sticker that reads "Freedom isn't free"? This proclamation is referring to the brave men and women serving our country in the military, but the same sentiment applies to us who desire to mature in Christ and experience more spiritual and emotional freedom.

Bible teacher Beth Moore has experienced freedom at a cost firsthand. When someone asked her how she gained the maturity and victory she currently has in life, she thought about it for a moment and then responded, "Disaster."

It seems like an upside-down way of looking at life, doesn't it? Trouble ultimately produces hope. Suffering leads to greater character. Disaster leads to maturity. Attacks from Satan lead to strength. Why? Because freedom isn't free. It's typically paid for and bought with pain, problems, and crises that make us want to throw up our hands and scream.

So what should our response be? We rejoice. How is it possible to rejoice in our sufferings? We must have the confident hope that something good is coming from our turmoil. We must choose to believe that a greater freedom is on its way, not in spite of the troubles we're experiencing but because of them.

Lord, even though it's difficult sometimes, help me
to remember that the trials I face are providing for
me a greater freedom when I submit to You. Amen.

Reducing Love to Feelings

Now that you have purified yourselves by obeying
the truth so that you have sincere love for each other,
love one another deeply, from the heart.
1 PETER 1:22 NIV

There was a time in my life when I believed that I could recognize true love because it was always characterized by exhilarating feelings, and the absence of strong emotions meant I was in the wrong relationship. I now know that if we reduce love to emotion, it makes for a very unsteady relationship, because emotions, like the waves of the ocean, roll in and roll out. One moment they are here, the next they are gone. A wise woman acknowledges this so she doesn't allow her fickle emotions to choose the temperature of her relationships. Instead, she chooses love by doing love. And while she is doing love out of commitment, she does not fear, because she knows that as sure as the tide rolls in and out, the pleasant feelings of love will return again, too.

Don't be deceived by reducing love to feelings. If you do, your relationships will be tossed by the winds of every circumstance. But when you make love a choice, you will steady yourself and choose for yourself a firm foundation whereby the most difficult challenges cannot destroy love.

Lord, please forgive me for those times when I allow my emotions
to drive my reactions in relationships. Please help me to pursue
love by serving my loved ones. Thank You that the emotions
of love often follow the actions of love. Amen.

Filling in the Blanks of God's Promises

Your love, Lord, reaches to the heavens, your faithfulness to the skies.
PSALM 36:5 NIV

Sometime ago a woman contacted me to tell me about a man she was interested in. She wondered if she should move cross-country to live near him. As we talked, I realized she didn't have a relationship with her love interest. "But I know he likes me," she said.

"How do you know?" I asked.

"Because I ran into him one night when I was out with friends and he said, 'I remember you. I met you last summer.' "

Of course, this woman had no basis for moving cross-country. It's just that she wanted this man so badly that she was filling in the blanks of what she didn't know with information that comforted her longing heart.

Sometimes we fill in the blanks with God, too. Maybe He reveals something He is going to accomplish in our lives, such as a new job or the birth of a child. We then make the mistake of filling in the blanks of what He said with details He never gave us. We will get a job living in Cincinnati, or we'll have two boys and a girl.

We need to be careful not to add on to what God said lest we become discouraged and blame Him for being unfaithful. When life doesn't make sense, we can hold firmly to the certain promises He has given. He will always do what is absolutely best for us according to His agape love, and His perfect character and love demands the perfect handling of all that concerns us.

*Lord, please help me to trust You when I don't
understand all that You are doing. Amen.*

God's Love Is Bigger Than Your Circumstances

Who shall separate us from the love of Christ? Shall trouble or hardship or persecution or famine or nakedness or danger or sword? As it is written: "For your sake we face death all day long; we are considered as sheep to be slaughtered." No, in all these things we are more than conquerors through him who loved us. For I am convinced that neither death nor life, neither angels nor demons, neither the present nor the future, nor any powers, neither height nor depth, nor anything else in all creation, will be able to separate us from the love of God that is in Christ Jesus our Lord.

ROMANS 8:35–39 NIV

If these things cannot separate us from God's love, then they aren't an indication of the absence of God's love either. But have you noticed that we still doubt God's love based on what happens in our lives? If we get what we want, we believe God has accepted us and loves us. If we do not receive what we long for, we believe He has abandoned or rejected us. What desperate tragedies of the heart befall us when we measure God's love by our circumstances! We pierce ourselves through when we believe that God only receives and loves us when life goes our way. We must remember that this is not heaven; the final story will be told later. Until then, life sometimes is hard. But still, nothing can separate us from Christ's love. Nothing.

Lord, help me to remember how much You love me this day no matter what I face. Amen.

Living between the Pain of Earth and the Hope of Heaven

For just as we share abundantly in the sufferings of Christ,
so also our comfort abounds through Christ.

2 CORINTHIANS 1:5 NIV

God never promised anyone a life without pain. Oh! What wretched depths of despair we descend into when we expect that life will be filled with only happiness because we know the Savior. We begin to think that we are unloved by Christ, or we believe He is mean, powerless, or passive—and our hope fails. We must remember that God's plan for our lives includes pain: "In this world you will have trouble," but it also includes hope, "Take heart! I have overcome the world" (John 16:33 NIV).

Until Christ returns, we live in the in-between, where His glory has not been fully revealed and we suffer. We must remember that in spite of what happens to us, God is good and He loves us, and He will ultimately make things right. Until then, we share in the sufferings of Christ and we wait. And with the power that comes from the Holy Spirit, we choose gratitude over self-pity and complaining. We cast our broken hearts, broken lives, and cares at His feet because He cares for us (see 1 Peter 5:7). We give Him our burdens, and in exchange, we receive rest (see Matthew 11:28).

Living the abundant Christian life isn't about what happens to us. It's about how we respond to what happens to us.

Lord, thank You that even though life is sometimes difficult, You have given me all I need to be an overcomer through faith in You. Amen.

God's Empowering Grace

The boundary lines have fallen for me in pleasant places;
surely I have a delightful inheritance.
PSALM 16:6 NIV

I once met a woman who lamented over a friend's success. "She is receiving promotion after promotion. She is doing in her ministry career what I want to do in mine. I have prayed. I have asked God to help me use my gifts and talents serving Him the same way she is serving Him, but nothing has happened. Any time I try anything, I get shut down. I feel like God has forgotten me and I don't have any value in the body of Christ."

As I spoke with this woman, I thought that the kingdom of God is like a farmer's field and each of us has been given a patch to work and to tend. One person has been given a large patch, another has been allotted a smaller assignment. One person works in a noticeable part of God's field, another in a less visible part—but all assignments are important.

What this woman failed to see is that God's grace—or His unmerited favor—empowers us to do what we need to do. Grace will enable you to accomplish your God-given assignment. But where grace is absent, you won't be able to move that mountain. Therefore, don't waste your precious time envying someone else's accomplishments or worrying about how you are being shortchanged. Know that the Lord has a plan for you to serve Him in a unique way. Rest in this truth.

Lord, thank You so much that You will empower
me to do that which You have called me to. Amen.

When You Feel like You Are Blowing It

For the word of God is alive and active. Sharper than any
double-edged sword, it penetrates even to dividing soul and
spirit, joints and marrow; it judges the thoughts and attitudes
of the heart. Nothing in all creation is hidden from God's sight.
Everything is uncovered and laid bare before the
eyes of him to whom we must give account.
HEBREWS 4:12–13 NIV

Have you ever had a sense when you read the Bible that you just weren't measuring up? That you were totally blowing it? That happened to me once as I read the New Testament. Then this thought came to mind: *The conviction you are sensing is the purification of the human heart through the Word.* I suddenly remembered Hebrews 4:12–13, which says that God's Word judges the thoughts and intentions of the heart. Suddenly it hit me: *The conviction I feel is God's love in action, transforming me through His Word.*

It's never His desire to burden us down with guilt that leads to death, but to reveal our sin so we can experience life! It's to show us where our thoughts and intentions are wrong so He can lead us to what is right.

Ah! Joyous liberty!

Thank You, Lord, that my soul and spirit are laid bare and exposed
before You. You know everything about me. You see the thoughts
and intentions of my heart, and You purify me as Your Word judges
both. This is the purification of my heart through Your Word
as it corrects me and shows me where I am blind. Amen.

Feeling Disappointed?

*Though the fig tree does not bud and there are no grapes on the vines,
though the olive crop fails and the fields produce no food, though
there are no sheep in the pen and no cattle in the stalls, yet I will
rejoice in the LORD, I will be joyful in God my Savior.*
HABAKKUK 3:17–18 NIV

One of my best friends can always tell when her kids have been in
the kitchen after school because there are little fingerprints on the
refrigerator. How can you tell that the enemy of your soul has been
at work? You can see his fingerprints of disappointment which lead
to discouragement, then depression, and finally defeat. According to
author Vicki Kraft, the best time to stop the slippery slope to negative
emotions is when feelings of disappointment come knocking. The
solution? Praise God.

Praise Him that He is at work. Praise Him that He hasn't left you.
Praise Him for what He has done. Praise Him for what He is going to
do. Praise Him in song. Praise Him with a shout. Like the psalmists did,
don't ignore your disappointment, but don't wallow in it in unbelief,
either, by lifting your burden to God without throwing in a healthy
dose of thanksgiving.

*Lord, although life is sometimes difficult, and sometimes I am
disappointed, I praise You for all the amazing things You have
done in my life so far and all that You will accomplish in my
life in the future. How good You are! Amen.*

How to Experience Peace While You Work

*You will keep in perfect peace those whose
minds are steadfast, because they trust in you.*
ISAIAH 26:3 NIV

There are some women who balance the demands of work or their calling with extraordinary grace. They calmly endure crises with joy, they patiently wait for God to act when things go awry, and they confidently navigate numerous daily pressures. Then there are those of us who panic, burn ourselves out trying to control the future, strive while we work, and worry ourselves into fitful nights without sleep.

There have been many seasons while I have worked that I have experienced peace, but there have been others when work demands and seemingly impossible tasks threatened to steal all joy. How can we work without striving so we can experience internal rest and peace while we work? How do we push forward through the day and face its demands without becoming a victim of panic or worry?

In his study on Hebrews, John MacArthur writes: "Rest does not mean free from all nuisances and hassles; it means freedom from being so easily bothered by them. Rest means to be inwardly quiet, composed, peaceful. To enter God's rest means to be at peace with God (Romans 5:1)[,] to possess the perfect peace He gives (Isaiah 26:3). . .to maintain our confidence in it or him."

Internal rest is found in belief and trust in God (see Hebrews 3:18–19)—even while we work. Do you want to experience internal rest and peace while you work? Choose to trust God and believe that all that concerns you is under His control. Let Him carry your burdens.

Lord, thank You that I can trust You with all that happens to me today. Help me to enter Your rest through trusting You. Amen.

Relationship Wisdom

Who is wise and understanding among you? Let them show it by their good life, by deeds done in the humility that comes from wisdom.
JAMES 3:13 NIV

If you are having relationship trouble, here are some truths to ponder. Wisdom produces good conduct, and you can recognize it in your relationships because, according to James 3:16, it is:

- Pure
- Peaceable
- Gentle
- Open to reason
- Full of mercy and good fruits
- Impartial
- Sincere

But jealousy and selfish ambition (both self-centered in nature) produce bad conduct in relationships; they create disorder (see James 3:17–19). Both jealousy and selfish ambition create passions in us that are not guided by wisdom. You can recognize these evils in your relationships because they result in quarrels and fights.

If you have a consistent history in your relationships of quarreling, fighting, and relational disorder, check your heart for selfishness or jealousy. If you need to confess sin in your heart, do, then ask God for wisdom and empowerment from the Holy Spirit to practice good conduct. If you are aligning with those who are characterized by selfishness, ask God to give you the wisdom on how to proceed in your relationships. It all comes back to the heart.

Lord, help me to show only love and acceptance to others, to love them unselfishly and rely on You. Amen.

God Is Bigger Than the Wrong Done to You

"But if you do not forgive others their sins,
your Father will not forgive your sins."
MATTHEW 6:15 NIV

It can be tough to forgive. It presses us to the edge of ourselves where we are forced to acknowledge that God is greater than the wrong that has been done to us. When we choose to forgive, it keeps God's power in perspective.

Someone may stop loving you, insult you, steal from you, or abuse you, but that person will never be able to destroy the love that God has for you or His sovereign rule over all that concerns you. God's redeeming love is bigger than your enemies. This is what Joseph acknowledged after his brothers threw him in a pit and sold him into slavery: "You intended to harm me, but God intended it for good" (Genesis 50:20 NIV).

Think about something someone has done to you that has demanded forgiveness. Do you believe God is bigger than the wrong? Are you convinced His love and His rule are redemptive? If so, let the person who has wronged you off the hook. Stop thinking that he or she has ruined your life and that you will never recover—because God is a redeemer.

Lord, when someone wrongs me, I may want to lash out or hold
a grudge. Help me to remember that there is nothing that will
happen to me that You cannot redeem for my good and Your glory.
Help me to live in the freedom of this truth. Amen.

Just Enough Light for the Step You're On

Your word is a lamp for my feet,
a light on my path.
PSALM 119:105 NIV

In his book, *The Fulfillment Factor*, Mike Kendrick writes: "Having a vision for your future isn't like having a GPS in your car. You can and should make long-term plans, but God will never give you every detail about your future. You won't be able to see the entire 'map' of your vision up front. Only a few of the main intersections will be marked."

The Bible echoes Kendrick's sentiments. Scripture says that God's Word is a light unto your path. It doesn't shine like you're in broad daylight, casting clarity on every step from where you are to where you'll be next year. Instead, the Lord—and His Word—will give you just enough light for the step you're on. If we insist that God reveal every step between where we are and the fulfillment of a revealed promise, we rob ourselves of the abundant joy that comes from walking with Him, of moving when He moves, of responding to His direction on a moment-by-moment basis, and of seeing Him orchestrate the events of our lives in surprising ways. This is what it means to keep in step with the Spirit (see Galatians 5:25).

Can you rest in the unknown today and trust God for the future? Do you need to give your fears about what you don't understand to Him?

Lord, You have never let me down; You won't disappoint me now.
Help me to trust in You for the unknown future. Amen.

Giving Up Your Pennies for Something Good

*And my God will meet all your needs according
to the riches of his glory in Christ Jesus.*
PHILLIPPIANS 4:19 NIV

Years ago, I watched a movie in which a tiny girl held a handful of shiny pennies. An adult approached her and held out a five-dollar bill, inviting her to trade. Convinced she already had what was best because it looked like the most, she told him no and hugged her pennies close.

This reminds me of how we can be when Christ comes to us with an invitation. He stands before us and asks us to join Him in a new work, passion, or calling. But we often hold on to the old when we could have something better. To let go of the old, we have to choose to trust God. But sometimes we need convincing, which is why God may move at a turtle pace with us. It's not that He can't change our circumstances more quickly, but we first have to be moved from unbelief to belief to receive from Him and to do what He has called us to. That often takes time.

Even though scripture doesn't explain why it took so long for Abraham to have a son, Isaac to marry, Joseph to be released from prison, or Hannah to have a child, my guess is that God was doing as much in their circumstances as He was also doing in their hearts. He was transforming them and preparing them to lay down their handfuls of pennies.

Do you need to relinquish something today?

*Father God, I am guilty of holding a tight fist sometimes.
In my head and heart I know this shiny thing that I hold on
to pales in comparison to the perfection that You offer me.
Loosen my grip. Forgive me when it tightens. Amen*

Don't Get in That Tit for Tat

Keep reminding God's people of these things.
Warn them before God against quarreling about words;
it is of no value, and only ruins those who listen.
2 TIMOTHY 2:14 NIV

I wish I could say I have always handled disagreements with Paul's words of wisdom. I haven't. But recently I had another opportunity to get in a tit-for-tat argument over words and trivialities online while ignoring the command to love. I was reminded what a waste of time, energy, and emotion it would be, not to mention, foolish.

Why am I telling you this? Because we all have opportunities to argue over small spiritual matters that aren't worth arguing about. And Paul's words weren't just for Timothy. They are especially powerful for us today because we not only speak but text, message, tweet, and post. In a day when the readiness to become offended is at an all-time high, it takes wisdom and carefulness to know when and how to insert one's beliefs or opinion into a conversation. We must remember that the most godly and loving thing to do is to sometimes say nothing at all, especially when dealing with someone who is contentious. And when we do speak, we should always be kind.

Lord, help me to be a wise woman who is careful to speak and
slow to get angry so that I can show others that You are real. Amen.

It's Not about the Dream

Do not love the world or anything in the world. If anyone loves the world, love for the Father is not in them.
1 JOHN 2:15 NIV

When God called me to write, I knew if I wanted to be effective for Him, I had to write out of my relationship with Christ. And what could be better than marrying my passion for words with my passion for Jesus?

Sadly, after a few years in ministry, my love for Christ was overshadowed by building a bigger platform. After all, I had repeatedly heard that that's what successful Christian authors and speakers do. They write a lot of books, build their e-mail lists, and make money so they can fund their ministries to reach more people for Christ. Don't get me wrong. There is nothing bad about wanting to reach people for Christ; there is something wrong with loving your mission more than you love the Messiah. There is something wrong with being led by your own goals instead of being led by the Spirit. Because, "For those who are led by the Spirit of God are the children of God" (Romans 8:14 NIV). If goals or outcomes become our idols, we are out of God's will. If our dreams are more important to us than the one who gave us the dreams, we are serving out of the wrong motives.

Lord, take the desires of my heart and do with them what You will. Change them if You need to; I want to walk only in Your will. Amen.

Is the Grass Really Greener?

No good thing does he withhold from
those whose walk is blameless.
PSALM 84:11 NIV

A few years ago when I was still single, I ran into an old friend at a coffee shop. After our conversation, which included the topic of her family and what I had been doing in my career, she walked away with a smile and a wave, and I felt a sickening emotion rise up in my heart: envy. I was shocked by how I felt, then I prayed, *All right, Lord. Why do I feel this way?* God revealed to me that I felt cheated. My friend had what I wanted: a family. I felt deprived of what I longed for most. I asked the Lord to reveal truth to me about my attitude.

In the next few moments, I realized a couple of things: Because envy involves feeling cheated, envy has a distorted view of God's character. Therefore, the person who envies disbelieves God's goodness, His love, or that He is in control. When we envy, we also reject the truth that God is intimately involved in all the affairs of our lives.

Envy believes the lie that God's good gifts are not enough. The person who envies denies that the provision God has given her is pleasant (see Psalm 16:6). The provision God has assigned to each of His children is actually very personal. It would be unfair for Him to treat everyone the same because it would deny the unique way He has created each one of us.

Lord, thank You that You are good and that You have
personally picked the blessings I have in my life.
Help me to be grateful and not envious. Amen.

What's Your "But God" Story?

But God demonstrates his own love for us in this:
While we were still sinners, Christ died for us.
ROMANS 5:8 NIV

Some people believe God set the world in motion, then stepped back just to watch it spin without intervening in the lives of men. A simple search for the phrase "but God" in scripture shows otherwise. According to Khouse.org, the exact phrase "but God" is used 64 times from the Old Testament to the New.

- In Genesis 20:3, Abraham gave his wife, Sarai, to Abimelek, but God intervened and came to Abimelek in a dream telling him that he was as good as a dead man since Sarai was married.
- In Genesis 41:16, Joseph couldn't give Pharaoh the interpretations for his dreams, but God could (and did).
- In Genesis 45:5, there was a famine, but God sent Joseph ahead of his family through a nasty betrayal to save the lives of many people, including his brothers who had betrayed him.
- In Jonah 1:17, Jonah ran from God, but God provided a great fish to swallow Jonah.
- In Acts 2:24, Jesus was put to death, but God raised him from the dead.

How awesome! But God! God was involved in the lives of men and He is still involved now, intervening, guiding, and ruling. What's your "but God" story?

Lord, thank You that You are always at work in my life.
Help me to notice all the ways You intervene to guide me,
lead me, and provide for me. Amen.

When You Worry about What Other People Think

Fear of man will prove to be a snare,
but whoever trusts in the LORD is kept safe.
PROVERBS 29:25 NIV

In the original Hebrew language, the word *snare* in Proverbs 29:25 is the word *mokashe*, and it means "trap." No one wants to fall into a trap, but that is exactly what allowing the fear of people to rule us will do. Fearing what they think. Fearing their retribution. Fearing their shame. Fearing their judgment. Fear gives others the ability to control us.

Maybe you can relate. Maybe you have allowed the fear of others to cause you to choose a poor path, turn down a job offer, reject a marriage proposal, or run from a promotion.

Matthew Henry has something beautiful to say about fearing those who are no greater than ourselves: "Abraham, for fear of man, denied his wife, Peter his Master, and many a one his God and religion. We are encouraged to depend upon the power of God, which would keep us from all that fear of man which has either torment or temptation in it."

When we trust God instead of allowing the fear of others to rule us, then we will be able to say with confidence, "If God is my salvation, I will trust and not be afraid."

Lord, help me to live for an audience of one.
Help me to know that I need to focus on pleasing You.
Give me courage and strength to say yes to You. Amen.

Truth That Is in Plain Sight

"Then you will know the truth,
and the truth will set you free."
JOHN 8:32 NIV

In the original Greek language, the word for truth in John 8:32 means that it's truth that is plain in sight; it's obvious. It's truth that is right before your eyes.

When I read this, I thought, *Wait a minute! Truth that is right before your eyes? We hardly feel like truth is right before our eyes! It seems like it's hidden and so very difficult to apprehend. Why is this?* As I mulled this over, the thought that immediately came to mind is that our hearts are often so unbelieving.

God tells us who He is; we doubt it. He confesses His love for us in scripture; we ignore it. He tells us how to live; we do things our own way. And so it is with us like it was with the disciples when Jesus asked them, "Do you not yet see or understand? Do you have a hardened heart?" We see but we don't see. We hear but we don't listen. We know it but we don't understand. All of this means that we miss the Truth that is right in front of our eyes; we remain bound when we could be set free. It's not the person who just intellectually knows the truth who is set free; it's the person who knows and believes that is set free.

Lord, help me to believe You so that I can see You at work.
Give me a tender heart so that my spiritual eyes will be open. Amen.

Only God Gets to Be the Cake

"You shall have no other gods before me."
EXODUS 20:3 NIV

I once heard a woman on television say she wanted another child because, "I know another child will make me happy." She already had eight. If she birthed more babies, a hunch tells me she discovered Number 9 couldn't do anything for her that Numbers 1–8 hadn't. This woman had made an idol out of motherhood.

In my thirties, it slowly dawned on me in a way it hadn't ever before that all my biggest and brightest dreams fulfilled—and even the greatest gifts life offers, such as the love of family and friends—will never fully satisfy. All of our greatest earthly desires are like icing on the cake of life, not the cake. And they can never be the cake. It's not possible. Only God gets to be the cake. It's the way He designed it.

When we admit that a new home, the best furnishings, a six-figure job, a loving spouse, or even another child cannot fill us, we are in a *very good place*. At first, it may make us feel desperate because we come face to face with our emptiness. But it's a good kind of desperate because it can lead to peace and rest.

Until then, we are like little children who scream in a panic while grasping at the sky, "I want!" But after we admit nothing in this world can satisfy like Christ, we can lie down in the gentle grass of "God's enough." And then comes rest from striving.

Thank You, Lord, that You are enough. Help me to remember that You are the only place I can find true satisfaction. Amen.

Going against the Flow

Whoever claims to live in him must live as Jesus did.
1 JOHN 2:6 NIV

In 2011 NBC News aired a story about an unemployed man who was mining for gold and diamonds on a busy sidewalk outside a handful of prominent Manhattan jewelry stores. The news showed him peering into a crack in the sidewalk while holding a magnifying glass and a tiny broom.

The report stated that some people who walked into the jewelry store later emerged with tiny pieces of lost gold and diamonds, which had fallen off clothes and rings, attached to their shoes. These tiny treasures were then deposited in the sidewalk cracks.

This ingenious man saw what others couldn't see.

When God has called you to do something for Him, you may see what others can't. God will give you a plan for the future. He will call you to a particular task, and others won't be able to see—or envision—what you see. And because they can't see what you see, they may think you are unwise or uninformed, which means you will have to go against the flow.

Jesus' walk was characterized by obedience to His Father even when others didn't agree. He went against the flow. Will you follow His lead?

Lord, it can be scary to follow You when others are saying that it's not a good idea. But, Lord, make me a woman of faith who stands for courage and for what's right even when it doesn't make sense to the world. Amen.

Don't Give Up

*In all these things we are more than
conquerors through him who loved us.*
ROMANS 8:37 NIV

There are times in every woman's life when pursuing a calling—whether it's raising children, running an organization, or attending college—can become tiring. When this happens, some people want to throw in the towel and give up. Maybe you have felt the same. You feel weighed down, beat up, and discouraged. You feel like you are running in so many directions that you are exhausted.

A few years ago, I collected about thirty smooth river rocks and washed them. Next, I wrote a word or short phrase on each one with a marker to remind me of God's faithfulness and placed them in a basket on my kitchen table.

Since then, every time I have picked up one of these rocks and held it in my hand, a phrase like "Move to Colorado," "Provision for ministry," or "Teaching job in Texas" has reminded me of God's pro-vision. On a few occasions, these rocks—and the memories they represent—have given me the courage to go on when I felt like call-ing it quits. No doubt, remembering God's faithful acts is a powerful way to bolster endurance, and remembering our faithfulness toward Him can do the same.

*Lord, you have been so faithful to me. Help me to take
the time to remember the ways you have practically
demonstrated your love for me. Amen.*

The Guarantee of Finding Him

*"You will seek me and find me when
you seek me with all your heart."*
JEREMIAH 29:13 NIV

In this verse, God reveals that He doesn't hide where He can't be found but invites us to look for Him and find Him. In the original Old Testament Hebrew, the word *seek* specifically involves seeking God through prayer and worship. Contrary to what some people say, God isn't found by following a long list of legalistic rules and religious regulations. Instead, He's found in sincerity of heart by focusing on nurturing your relationship with Him.

There are few guarantees in life, but this scripture provides one: when you seek God with all your heart, you will find Him. There's no wondering if you'll find Him, if you'll be able to make your way to Him, or if you will be allowed to find Him. There's no question. He will show Himself to you when you genuinely search for Him through prayer and worship.

In *The Case for Faith,* journalist Lee Strobel interviews Peter Kreeft, a world-class philosopher, who makes the following statement: "The Bible says, 'Seek and you shall find.' It doesn't say that everybody will find him; it doesn't say nobody will find him. Some will find him. Who? Those who seek."

*Lord, sometimes You seem elusive and sometimes I can't
sense Your presence, but I stand on the promise that You have
said I can find You when I seek You. Thank You, Lord. Amen.*

How You Can Keep Believing

For we live by faith, not by sight.
2 CORINTHIANS 5:7 NIV

Some people say Christianity doesn't work because it doesn't eliminate life's problems. It's not like rubbing a genie bottle. Instead, sometimes being a believer means that God will take us places we never had any intention of going. It means that sometimes being a disciple hurts—just like it hurt Christ.

In John 15:20 (NIV), Jesus said, "Remember what I told you: 'A servant is not greater than his master.'" Since these things are true, some people ask, "How can you keep believing in the face of evil, persecution, heartbreak, disappointment, and crushed dreams? How can you continue to trust Christ and believe God exists when the circumstances are sometimes so contrary?"

We can because that is what faith does. It believes. In spite of what we can't see. In spite of what we don't understand. Faith always bends its knee to the God who made everything and knows everything. And faith remembers that this is not heaven, that this current life is a dot on the timeline of eternity. And faith is confident that in time God will make all things right. Maybe not this moment, maybe not next week, and maybe not next year. But when Christ returns, justice will be served, every wrong will receive its recompense, everything will be made beautiful, and everything will be made new. That's how we can keep believing.

Will you choose to believe God today in spite of your circumstances?

Lord, give me the faith to follow You no matter what happens in my life. Amen.

Why It's Okay to Say No

Whether you turn to the right or to the left, your ears will hear a voice behind you, saying, "This is the way; walk in it."
ISAIAH 30:21 NIV

In the past, there were days I was under the illusion that I was Wonder Woman. If I could reasonably fit nine things on my to-do list, I would add five more. Over the years, God has often reminded me that I can't do everything, and if I want to be effective in fulfilling His plans for my life, then I can only do one or two things well. Because, as Pastor Andy Stanley says, "Devoting a little of yourself to everything means committing a great deal of yourself to nothing." This means there will be times when I have to say no.

Not only that, but if you don't say no, you could be stealing someone else's opportunity. Imagine that the women's ministry director at your church asks you to lead a Bible study. You don't really want to because you know you have too many things on your plate. But she insists, and the next thing you know, you find yourself saying yes, when you should be saying no. Could it be that God actually called another woman to lead, and when you said yes, you stole her opportunity?

Lord, help me to always follow Your leading when I should say no, so I will always do my best work for You and won't steal someone else's chance to serve. Amen.

Perhaps Your Desire Is from God

"Everything is possible for one who believes."
MARK 9:23 NIV

What desires has God placed in your heart? What do you want to accomplish? What dreams do you want to reach? Whom do you want to help? What do you want to do for Christ?

Take an inventory of your "I can't" statements. "I can't because _____." If God has placed it in your heart, He will enable you to do it because it's His desire. It doesn't mean it won't be difficult, but you can accomplish it through Him.

Before I pursued a career as I writer, I used to think, *Well, that desire can't be from God because it's something I want to do.* I somehow got the crazy idea that being a Christ follower meant my desires would never line up with His. I didn't know that God has given each of us gifts and talents that are to be used—and we are often passionate about using them!

If God has placed a dream in your heart, if it involves your gifts and talents, if it's going to help others, if it will glorify Him as you shine in the glory He has given you, then think again. If it's not sinful, if it doesn't violate His laws, and if it's a "I would really like to do that one day" nagging that doesn't disappear, perhaps it's God who put the desire in you for His glory.

*Lord, show me how to use my gifts
and talents to glorify You. Amen.*

Practicing Good Boundaries

The righteous choose their friends carefully.
PROVERBS 12:26 NIV

When I was in college, I knew a young woman who dated a guy named Rick. Unfortunately, the romance with Rick ended badly. Later on, that same young woman dated another guy named Rick. Sadly, that relationship went south, too. After that, the young woman developed a cynical attitude about all men named Rick. "I am never dating a guy named Rick again." This made sense to her because all guys named Rick are bad, right? Of course not.

It's understandable that when we become hurt, we may want to protect ourselves by becoming cynical rather than trust God with our pain. But this is unwise. A better idea is to practice discernment. A cynical person makes blanket statements about people. "All people are rude," "All men are losers," "All women are cheaters," or "All guys named Rick are jerks." But someone who is wise and discerning evaluates each situation on a case-by-case basis to determine if the person is safe, and if God wants that person in her life.

Even Jesus, who knew the evil intent of men's hearts, wasn't jaded or overly self-protective. He wasn't cynical but was discerning. He did not make the mistake of being overly self-protective or nasty. He was tender when needed and firm when necessary. When we practice discernment by listening to the Holy Spirit and receiving wise counsel, we can become empowered to practice good boundaries.

Lord, thank You that I don't have to become cynical or overly self-protective in relationships. Please give me Your wisdom. Amen.

Forgiveness Isn't like a "Stoptional"

Then Peter came to Jesus and asked, "Lord, how many times shall I forgive my brother or sister who sins against me? Up to seven times?" Jesus answered, "I tell you, not seven times, but seventy-seven times."
MATTHEW 18:21–22 NIV

I once rode in the car with my humorous husband when he ran a stop sign. I said, "Oops! Missed that one." He laughed and responded, "That's what I call a Stoptional."

Sometimes we treat God's commands like Stoptionals. Sure, He told us not to do a particular something like gossip, lie, steal, or harbor bitterness, but it's not a big deal if we don't follow through, right? Because, well. . .sometimes God allows some of His commands to be optional, right? And of course there is always grace.

One of those commands we sometimes feel is optional is His command to forgive. We convince ourselves that we can love God but still harbor a little hate for that person who rubbed us the wrong way, wounded us, mistreated us, abandoned us, robbed from us, attacked us, left us, or lied to us, right? Wrong. In fact, God says it's impossible to love God but not love our brother—or sister (see 1 John 14:19–21).

It's impossible to love God and harbor unforgiveness in our hearts. Forgiveness is an indicator of whether Christ's love dwells within us. Habitual forgiveness is a sign we belong to Him. Christ says that if we don't love, we don't belong to Him. Tough—but true—words.

Do you need to make the choice to forgive someone today?

Lord, help me to always be quick to forgive as a demonstration of my true faith. Amen.

Every Day of the Year

This is the day the LORD has made;
we will rejoice and be glad in it.
PSALM 118:24 NKJV

I once heard a radio personality describe the summer season as a weekend with June being Friday, July like Saturday, and August as Sunday. Many people would be just a bit depressed when August comes around since it means summer is gradually coming to an end and all the fun activities and vacations will also end. August also usually means some of the hottest weather of the season for many regions, and the same people who dread thinking of colder weather also complain about excessively warm days.

Perhaps we need a renewed perspective about August and, figuratively, about Sunday. Interestingly, while Sunday is seen as the last day of the weekend, it is actually the first day of a new week. Yet since Monday brings work and responsibility, we like to put it off as long as possible. But, if our lives are grounded in Christ, we need to ask Him for an uplifted outlook whether we face scorching hot August days or blustery winter winds. We cannot stop the progress of the week nor the parade of the seasons. Would we want to? Heaven is the only place where a continual "now" will be good for us. On this earth, God is at work in us throughout every day, every month, and every season of life. That's good news on this first day of August.

Lord, make me willing to submit to Your work
in me on every slot in my calendar. Amen.

Your Daily Earful

"O LORD, there is none like You, nor is there any God besides You, according to all that we have heard with our ears."

1 CHRONICLES 17:20 NKJV

What was the first thing your ears heard this morning? After your alarm, that is. What did you listen to while you brushed your teeth, drove to work, made a run to the grocery store, or picked up the kids from a summer activity? Chances are, you were listening to some form of music while you were completing some of these duties. In fact, according to a 2014 survey conducted by Edison Research, most US citizens listen to about four hours of audio per day.

Four hours is one-sixth of your day. It's a lot of time for mental stimulation or acquiring information or receiving inspiration. What is filling your ears, penetrating your heart, and affecting your mood? Challenge yourself this month to increase the amount of time you spend listening to Christian music and programming. A mind can only take so much of the talk show rants and human-interest stories and catastrophic news, not to mention the detriment of sexually charged dialogue and politically correct but biblically incorrect commentaries. Go through the playlist on your device and examine it through the grid of God's Word. Set your satellite or traditional radio stations to choices that will glorify Christ and edify you. And then watch your attitude take on a new look.

Dear God, I ask for forgiveness where I have dishonored You with my listening and for grace to make the changes that are needed. In Jesus' name, amen.

It's Time to Share a Watermelon

Then God said, "Let the land sprout with vegetation—every sort of seed-bearing plant, and trees that grow seed-bearing fruit."
GENESIS 1:11 NLT

You may not know this if you live in the Northern United States, but today is National Watermelon Day. Several southern towns hold annual watermelon festivals, and some also have special parades. But if you're thinking that this elongated fruit is just a slice of Americana to serve ice-cold at Fourth of July picnics, think again.

Watermelon is thought to have originated in the Kalahari desert of Africa. And it sure makes sense to have watermelon in a desert—its juicy pulp is just the thing for people with depleted water sources. In fact, the very first recorded watermelon harvest was in ancient Egypt. Watermelon was brought to America by European colonists and African slaves. Since a large number of these slaves were sent to plantations in the South, perhaps this is why it became an iconic southern food.

We know that watermelon originated with God, the Master Creator. He commanded the earth to bring forth vegetation and it did. One of those bits of new vine produced watermelon, and over the years it has been a staple at family gatherings, church dinners, and community get-togethers. So, through the years, watermelon has been a very social fruit, associated with good times and sharing. And since today is set aside in honor of the colorful watermelon, why not join in the celebration and enjoy one right now!

Lord, thank You for creating the watermelon
and giving me someone to share it with. Amen.

Friday Delight

*So I decided there is nothing better than to enjoy food
and drink and to find satisfaction in work. Then I realized
that these pleasures are from the hand of God.*
ECCLESIASTES 2:24 NLT

It's Friday! Are you glad? I hear that glad chorus and my voice is right in there with yours! Friday is a day when you think you can endure just about any difficulty at work because the weekend is about to arrive. Friday is a feeling of anticipation, a reminder that life exists beyond the alarm clock and the time clock; it's the joy of knowing that the stress of deadlines and appointments will recede for a couple of days. Not every day can be a Friday, of course, because we need the discipline of the other days in order to accomplish the real stuff of living. But I would certainly not want to have a week without Friday.

Friday has its own kind of energy, an inertia that moves it along and makes it buoyant in our minds. We expect it to be a good day, and many times it is. It certainly was for Daniel DeFoe's character, Robinson Crusoe, who discovered his native friend on that day and named him in honor of it.

It was God who created time and planned for us to work six days and rest on one. When we have gotten our work done, a little Friday joy is good. And when we acknowledge Him in every day of the weekend, the relaxing won't leave us hung over either!

*Thank You, Lord, for Fridays and the joy they bring.
I delight in this good gift. Amen.*

Balanced and Blessed

For every creature of God is good, and nothing is to be refused if it is received with thanksgiving; for it is sanctified by the word of God and prayer.
1 TIMOTHY 4:4–5 NKJV

Have you had your seaweed today? Or your soy milk? Or your vitamin supplements?

Whole food stores and wellness centers are springing up everywhere, like veritable mushrooms in a forest of supermarkets. And is it any wonder? With the rise of disease attributed to detrimental lifestyle and bad diet, consumers are looking for ways to be healthier and live longer. We are figuring out that what we put into our bodies really does matter.

Now, I was raised in the South. And like any good Southern girl, I say if you can't fry it, it isn't worth eating! Slather butter on the biscuits, pour sugar in the tea, and pepper everything really well to make it edible! And if it kills me, bury me with my cast-iron skillet in testimony!

But the only problem with that way of eating on a long-term basis is that it does kill people. Our bodies just weren't made to filter out that much sludge all the time. We are responsible for making good choices in caring for our bodies, which are the temple of the Holy Spirit. So let's seek balance in our eating and exercising and vitamin taking and trust God with the rest.

Dear God, I'm glad for every green plant You created and every source of meat You provide and every vitamin You infused into the nutrients of the earth. Bless my body with health as I honor You with my choices. Amen.

Thank God for Sisters

*"Again I say to you that if two of you agree on
earth concerning anything that they ask,
it will be done for them by My Father in heaven."*
MATTHEW 18:19 NKJV

Today is National Sisters Day!

The first Sunday of every August has been chosen as the day to honor the special bond of sisters. Now, if you're like me, you don't have one. A sister, that is. Both of my siblings are brothers. And I love them dearly. But they, clearly, are not women. So for me, this day is more about celebrating the sisterhood of friendship. Who else but another woman, a "sister," can really know how it feels to give birth or go through menopause or feel your heart break as you leave your child at college? Who else can sympathize with the absurdity of diets, the ignominy of mammograms, or the agony of widowhood? Who else will cheer for you, pray with you, and talk straight to you? Who else will answer your texts and put up with your complaints and listen to your woes?

No one but a sister, sister! If you have one, either by blood or by choice, you have a real treasure. Reach out to her today—call her, text her, Facebook-message her, Snapchat with her! And don't forget that two women united in prayer are a formidable force! Make your sisterhood a prayer partnership and stand together for your families and your future and your faith journey. He will make your bond even stronger.

*Father, thank You for my sisters, either of family
or of the heart. Let us stand together in You. Amen.*

The Right Assurance

And we know that all things work together for good to them that
love God, to them who are the called according to his purpose.
Romans 8:28 kjv

"God won't give me more than I can handle." You hear this phrase a lot. Is it true? Does the Bible say this?

The origin of this phrase is 1 Corinthians 10:13, which is actually dealing with the idea of temptation and says that God "will not allow you to be tempted beyond what you are able, but with the temptation will also make the way of escape, that you may be able to bear it" (NKJV).

Sadly, this verse is used by many who do not know Christ but who find some measure of mental comfort in the idea that, no matter what they are experiencing, even if it is the consequences of sinful choices, God is not allowing them to bear too much. This just isn't so. Proverbs 13:15 (KJV) declares that "the way of transgressors is hard." The crushing consequences of sin will break you and cast you aside.

Only the ones who are following Christ can lay claim to the promise that God will work all things together for good. Those who trust and obey can rest in the assurance that everything (the good and the bad) fits together in the pattern He has laid out for them.

Lord, thank You for helping me bear my burdens and
for keeping track of the things in my life. I know You are
working all things for my good. In Jesus' name, amen.

Trading Complaints for Praise

Praise the LORD, for the LORD is good;
sing praises to His name, for it is pleasant.
PSALM 135:3 NKJV

No one likes a complainer. But most of use like to complain. Just being able to grouse about something seems to make us feel better, or at least vindicated in our irritation. Yet Philippians 2:14 (NKJV) tells us to "do all things without complaining."

This is a hard one for me. When things bother me, I talk, and when something isn't right in my day, my natural inclination is to comment on it. And that leads, sometimes, to more negative observations.

God knows that we become what we focus on. He desires that we be people of praise. Remember the Hebrews in the wilderness and how they complained and murmured every time something went wrong? Eventually, it affected their faith and they did not believe they could defeat the giants in Canaan, and God let them wander around for forty years until they were all dead. No doubt, many of them saw their sin, but it was too late to change the consequences.

The antidote for complaining is praising. Praise is the language of Christians. When we are praising, we are focusing not on ourselves but on Christ and His glory. And of course, this is where we find the most happiness.

Dear Lord, remind me to praise today when I feel like
complaining. Show me how to switch gears and keep
an attitude of praise to You all day long. Amen.

Biopsies and Bravery

"For the life of every living thing is in his hand,
and the breath of every human being."
JOB 12:10 NLT

What about biopsies? Have you had one? If not, chances are good that you will before your life is over. There seems to be a point in all our lives when the doctors can't diagnose from the outside but have to extract a little piece of the inside of us to look at. This gives them more accurate information about whatever is growing or not growing inside of us. And that's a good thing. If something inside has gone rogue, we surely want the medical team to find out.

But still it's a difficult thing to endure the procedure and then wait for the results. In the interim, all sorts of fears play out in the mind. But why should a Christian be frightened about medical tests? Aren't we supposed to want to go to heaven? Why shouldn't we be happy about whatever report the doctor brings back?

The answer is that God implants the desire to live deep within us and He doesn't take that out when we receive Him as Savior. A biopsy reminds us that there may not be a tomorrow for us to enjoy with friends and family. But biopsies also remind us that God is in control and can see every detail of our bodies from the inside out. Whatever the doctor finds will be news that has already passed heaven's copy room.

Heavenly Father, when I have my next biopsy,
please renew my faith in Your promise and help
me to trust Your knowledge. In Jesus' name, amen.

A Mother's Trust

Keep me as the apple of Your eye;
hide me under the shadow of Your wings.
PSALM 17:8 NKJV

Have you heard of Betty Stam? She and her husband, John, serving as missionaries with the China Inland Mission, did not have time to escape with their infant daughter before the invasion of the Red Army. Their captors plundered their home, seized their money, made them write a ransom letter, and then marched them away to another city, where they were stripped of their outer clothing and the next morning paraded down a city street lined with jeering onlookers. At the place of execution, they were forced to kneel in the dust and then beheaded.

But, walking up Eagle Hill that December day in 1934, Betty was leaving behind, hidden in some blankets, her three-month-old baby, Helen Priscilla. She left her with some diapers, milk powder, and ten dollars. She had no way of knowing that the baby would survive for twenty-four hours all alone and would be found by Chinese Christians and taken to her maternal grandparents in another part of China. What kind of mental anguish must she have endured as she walked away from that room, knowing she would likely never return and wondering what would become of her child? We will never know what she thought or how she prayed. But we mothers of today can trust our children to the same God who watched over little Helen Priscilla. They are in His care, and when we are gone, He will still be there.

Father in heaven, give me faith to
trust my loved ones to Your care. Amen.

Who Made It All

...children of God without fault in the midst of a crooked and perverse generation, among whom you shine as lights in the world.
PHILIPPIANS 2:15 NKJV

When you really get to talking with fellow students or coworkers, it is astonishing to discover how unbiblical ideas about the origins of the earth have taken deep root in our society.

Now, it is very important to be focused on showing Christ's love rather than correcting every wrong idea held by others, yet drawing attention to the fact of God's creative work is actually very significant. Evolution is a complicated theory, but at its core is an unwillingness to acknowledge the sovereignty and authority of a Creator. Those who do not want to be subject to Him simply deny that He even exists and find another way to explain this world with its genetic complexities and majestic wonders. Charles Darwin and others after him do not embrace the fact that humanity came into existence because of a loving God who gave us breath and free will and an eternal destiny. They cannot, for it would cause their entire structure of thought to tumble. And today, there are generations of people who simply accept what they have been told. But we know the truth and are called to give witness to it. Not in a strident and rude manner but in a confident and peaceable way. This is the way we shine as lights, illuminating the truth.

Heavenly Father, let me always bear witness to Your creative work and glory. Amen.

More Than a Piece of Fruit

Thank you for making me so wonderfully complex!
Your workmanship is marvelous—how well I know it.
PSALM 139:14 NLT

You know about the fruit analogies for body shapes, right? Are you an apple or a pear? Do you know the advantages and drawbacks of your type? What about the health risks? Did you know that "apples" tend toward heart disease and "pears" lean more toward hormonally fed cancers? What if you're not a truly defined apple or pear but more of a squash or a string bean? Is there honestly anything more degrading than comparing ourselves to fruits and vegetables?

A woman is much more intricately designed than a piece of fruit. And the basic shape of our bodies is something over which we have no control; genetics handles that. We do have a say in what we eat and how we dress and whether we put much effort into exercise and upkeep. But who among us has not failed in these areas at some time or other?

Women were designed by God to be beautiful. And He likes variety. If we're speaking about the plant world, think about the many species of flowers around the globe. They come in every imaginable shape and color and petal dimension. And each of them has its own unique glory. Maybe we should be more like the flowers—stay connected to the Source of our being, accept the sunshine and rain, and reflect His glory in how we grow.

Lord, give me the right perspective of my body and beauty;
may I honor You with my being. Amen.

Whichever Hand You Use

He has made everything beautiful in its time.
ECCLESIASTES 3:11 NKJV

They've been called lefties or southpaws and probably a few other names. They have been forced to adapt to a right-handed world in the way they write, use scissors, play sports, etc., yet they are more likely to be geniuses.

Today has been specially designated to draw attention to the hardships of left-handers who make up about 10 percent of the population. And while it is good to be sensitive to the specific issues faced by others, perhaps we can use this day to emphasize something else that is true for all of us.

The Bible tells us that each human being is uniquely precious to God. And He endows us with the traits we need to fulfill His purpose for our lives. Left-handedness is one of those gifts. In Judges 20:16, scripture records the existence of an elite group of warriors in the tribe of Benjamin. These seven hundred men were all left-handed, and "each of them could sling a rock and hit a target within a hairsbreadth without missing" (Judges 20:16 NLT). These guys used their differentness as an advantage.

You may not be left-handed, but there is something about you that is different from others around you. Give that to God and let Him develop it into something special He can use to strengthen you and bless others.

God, I thank You for the unique gifts You have given me.
Help me use them for Your glory. Amen.

Winning Big

"He who is faithful in what is least is faithful also in much."
LUKE 16:10 NKJV

Why shouldn't I play the lottery? If I can exercise self-control and spend only a few dollars a month on tickets, what is the harm? Even if I never win, I am not losing a lot of money, and I am certainly not keeping food out of my children's mouths. Why can't I take a small risk and keep the door open to winning big?

Our culture has become so accustomed to the lottery mind-set that the idea that playing the lottery might be biblically wrong is unheard of. While there is no verse that specifically mentions the lottery, God gives us some principles in His Word that can guide us.

All the earth's resources belong to God, and He will give them to us if we need them to fulfill His will. ("The earth is the LORD's, and the fullness thereof" [Psalm 24:10 KJV]; "The silver is mine, and the gold is mine" [Haggai 2:8 KJV]; "Every beast of the forest is mine, and the cattle upon a thousand hills" [Psalm 50:10 KJV].)

Accumulating wealth is not to be our focus. (Matthew 6:19–24)

Coveting is a sin. (Luke 12:15; 2 Timothy 3:2; Colossians 3:5; Exodus 20:17)

Moneymaking schemes are like traps and usually lead to sin. (1 Timothy 6:9)

We are to trust Him, not in "uncertain riches." (1 Timothy 6:17; Proverbs 11:28)

God will take care of our needs if we honor Him. (Matthew 6:31–33)

Lord, help me be wise in how I use the money I am given.
I want to be a faithful steward. Amen.

Stay Connected

Give all your worries and cares to God,
for he cares about you.
1 PETER 5:7 NLT

A lot of people today say they pray, especially when someone is sick or there has been some kind of tragedy, but prayer is more than a good luck wish or an emergency contact number. Prayer is the channel through which we interact with our heavenly Father; it is the way we process the events and emotions of our lives and how we can see His will come to pass in our families.

Prayer is your lifeline. It is the vital connection that keeps you in touch with the Father. Imagine being disconnected from your devices all day, every day, for a week. At the end of that time, you would feel uninformed and shut out, cut off from the people who are most important to you. Perhaps God feels a little bit like that when we keep the channel of prayer closed on an ongoing basis. For, at its simplest, prayer is talking to Him. And when we don't talk to Him, we shut Him out of the details of our lives. Of course, being omniscient, He is aware of what is going on anyway, but He wants us to invite Him in, to want to share our days with Him.

Have you prayed today? Don't see it as an obligation or a guilt inducer but as a chance to communicate with the one who loves you more than anyone else and who can do more about your situation than anyone else.

Lord, thank You for being interested in
everything that concerns me today. Amen.

Grace in the Workplace

Always be humble and gentle. Be patient with each other,
making allowance for each other's faults because of your love.
EPHESIANS 4:2 NLT

According to a 2014 survey conducted by Nielson and Everest College, 80 percent of Americans (that's 8 out of 10) are stressed out by a least one thing at work. One of the reasons cited for the stress was annoying coworkers.

Do you clash with someone at work? There are a lot of possible reasons. It could be anything from a difference in basic temperament to opinions of neatness to a radically opposite approach in doing the inventory. We all have our own ideas and opinions, some of them good and plainly beneficial; others sounding ridiculous to the people who work with us. And sometimes the clashes result from sticking to one's Christian testimony. How do we handle these awkward moments?

Gentleness. If it's not a big deal, let it go. If you can give in to the other person's way of doing it without having to be untruthful or go against policy, then do it.

Humility. We don't always have to have the last word or prove our point to the letter.

Mercy. We can choose to get along, even if we don't agree, and refuse to let the irritations become huge tension points.

Let's not be holy snobs or know-it-alls, but rather let's practice the traits of gentleness, humility, and mercy and make the workplace a better place to be.

Lord, give me grace to honor You in my relationships
with my coworkers. In Jesus' name, amen.

An Exclusive Place

But now they desire a better, that is, a heavenly country.
Therefore God is not ashamed to be called their God,
for He has prepared a city for them.
HEBREWS 11:16 NKJV

There are many old songs about heaven that speak of it being a city. Those songwriters of yesteryear used phrases like "the pearly white city," "the city built foursquare," and "the city that never knows night." The Bible tells us that heaven is a city, a place built for God's children and populated with saints from all the ages.

Have you realized that those who make it to that city never say the word *good-bye*? There are no endings there. There are no deaths or partings or moving vans. Existence there will be an ongoing, joyous present. Think about the joy of arriving home for Christmas or coming to a family reunion, that moment when you walk in the front door to warm hugs and happy cries of welcome—that's the delight of every moment of eternity. Isn't it a comfort to know that we have this place waiting for us when this life is over?

Heaven is prepared for those who are in relationship with God. The only way to get there is by accepting the sacrifice of Jesus Christ's work on the cross. Salvation is an inclusive invitation to an exclusive place. Have you made plans to go?

Heavenly Father, thank You for preparing a heavenly
city where I can live for eternity. By Your grace, I will
be there with You when I die. In Jesus' name, amen.

Fear Not; He Is Peace

"You will keep him in perfect peace, whose mind
is stayed on You, because he trusts in You."
ISAIAH 26:3 NKJV

What are you afraid of? Spiders, darkness, cancer, being alone? All of the above?

Every human being has fears. Maybe you've seen the slogan going around back in the 1990s that said "No Fear." It was plastered on T-shirts and bumper stickers and soft drink cups. But it seems that their confidence was slightly misplaced; the company filed for Chapter 11 bankruptcy in 2011. They did have a reason to fear after all.

Most of us are smarter than to deny that we have any fears. Bravery has been defined not as a lack of fear but as action in spite of fear. Anyone who has worn a uniform that put her on the front lines of battle whether in the jungle, desert, or city streets understands this principle.

But Jesus promised us more help than simply bluffing our way through the things that frighten us. He gave us the promise of peace. In John 14:27 (KJV), He said, "My peace I give unto you." This heavenly peace keeps our hearts and minds and gives us the strength to do things we never thought we could while multipling to more than fit whatever need we have. And Satan has no fiery dart that can penetrate it.

Lord, thank You for Your peace. Keep my
heart and mind through Christ Jesus. Amen.

National Aviation Day

If I take the wings of the morning, and dwell in the uttermost parts of the sea, even there Your hand shall lead me, and Your right hand shall hold me.

PSALM 139:9–10 NKJV

There once were two brothers who wanted to fly. After receiving a toy "helicopter" from their father after one of his trips, they played with it until it broke and then built their own. They pointed back to this incident as their first inkling of interest in flight.

Then, on December 17, 1903, four miles south of Kitty Hawk, North Carolina, the Wright brothers made the first controlled, powered, and sustained heavier-than-air human flight. And the rest, as they say, is history.

Today is marked to celebrate the history and development of aviation and those who made it possible. It is truly remarkable that man has developed the ability to soar into the air and travel to distant places and even blast off to the canyon of space and walk on the moon.

But long before Orville and Wilbur built their flying machine, the psalmist David understood the concept that God is everywhere and no winged thing can get away from Him.

So, today it is fitting and proper to celebrate the accomplishments of great men, but let's not forget to honor our God, who stretches out the heavens like a curtain (see Isaiah 40:22) and walks on the wings of the wind (see Psalm 104:3).

O God, You are mighty in all You do. Today, I praise You because You are Ruler of the heavens and all those who are below. Amen.

A Day for Your Best

"Keep the Sabbath day holy. Don't pursue your own interests
on that day, but enjoy the Sabbath and speak of it with delight
as the Lord's holy day. Honor the Sabbath in everything you do
on that day, and don't follow your own desires or talk idly.
Then the Lord will be your delight."
ISAIAH 58:13–14 NLT

Sunday has lost its special aura. The "come as you are" philosophy of many churches has made us lose the beauty of dressing up to attend God's house. The "early service" habit has let churchgoers get their duty done quickly so they can rush off to spend the rest of the day doing something other than worshipping and resting. The proliferation of restaurants open on Sunday has made us forget that Sunday dinner at home used to be the best meal of the week.

Now, in the days of the Old Testament, the people brought sacrifices to the Lord as an offering. These items had to be the best—the healthiest grain and produce, the most perfect lamb of the flock. There could be no defect or blemish in the offering presented to the Lord God.

Today, we are under the New Covenant, which did not abolish the old but rather fulfilled it, as Jesus said. One day in seven is still to be set aside for rest and worship, according to the pattern established by God at the beginning and set forth in the Ten Commandments. If we return to these values, perhaps we would see the beautiful benefits that accompany honoring this day of the week.

Heavenly Father, show me in what ways I can better
honor You in my Sunday rest and worship. Amen.

Still Contributing and Blessing

The silver-haired head is a crown of glory,
if it is found in the way of righteousness.
PROVERBS 16:31 NKJV

One of the indicators of whether a culture will survive is the degree of value it places on its older generation. Those who have lived long and experienced much have great wisdom to share. They are of inestimable value to those who follow.

In the twenty-first century, people are living longer and longer. Retirement is no longer the downward slope to the grave but the beginning of an exciting new era for many. Modern medicine has made it possible for people to defeat major illness and debilitating conditions and still enjoy some very full years of life. And because of this, senior citizens are still very much part of the public scene. Many of them continue working a regular or part-time job, while still others volunteer at a hospital or library or some other place that can use their cheery smiles and good-natured spirits.

Today is National Senior Citizens Day. It is an annual observation of the contributions made by this special demographic to our towns, communities, churches, and civic organizations.

Life is beautiful in all its seasons, and when we recognize and celebrate that fact, there is great benefit. So today, thank a senior citizen you know for how he or she is making the world a better place.

Dear God, I ask Your blessing on the senior citizen
generation. Draw them into relationship with You
and provide for their needs. In Jesus' name, amen.

A Noticeable Witness

"For whoever is ashamed of Me and My words, of him the Son of Man will be ashamed when He comes in His own glory, and in His Father's, and of the holy angels."
LUKE 9:26 NKJV

Perhaps Norman Rockwell illustrated it best in one of his famous covers for *The Saturday Evening Post*: a woman and child bowing their heads over their meal in a diner while being observed by some rather callous-looking fellows to the side. Back in the 1950s when this painting graced the front of the popular magazine, the concept of "saying grace" over a meal was still a common practice. And while Rockwell highlights the fact that some will smirk, the obvious message of his depiction is that the naysayers are the ones who were to be pitied.

Do you ask a blessing over your food when you eat in a public place?

Make the commitment to letting there be no doubt in anyone's mind that you are thanking God for the food He has provided. Be a noticeable witness. Is it a sin not to pray before eating? Probably not. But it is certainly honoring God to do it and makes a statement to all who are watching that you acknowledge Someone higher than yourself even in something as ordinary as eating. So today, be bold in your witness by gently bowing your head and thanking God for the food that in reality does come from His hand.

Father God, thank You for taking care of me and giving me food to eat. Help me never to forget to publicly acknowledge Your goodness. Amen.

Not Hot but Holy

A beautiful woman who lacks discretion
is like a gold ring in a pig's snout.
PROVERBS 11:22 NLT

It used to be that using the word *hot* referred to the state of being warm in temperature. Now, however, saying something or someone is "hot" has a different meaning.

In our present culture, being hot is the status many teen girls want above all others. It seems to be a verbal affirmation. It is thought to be a high compliment.

But, in reality, it is not. Being called hot is simply the equivalent of an animal's mating response. Because, after all, that is what it is. The word *hot* implies sexually "hot" or arousing the senses. It is most likely a thinly veiled reference to a female animal who is in heat.

Should we want boys thinking this about our daughters? Should we want our daughters to yearn for this status?

God's Word has a lot to say about lust, and those who incite it are guilty, too. The Bible says in 1 Peter 2:11 (NKJV) that we should "abstain from fleshly lusts which war against the soul." The apostle Paul told the young man Timothy to treat young women as his sisters "with all purity" (1 Timothy 5:2 NKJV). We must mentor our daughters so that they will see their bodies not as tools with which to gain admiration but as temples of the Holy Spirit set apart for God's glory.

Dear God, help me to remember that my body belongs
to You and is set apart for Your purposes, not to be
hot but to be holy. In Jesus' name, amen.

Solid and Unfading

No prophecy of Scripture is of any private interpretation,
for prophecy never came by the will of man, but holy men
of God spoke as they were moved by the Holy Spirit.
2 PETER 1:20–21 NKJV

What is the foundation for your code of behavior? The other day I told someone that I tried to base the way I live on the Bible. Her response was that the Bible had changed too much through the millennia and that even Protestants and Catholics don't agree on the canon of scripture, so it was hard to tell what God really intended for us to follow. Her solution? She believes God will judge each of us on what we believe to be right, and if we are not violating our own consciences, then we will be all right in His eyes.

That, my friend, is shaky ground. I would surely not want to stand before the Judge of all and present that as my explanation.

God has preserved His Word. He inspired holy men of old to write. He guided those who did the copying and the translating. And He guided those who agonized over which books should be included in the canon, the sixty-six books which have been handed down to us.

Remember, "The grass withers, the flower fades, but the word of our God stands forever" (Isaiah 40:8 NKJV); "All Scripture is given by inspiration of God, and is profitable for doctrine, for reproof, for correction, for instruction in righteousness" (2 Timothy 3:16 NKJV).

Lord, You have given us Your Word. Thank You for it. Use it
to light my path and guide my steps. In Jesus' name, amen.

Double-Sided Tongues

*But no man can tame the tongue. It is an unruly evil,
full of deadly poison. With it we bless our God and Father,
and with it we curse men, who have been made in the
similitude of God. Out of the same mouth proceed blessing
and cursing. My brethren, these things ought not to be so.*

JAMES 3:8–10 NKJV

There is a problem with the speech of this generation. It can be crude, unloving, and terribly profane. Yet it can also be affirming, positive, and churchy. And many people see nothing wrong with this dichotomy.

But God's Word says that there is something really awry with this kind of person. James compares speech to the fruit hanging on trees and water coming from specific sources. Everyone is fully aware that figs grow on fig trees, not olives, and that salt water cannot come from a fresh spring. Yet today, we don't blink our eyes when a Christian uses a bad word here and there. We make excuses on the grounds that "she was really upset" or "everyone slips once in a while." But what is really alarming is that our mouths reveal what is in our hearts. In Luke 6:45 (NKJV), Jesus said, "Out of the abundance of the heart [the] mouth speaks."

So is it really okay to use bad language once in a while? Only if it is okay to harbor evil in your heart once in a while! God wants to cleanse and renew our hearts so that our speech will reflect the good treasure that is inside us.

*Lord, search my heart and cleanse me of any evil You
find there. Renew my speech so that I may use my words
to edify others and glorify You. In Jesus' name, amen.*

Loving the Lost Things

*"For the Son of Man came to seek
and save those who are lost."*
LUKE 19:10 NLT

They say "every dog has his day." Today is it, the day in which dog lovers the world over acknowledge the ways dogs protect, work, and comfort their owners and families every day. This is National Dog Day. It is also used to draw attention to the number of dogs that need to be rescued from animal shelters. All citizens, even those who do not own dogs, are encouraged to donate five dollars to their local shelter.

So there you have it, a celebration founded by someone who has a heart for the dogs of the world. If not unbalanced in its approach to humans as well, this kind of compassion is a reflection of the heart of God.

When it comes to people, God loves each of us, no matter our pedigree or "breed," our size or our temperament. And He goes after the ones no one else wants. He loves the castoffs and misfits, the oddballs and the eccentrics. He has a place for each one. He sees the uniqueness of each individual life.

God cares about the animals. He wants us to care for them and enjoy them. But people are worth so much more. And while there is only one "dog day," any day is a great time for people to be rescued and celebrated and made part of His big family.

*Lord, You made the animals for our pleasure and use;
I'm glad of that. But I'm most thankful for Your love for each
of us and the privilege of being part of Your family. Amen.*

The Gift of Sleep

In peace I will lie down and sleep.
PSALM 4:8 NLT

God infuses variety into our body clocks just like He does with other aspects of our personhood. So for every night owl, there is somewhere a morning lark or a hummingbird (those in the middle). And that way, all the jobs on earth get done and there is always someone awake with the needed energy and creativity. It would really be sad if no one could take the midnight shift at the hospital or if no one could get up at four in the morning to milk the cows!

Still, no matter the rhythm of one's internal clock, all of us need sleep. Our bodies require sleep to renew themselves and recharge for the next day. According to the National Sleep Foundation, while we are sleeping, tissue growth and repair occurs, energy is restored, hormones are released, appetite is balanced, and the immune system gets a charge. It is normal to spend about one-third of our lives sleeping.

And when you think about it, God did plan the nighttime for our benefit, right? In the beginning, He separated the darkness and light and gave each a place in the cycle of a twenty-four-hour day. And though He never needs to rest, we do. We cannot do the 24-7 thing; we weren't meant to. And as long as God sustains the earth, there will always be tomorrow in which to work.

Lord, let me praise You by getting the proper rest
for my body so that I may be at my optimum level
of energy and creativity for Your glory. Amen.

Smile Away!

Be glad in the LORD and rejoice, you righteous;
and shout for joy, all you upright in heart!
PSALM 32:11 NKJV

Everyone today wants a beautiful smile. And providers have cashed in on this desire! It's a very cool thing for adults to have braces, and whitening procedures are now considered practically a necessity. Yet, though we may have the teeth for it, most of us probably don't wear a smile very often. I wonder why. Smiling, we are told, uses fewer facial muscles than frowning. Smiling is a gift that costs us nothing. Smiling is the fastest way to communicate welcome, joy, and kindness. "Smile and the world smiles with you; cry and you cry alone."

I think Jesus smiled a lot. We don't know what kind of temperament He had in His earthly form, but I believe He had the best traits of all the types—sanguine, choleric, melancholy, and phlegmatic. Certainly, His personality wasn't warped by the selfishness of sin and He always had time for others. It is my opinion that He had a sense of humor. I think He took delight in the world around Him and the people in it.

We are reminded often to be Christlike in our attitudes, words, and conduct. But what if we were to add to that list a challenge to be like Him in smiling at others? Of course, we don't know for sure, but there could certainly be nothing wrong with giving encouragement to others we meet throughout the day by letting our faces reflect the joy of the Lord in our hearts.

Lord, I want to be like You. Help me give others the
gift of my smile so that they can see You in me. Amen.

Liar!

*"When he speaks a lie, he speaks from his own
resources, for he is a liar and the father of it."*
JOHN 8:44 NKJV

No one likes to be lied to. And after awhile, a liar is not believed. We've all heard the story of the little boy who cried "wolf" one too many times.

But there is one liar to whom we listen over and over. Yeah, you guessed it! Satan, the father of lies.

Why do we perk up our ears when he comes slithering around? Has he ever had anything good to say, anything that was totally truthful or helped us in our walk with Christ? Do we think he has changed in the last thousand years? Is he now trustworthy?

Not on your life. Jesus dealt with his treachery by quoting the Word of God and telling Him to "heel." He could do that because, as the Son of God, He has authority over all things and everyone. We do not have that type of sovereignty, but we do have power in the name of Jesus and in His shed blood. James 4:7 (NKJV) admonishes us to "resist the devil and he will flee from you." He has no lie or ploy that can stand against Christ's authority over him. When we are being attacked, we can be confident that "greater is he that is in [us], than he that is in the world" (1 John 4:4 KJV).

*Lord Jesus, You are the Victor over Satan. I resist him
through the authority of Your name. Thank You
for being my Savior and Lord. Amen.*

God Is Good

Praise the LORD, for the LORD is good;
sing praises to His name, for it is pleasant.
PSALM 135:3 NKJV

We hear it in church. We say it to others. We want to believe it. God is good. All the time.

The Bible says it so we know it is true. Jesus lived it so we could see it in living color. But sometimes, when life yanks hard and pulls the rug out from under us, we begin to doubt. And that is probably a normal human temptation. Though we know that good parents discipline their children and sometimes allow them to learn "the hard way," we expect God, our heavenly Father, to do it differently.

So we need reminders. And He put them in our world everywhere we turn, at unexpected junctions and in the most ordinary places. Warm sunshine, brilliant flowers, rainbows after storms, newborn babies, friendships, families, food, air to breathe, pets, church dinners, sunrises, sunsets, beaches, forests, prairies, mountains, the moon and stars at night and puffy clouds in the day. All around us are hints that God is good and that His works are beautiful and life-giving.

When disease or tragedy or hardship enters our lives, we can rest assured that God is not the author of these destructive things and that someday He will cleanse this globe of its misery and set everything right. Until then, He has given us His strength, His hope, and His promise. That is enough to keep us going.

Father God, I praise You. You are good. Your works
are wonderful. I know You love me. Help me to trust
Your plan and purpose for me. In Jesus' name, amen.

Yielding: A Better Way of Life

Yes, all of you be submissive to one another, and be clothed with humility, for "God resists the proud, but gives grace to the humble."
1 PETER 5:5 NKJV

Whatever happened to following the yield sign?

My daily commute takes me by a yield sign both going to work and coming back home. On the way out in the mornings, I am the one who is supposed to yield; on the way back, I am the one who is supposed to be yielded to. Without sounding like I am tooting my own horn here (to use a driving analogy), I try my best to obey, but rarely does anyone yield to me when I am coming the other way. It's like the sign isn't even there!

Now, a traffic sign which cautions us to yield is there for the good and benefit of all. The sign isn't there to suppress one or more drivers in the other lane; it's there to keep the flow of traffic moving smoothly and safely and to avoid a serious crash.

And so it is in our lives, whether in the home, in the church, on the job, or whatever other organization one is in. There has to be someone (and usually more than one) who yields. It isn't to put someone down (at least, not if the thing is managed correctly) but to create harmony and efficiency and progress. The Bible calls it submitting, and it would do us all much good to take a fresh look at what God has to say about it.

Heavenly Father, I submit myself to You and ask that You give me the grace to know when I need to yield in my daily life. In Jesus' name, amen.

Testing the Hull

*My brethren, count it all joy
when you fall into various trials.*
JAMES 1:2 NKJV

When the navy finishes a submarine, the integrity of the hull is tested on a "sea trial." If there is any weakness, the pressure of the deep waters will expose it.

In the same way, when God applies a little pressure in our lives, it exposes our weaknesses. That's often when the whining and blaming begin, and sometimes sin finds its way squeezing out in the form of alcohol, affairs, or just plain bitterness.

Most Christians know the story of suffering Job, but did you know Job's righteousness was the *reason* God pointed him out to Satan (see Job 1:6–12)? Job was living exactly as he should, and God allowed Satan to take everything from him—children, livestock, lands, home, and health. And yet, "In all this Job did not sin nor charge God with wrong" (Job 1:22 NKJV).

What kind of reaction do you have during tragedy? Do you blame God? Turn to sin? Or hold fast to the truth, despite the pain?

First Peter 1:6–7 (NLT) says, "So be truly glad. There is wonderful joy ahead, even though you must endure many trials for a little while. These trials will show that your faith is genuine. "

*Father, as I walk through trials that inevitably come,
remind me that through Your sovereignty,
I will come forth as gold. Amen.*

The Workers Are Few

The Spirit who lives in you is greater
than the spirit who lives in the world.
1 JOHN 4:4 NLT

Bailey was excited about her salvation. She told her Christian friend, "Now the real work begins." But her friend replied, "No, the work was done on the cross. You just have to learn to rely on that."

Satan has done a fantastic job of paralyzing Christians with this lie: "I'm not good enough." Satan is called "the accuser of [the] brethren" (Revelation 12:10 KJV), and his most powerful tool is to continually and persuasively remind you of your shortcomings.

So many Christians avoid serving the church because they feel inadequate, uneducated, and unworthy. Jesus said, "The harvest is plentiful but the workers are few" (Matthew 9:37 NIV).

The truth is we are no longer enslaved to sin. Through the Holy Spirit we have the power to overcome and carry on. Romans 8:37 (NIV) says, "We are more than conquerors through him who loved us." The Holy Spirit is always full of grace for the believer. Every conviction is for growth, sharpening, and disciplining, never guilt and shame.

Satan is right about one thing—we're not good enough; we fail over and over. But here is the difference: our confidence is in Christ, not ourselves. And He has set us free!

Lord, thank You for setting me free. Speak into
my heart and continually remind me that I am clean
in Your sight because of Your work, not mine. Amen.

Revival Begins with Repentance

"Produce fruit in keeping with repentance."
MATTHEW 3:8 NIV

A. W. Tozer said, "Have you noticed how much praying for revival has been going on of late—and how little revival has resulted? I believe the problem is that we have been trying to substitute praying for obeying, and it simply will not work."

Could it be that Jesus is waiting for His church to repent? To the Ephesian church He said, "Consider how far you have fallen! Repent and do the things you did at first" (Revelation 2:5 NIV).

Why do we sit back in our comfortable darling sins and wonder why God hasn't sent a fresh wind of His Spirit? Could it be that our desire for revival is only rhetoric? Do we really want to see the power of God moving among us?

William Gurnall said, "Holiness has a mighty influence upon others. When this appears with power in the lives of Christians, it works mightily upon the spirits of men; it stops the mouth of the ungodly."

In a country where the majority is Christian, our light should be brighter than it is. Now is the time to wipe off the cobwebs of our stained-glass windows and let the light and beauty of Christ shine through.

Lord, my desire is to be a light in this dark world.
Give me the strength to give up the sin in my
life that I cling to, and repent. Amen.

Rewards of Labor

And when the Chief Shepherd appears, you will
receive the crown of glory that does not fade away.
1 PETER 5:4 NKJV

As America celebrates the labor of those who built our nation, it's important to remember spiritual work as well.

The missionary Jim Elliot wrote, "He is no fool who gives what he cannot keep to gain that which he cannot lose." Earthly work may provide worldly comfort, which will eventually pass away, but work for the kingdom promises everlasting results—rewards from God.

The Bible encourages believers to accumulate heavenly riches. Jesus said, "Store your treasures in heaven, where moths and rust cannot destroy, and thieves do not break in and steal" (Matthew 6:20 NLT).

In the book *Heaven*, Randy Alcorn writes, "In Heaven, the bride's wedding dress stands for 'the righteous acts of the saints' done on Earth (Revelation 19:7-8). Our righteous deeds on Earth will not be forgotten but 'will follow' us to Heaven (Revelation 14:13). . .because what we do on Earth will earn us those rewards."

The work we do in this life may not find its fulfillment in our lifetime, but our labor won't be in vain—first, we have the honor of participating in the redemptive work of Christ, and second, we will collect rewards that are incorruptible.

Father, I pray that the work I do in this life is pleasing
to You and points to Your glory. I eagerly await the
day I can present my crowns to You. Amen.

By the Power of Your Testimony

I will speak to kings about your laws,
and I will not be ashamed.
PSALM 119:46 NLT

In the restroom of a busy downtown high rise, a man with an obvious learning disability shared his testimony. "I won't always be this way," he said. "One day God is going to bring me to heaven, and I'll be made whole. He can take you there, too."

This man had every earthly excuse to stay home. He wasn't eloquent, handsome, or bright. But he recognized the value of the treasure he possessed and desired to share it.

Our testimonies have power. Revelation 12:11 (KJV) says, "[The believers] overcame [Satan] by the blood of the Lamb, and by the word of their testimony." Yours may not be dramatic or emotional, but it bears witness to Christ, no matter how simple.

Satan will whisper that your story isn't important, that no one wants to hear it. He'll bring up all your failings and hypocrisy. He'll quiet you any way he can.

Peter admonishes us, "If someone asks about your hope as a believer, always be ready to explain it" (1 Peter 3:15 NLT). Written, spoken, or videoed—your personal testimony is one of the most powerful tools you have for the kingdom, and no one can take that away.

Jesus, give me boldness, and let the whole world hear
from my lips Your wonderful works in my life. Amen.

Test the Spirits

The gullible believe anything they're told;
the prudent sift and weigh every word.
PROVERBS 14:15 MSG

Joyce was in the kitchen while her elementary-aged children watched a popular cartoon movie. Joyce was surprised to hear one of the characters say something about existentialism—an atheistic philosophy. *What is this doing in a kid movie?* she wondered. Joyce sat down to investigate and discovered an entire storyline blatantly expressing themes of godlessness and idol worship.

In a world that is increasingly antagonistic toward Christianity, parents can no longer trust the mainstream media to protect the minds and souls of children.

Satan is called "the prince of the power of the air" (Ephesians 2:2 KJV), and his greatest weapons to manipulate the mind are logic, philosophy, doubt, and desensitization.

What beliefs are your children absorbing through the movies and music you allow into your home? First John 4:1 (NKJV) says, "Beloved, do not believe every spirit, but test the spirits, whether they are of God." These spirits can be found in something as simple as a cartoon.

Pay close attention to the message of the entertainment you enjoy. Every plot and lyric has an underlying belief system or worldview that the writer wishes to convey, deeper than just entertainment value. Watch television with your kids and be on guard.

Father, open my eyes to the subtle messages that attack my children.
Give me discernment to detect themes as I see them. Amen.

The Reluctant Servant

He will also keep you firm to the end,
so that you will be blameless.
1 CORINTHIANS 1:8 NIV

In *The Hobbit*, Gandalf invites Bilbo Baggins on an adventure of a lifetime, but Bilbo responds, "We are plain and quiet folk and have no use for adventures. Nasty, disturbing, uncomfortable things! Make you late for dinner! I can't think of what anybody sees in them."

That's the way many of us treat the call of God. He promises to guide us and provide the power to overcome, but we would rather stay undisturbed.

Moses and Jonah were both examples of men who were reluctant to accept God's call. Moses was insecure—slow of speech and unassertive. Jonah was simply rebellious. Yet both men eventually fulfilled God's purposes. . .because God wanted them to. Neither Moses nor Jonah was eager, but after kicking and screaming, God finally used them to save the Jews and the Ninevites.

Philippians 1:6 (NKJV) says, "He who has begun a good work in you will complete it." God does the work, and for some amazing beautiful reason, He wants to include us!

No matter how incompetent we feel, we can rest assured that God will not let us fail. He will provide us with everything we need to accomplish His perfect plans.

Lord, thank You that I can trust You to bring about Your
purposes in me. Even though I am an imperfect person,
my incompetence does not hinder Your outcomes. Amen.

With All Your Strength

Let all that I am praise the Lord.
PSALM 146:1 NLT

Christian scholar Larry Taunton launched a national campaign to interview college atheists. He discovered, "Our former church-attending students expressed [positive] feelings for those Christians who unashamedly embraced biblical teaching. [Michael] told us, '. . .Christianity is something that if you really believed it, it would change your life and you would want to change [the lives] of others. I haven't seen too much of that.'"

It's not enough to love God with a passing "I love you a lot" sentimentalism. Jesus told us to love God "with all your heart and with all your soul and with all your strength and with all your mind" (Luke 10:27 NIV). God wants devotion like David's, who said, "Bless the Lord, O my soul: and all that is within me, bless his holy name" (Psalm 103:1 KJV).

This kind of passion characterized the apostles, missionaries, and evangelists throughout history whose fervent devotion spread like fire and changed the landscape of Christianity. We aren't called just to love God but to love Him with intensity.

As Puritan minister Samuel Ward said, "The fervency of the true zealot is in the spirit, not in show. . .such a man's wroth cannot be set forth with the tongues of men and of angels."

God, I pray that my passion for You is strengthened
and that it shows through my daily life. Put a fire
in my soul that burns like a beacon. Amen.

We Carry His Name

You will be called by a new name
that the mouth of the Lord will bestow.
ISAIAH 62:2 NIV

Ester DeBerdt Reed helped raise over $300,000 to provide new shirts for Washington's troops. To make the men feel special, the women sewed their own names on the shirts. Ester wrote, "Brave Americans, your disinterestedness, your courage, and your constancy will always be dear to America, as long as she shall preserve her virtue."

At a time of low morale, each man carried the name of a woman who prayed for him and valued his sacrifice. Perhaps he thought of her each time he dressed to face the enemy.

Like those soldiers, we also carry a name—the one belonging to the King of heaven. Jesus said, "He who overcomes. . . . I will write on him the name of My God and the name of the city of My God. . . . And I will write on him My new name" (Revelation 3:12 NKJV).

This name comes from the Captain of our salvation and the one who intercedes for us. Each time we face a battle of faith we can look to the name of Jesus as our banner. He has promised that all who follow Him will be victorious.

Jesus, what an honor to carry Your name! I pray during times of low morale that You would remind me who prays for me and who gives me the strength to carry on—the One whose name I bear. Amen.

Shame and Mercy

And all things are of God, who hath reconciled us to himself by
Jesus Christ, and hath given to us the ministry of reconciliation.
2 CORINTHIANS 5:18 KJV

Actor Johnny Depp is handsome, successful, and beloved by millions, but he struggles to find inner peace. He confessed to *Rolling Stone*, "You wake up in the morning, and you brush your teeth, and you're like, 'ugh, that [idiot] again. You're still here? What do you want?' Hiding: I think it's important. It's important for you—for what's ever left of your sanity, I guess."

Doesn't that describe the way we oftentimes treat God? We put on outward works and memorize Bible verses all the while hiding from God, fearful of judgement of our "secret sins."

Adam and Eve literally hid themselves from God's righteousness, and when God called, "Where are you?" longing for fellowship, Adam responded, "I hid because I was naked and I was afraid" (see Genesis 3:9–10).

Yes, the couple had consequences for their sin, but God provided mercy. He covered their nakedness with an animal sacrifice, and then He covered their eternity with the promise of an ultimate future sacrifice made by Him alone.

When we sin, there is no need to hide; we will always find mercy to cover our shame when we come to God in humility and repentance.

Lord, why do I run from You when I commit sin?
In Your arms I always find healing and forgiveness.
Thank You for making the way for reconciliation. Amen.

Mommies Need Forgiveness

He who covers his sins will not prosper, but whoever
confesses and forsakes them will have mercy.
PROVERBS 28:13 NKJV

Nikki's morning was going all wrong, and her oldest son, Declan, presented the moment for a mommy breakdown. When he boarded the bus for school, she felt guilty and terrible. Throughout the day, she prayed, and when Declan came home, Nikki gave him a big kiss and hug and apologized. Most importantly—she asked for his forgiveness.

Nikki exemplified something fantastic to her son that day. First, parents aren't perfect, and second, imperfect people need forgiveness and grace.

"I'm thankful that a bad mommy moment doesn't make me a bad mommy," Nikki said. "I'm thankful that when I have the opportunity to apologize to my kids that it is a lesson on how to apologize and the importance of it. And I'm thankful that for as many times as I get this mommy thing wrong, there are a million times I get it right."

Children are so forgiving that Nikki could have just let the incident go. But she used the opportunity to teach a principle. James 5:16 (NLT) says, "Confess your sins to each other and pray for each other so that you may be healed." That's a truth that this young man will never forget.

Father, I know I'm not a perfect mom.
How grateful I am for forgiveness! Help me
extend it to my family as they extend it to me. Amen.

It Doesn't Take Much

Let your speech always be with grace, seasoned with salt,
that you may know how you ought to answer each one.
COLOSSIANS 4:6 NKJV

Jay was walking through the grocery store parking lot when he saw a young woman on the verge of tears. He wasn't sure how to help, but he approached her saying, "God sent me over to tell you that He loves you and everything is going to be okay."

That was the message Tiffany needed. Jay was able to comfort her and invite her to church, and eventually she accepted Christ and was baptized.

Sometimes the Holy Spirit is subtle. Jay could have ignored the nagging feeling in his heart and reasoned that someone else would help. But he obeyed. He didn't do anything dramatic or dangerous, nothing to write a movie script about. He simply reached out with the love of Christ.

Peter tells us, "Always be prepared to give an answer to everyone who asks you to give the reason for the hope that you have" (1 Peter 3:15 NIV). Tiffany didn't even know the question to ask, but Jay was ready to give her the answer she didn't know she needed.

Would you be bold enough to intervene? Be obedient to the nudges of the Holy Spirit, and see how He uses you to work little miracles.

Lord, make me sensitive to Your Spirit so I can
minister to those around me—at the grocery store,
the bank, the park. . .everywhere. Amen.

The Want for Wonder

Praise the LORD God, the God of Israel,
who alone does such wonderful things.
PSALM 72:18 NLT

G. K. Chesterton said, "The world will never starve for want of wonders; but only for want of wonder." There are so many wonders in the world—places to see, goals to accomplish, exciting special effects—and yet many of us are still missing "awe."

The church is struggling, too. Almost all of us—Christian and non-Christian alike—have grown up with a view of God as loving, accepting, and forgiving, and we have learned to take those attributes for granted. We've lost the wonder of His majesty.

In the early days of the apostles, many Jews repented and were baptized. They devoted themselves to teaching and fellowship, and "a deep sense of awe came over them all" (Acts 2:43 NLT). They were amazed by God!

We can regain our wonderment through reading God's Word. The more we learn about Him and our own condition, the more we can appreciate His love. Proverbs 25:2 (KJV) says, "It is the glory of God to conceal a thing: but the honour of kings is to search out a matter."

Is it time for you to examine the character of God in a fresh way? Pray today that He would open your eyes to His wonderful mysteries.

Father, restore in me the wonder of who You are. It has been
too long since I have found myself amazed by Your love. Amen.

Don't Stop Praying

The effective, fervent prayer of
a righteous man avails much.
JAMES 5:16 NKJV

Augustine's mother, Monica, was a devout Christian, but her son was an undisciplined child. Even despite Monica's constant warnings to stay away from fornication, Augustine found himself father to a son and a member of a cult.

Years later, she begged him not to travel to Rome, but despite her advice, he went. She was able to persuade him to listen to the bishop. The words of the sermon lingered as he sat in a nearby garden. A child's song, "Take Up and Read," drew him to the Bible, and Saint Augustine was converted that moment.

Monica could have given up on her wayward son. But she was never willing to accept Augustine as he was in his state of godlessness. She kept praying until she got results.

Jesus tells us to pray relentlessly, like a man who knocks on his neighbor's door in the middle of the night for bread. He said, "Ask and it will be given to you; seek and you will find; knock and the door will be opened to you. For everyone who asks receives; the one who seeks finds; and to the one who knocks, the door will be opened" (Luke 11:9–10 NIV).

Don't give up on your prayers. The answer is closer than you know.

Lord, there are many burdens that have gone unanswered,
but I know nothing is impossible with You.
Give me the strength to come to You daily. Amen.

"I Like the Depression"

"Blessed are you who are poor."
LUKE 6:20 NIV

Sally Wall found her father's account of the Depression after he died:

I LIKE the Depression. No more prosperity for me. I have had more fun since the Depression started then I had in my life. I had forgotten how to live, and what it means to have real friends. . . .

I like the Depression. I am getting acquainted with my neighbors and following the Biblical admonition to love them. Some of them had been living next door to me for 3 years; now we butcher hogs together.

I like the Depression. I haven't been out to a party in 18 months. My wife has dropped all her clubs, and I believe we are falling in love all over again.

I like the Depression. Three years ago I never had time to go to church. I played checkers or baseball all day Sunday. Besides, there wasn't a preacher in Texas that could tell me anything. Now I'm going to church regularly and never miss a Sunday. If this Depression keeps on, I will be going to prayer meetings before too long.

Oh Yes! I like the Depression!

What is the Great Depression in your life? Could it be that, despite yourself, you're better off for it?

*Father, help me see my circumstances with an
eternal perspective and reap the treasures within. Amen.*

With All Your Strength

Whatever your hand finds to do,
do it with all your might.
ECCLESIASTES 9:10 NIV

"Now we have one day more," said Oxford chaplain Joseph Alleine in 1664. "Let us live well, work hard for souls, lay up much treasure in heaven this day, for we have but a few to live." Little did he know that only four years later, at age thirty-four, his time on earth would end.

Every single moment of life is a gift. We dare not waste one. "To live is Christ," said the apostle Paul (Philippians 1:21 KJV). Our lives were made to reflect God's glory, not just on Sundays or mission trips or during women's Bible study class, but in respecting our husbands and modeling decency and kindness for others. It's in the things we say, do, and think when no one is there to give credit. It's in the times we choose to do the right thing, even when it hurts.

Every moment has a purpose for God's kingdom. It's time to be zealous for righteousness in the course of everyday life, and God has promised a treasure trove awaiting us in heaven. The irony is that earthly life will also be filled with treasures—happy marriages, strong children, peace of mind, and joy unspeakable and full of glory.

God, I pray that my passion for You shows through my daily life.
Put a fire in my soul that burns so bright others can see it. Amen.

Pray for Your Enemies

See that no one pays back evil for evil.
1 THESSALONIANS 5:15 NLT

Paul is an active member of the military. He bought an "ISIS Hunter" sticker for his truck, but each time he considered putting it on his windshield, he felt called to pray for ISIS. "I'm a soldier. I'm not supposed to pray for the enemy," Paul said. "But I can't help but wonder if one of them may be a potential Saul who became the apostle Paul." Maybe one of those men will be dramatically converted because of Paul's prayers.

Our world is in turmoil, and there is a growing sense of aggression. The Middle East is filled with atrocities in the name of religion, and these sentiments are spreading around the world, even in the United States.

Christians are becoming targets, and the fear can make us want to build walls around our lives and look out for our own families and friends. It can be tempting to become an aggressor like those who would persecute us, but Jesus said, "Love your enemies and pray for those who persecute you" (Matthew 5:44 NIV).

War and military force is a reasonable response on a civic level, but on a personal level, we must seek to bring the Gospel to those who hate God, even as we once hated Him.

Father, there are those who despise me and use me, and I pray for them right now for Your grace and their salvation. Amen.

Make It Count

Like arrows in the hand of a warrior,
so are the children of one's youth.
PSALM 127:4 NKJV

When a young mom dropped off her children at school each day, she would encourage them, "Hey, let's make today count!"

Most of us realize that children are little sponges, so we get them the best educations and give them lessons in sports and music. But they are also sponges for understanding their purpose in the kingdom. While they are sopping up information, don't forget to instill their purposes as believers. Deuteronomy 6:7 (NIV) says, "Impress [God's principles] on your children. Talk about them when you sit at home and when you walk along the road, when you lie down and when you get up."

Your children are ambassadors for Christ even as young as they are! They are exposed to a mission field at school every day and a variety of differing denominations and beliefs, even at Christian schools. Your child could lead his friends to Christ on the playground. As Jesus said, "I thank You, Father, Lord of heaven and earth, that You have hidden these things from the wise and prudent and have revealed them to babes" (Matthew 11:25 NKJV).

How are you encouraging your kids to make every day count for the Lord? How are you helping them be a light?

Lord, I pray my children embrace the light I've given them and that they boldly bring the candle in the darkness wherever they go. Amen.

Striving Not Struggling

In all these things we are more than
conquerors through Him who loved us.
ROMANS 8:37 NKJV

Hudson Taylor was one of history's most successful missionaries, but it didn't start out that way. He longed to reach the Chinese and establish the China Inland Mission (CIM), but when he reached China, Hudson experienced language difficulties, homesickness, and personality conflicts with the other missionaries, and he was in financial crisis.

The final straw came when Hudson injured himself while trying to dye his hair black. A friend comforted Hudson in his depression, telling him to try "abiding, not striving nor struggling." Because Christ is "the only power for service; the only ground for unchanging joy." That was the spiritual surge Hudson needed, and by the time he died, the CIM had eight hundred missionaries.

How much sweeter would our own Christian lives be if we took the same advice and applied it to everything we do?

Stop striving in marriage. Stop trying to create perfect children. Stop trying to control every situation, and abide in Christ. Let the love of God flow through you, and trust Him to shine.

The Christian life will be filled with obstacles and struggles, but the Holy Spirit has given us the power to overcome. When we abide in Christ, those struggles become the fertilizer that brings about the fruit of the Spirit.

Lord, You promised that we are more than conquerors
through You. Help me to embrace the truth and
live in confidence of those promises. Amen.

Open the Cage

Do not stifle the Holy Spirit.
1 THESSALONIANS 5:19 NLT

There's an old African proverb that says "You don't have to defend a lion. Just open its cage."

It's true, isn't it? No one has to stand up for a lion or talk someone into backing off. The king of the jungle may be restricted by a cage for a time, but when you let it out, any taunters will run for their lives.

This is a beautiful picture of the power of Christ in the Christian. Jesus is called the Lion of Judah in Revelation 5:5, and each of us has been empowered by His spirit.

So many believers try desperately to *defend* Christianity by caging it up in modern philosophy and rhetoric or dressing the cage in camouflage. When all they really have to do is uncage the power! Proverbs 28:1 (NIV) says, "The wicked flee though no one pursues, but the righteous are as bold as a lion." We don't have to cower to please modern philosophy; be courageous and let the lion speak for itself!

There may be those who dare stand up to fight the lion in you, but stick to prayer and the Word. Don't back down—you're on the winning team.

God, forgive me for presuming that You need my help to reach the lost. Teach me to let the power loose and let it do what it was meant to do. Amen.

The Eccentric Blessing

*And David danced before
the LORD with all his might.*
2 SAMUEL 6:14 KJV

Billy Bray was an alcoholic until the Lord saved him at age twenty-nine. He remarked how inexplicably happy he was from the beginning, and it showed—he laughed, danced, and shouted "Glory!" wherever he went. "I can't help praising God," he said. "As I go along the street I lift one foot and it seems to say 'Glory!' and I lift the other, and it seems to say, 'Amen!'" When Billy died at seventy-three, his dying word was "Glory!"

Charles Spurgeon included Billy in his book *Eccentric Preachers* and commented, "It does not seem so very horrible after all that a man should be eccentric."

All Christians should have such enthusiasm. After all, we have been given eternal life and blessings unspeakable and full of glory.

When the apostles received the Holy Spirit, people thought they were drunk (see Acts 2:15), and Paul later said, "Don't be drunk with wine. . . . Instead, be filled with the Holy Spirit, singing psalms and hymns and spiritual songs" (Ephesians 5:18–19 NLT).

What if we all entered each other's homes proclaiming God's blessings and promises as we entered? Yes, people might think we're drunk or even call us eccentric. But perhaps, as Spurgeon said, that's not so bad after all.

*Father, let Your spirit shine through me, and give me
the courage not to care what others may think of it. Amen.*

Instant Feedback

The fear of human opinion disables;
trusting in GOD protects you from that.
PROVERBS 29:25 MSG

Our world is obsessed with instant fame. According to the official YouTube statistics page, the site has over a billion users, almost one-third of all people on the Internet. Anyone with an iPhone and a clever catchphrase or touching moment can become an overnight sensation.

Brian Robbins, the owner of the company that created YouTube channels for teens and tweens, told *The New Yorker*, "When you speak to kids, the number one thing they want is to be famous. They don't even know what for."

It's rare to find people who want to do the right thing with no expectations of praise, but that's exactly what Jesus encourages us to do:

"Don't do your good deeds publicly, to be admired by others, for you will lose the reward from your Father in heaven. When you give to someone in need, don't do as the hypocrites do—blowing trumpets in the synagogues and streets to call attention to their acts of charity! I tell you the truth, they have received all the reward they will ever get" (Matthew 6:1–2 NLT). He says the same thing about prayer and fasting.

When we perform for men's praises, we miss the rewards from God, which may not come in this life, but heavenly gifts are worth the wait!

Lord, I pray that my desire is for Your praise
only and that I set aside the praise of men. Amen.

The Blue and the Gray

*"No one lights a lamp and puts
it in a place where it will be hidden."*
LUKE 11:33 NIV

The Civil War is often recognized by the blue and gray uniforms that identified the opposing sides—blue for Union soldiers, gray for Confederates.

Few people know, however, that the colors were not assigned at first. Gray was often worn by Union volunteer units, and the opposite was also true. At the battle in Shiloh, the Orleans Guard Battalion wore blue dress uniforms into battle. The problem came when men would fire and kill their own soldiers. The Louisiana Guard wittingly made the decision to turn their coats inside out so the white lining would show.

Some Christians have suggested we should blend in with the world and find common ground. But just like with the Civil War uniforms, this theory has led to confusion, not commonality. The non-Christian doesn't see any difference between the world and the church.

Rather than blend, we should be set apart. That doesn't mean aloof, but it does mean different. Paul said, "Don't copy the behavior and customs of this world, but let God transform you into a new person by changing the way you think" (Romans 12:2 NLT). We have been given a light in the darkness. Why would we hide that light in order to look like the world?

*Father, I pray that my life stands out in stark contrast from the lost.
Create a light in me that burns brightly. Amen.*

None Wasted

*Always work enthusiastically for the Lord, for you
know that nothing you do for the Lord is ever useless.*
1 CORINTHIANS 15:58 NLT

Martin Luther was a devout monk whose love for the Word of God brought us the Protestant Reformation. Luther didn't always want to be a monk, however. He started out as a brilliant lawyer. But in a moment of fear, he vowed to become a monk if he survived a dangerous lightning storm. Despite his father's disappointment, Luther dedicated himself to the church.

Martin Luther's father felt his son's talents were being wasted, completely unaware that he would change the world forever.

Nothing we give to God is wasted, whether for praise, worship, or works of the kingdom. Sometimes that offering is in the form of sacrifice. Elizabeth Elliot and her husband, Jim, faced cannibals to spread the Gospel. Years after Jim's violent death, Elizabeth wrote, "I will offer to God both my tears and my exultation. Nothing we offer to Him will be lost." God has kept every tear in a bottle, and He knows their price (see Psalm 56:8).

God has promised that when we give ourselves for His sake, He will return "pressed down, shaken together, and running over" (Luke 6:38 NKJV). Whether our reward is in this life or the next, God's promise has been and will always be faithful.

*Lord, what treasures and gifts do I have that can be offered for You?
I wish to dedicate the best I have to Your service. Amen.*

Are Your Hands Too Full?

Trust in the LORD with all your heart.
PROVERBS 3:5 NKJV

"I've noticed as a parent it's very hard to pay for your kids to be on a team, and then let the coaches do their jobs," Tonya said. "Tonight I'm making a concentrated effort to yell *for* my kid and not *at* my kid."

That attitude is reminiscent of many Christians. God is the Maker of the universe; He knows all and sees all. And for some reason, we still think we know better.

Saint Augustine wrote, "God is always trying to give good things to us, but our hands are too full to receive them." Could it be that our hands are too full of the reigns of control?

It's wonderful that we fiercely love our families and favorite causes, but has our affection manifested into a self-appointed queenship, in which we see ourselves as comagistrate with God, where we sort of consult with Him instead of submit to Him?

Submission requires trust, and that can be difficult, especially if you've been disappointed before. But God has proven His faithfulness. Jesus said, "You believe because you have seen me. Blessed are those who believe without seeing me" (John 20:29 NLT).

Will you empty your hands? Let go of control and receive peace, joy, contentment, satisfaction, and confidence in its stead.

Jesus, give me the courage to give You control of my life.
You already have it. Now teach me to rest in that. Amen.

Grace Goes a Long Way

Therefore, my son, be strong in
the grace that is in Christ Jesus.
2 TIMOTHY 2:1 KJV

Robbie made a driving mistake that resulted in a confrontation. The other driver exited his truck yelling and gesturing. As Robbie approached to retaliate, the Holy Spirit said, *"This guy has more problems than you know."* Robbie's demeanor changed, and the confrontation was resolved quickly and kindly.

Later, the man called and thanked Robbie for being gracious. "He had been drinking," Robbie said, "and he was contemplating suicide. He told me the way I handled the situation may have saved his life."

With a little grace, Robbie turned the whole situation in a different direction. So much fighting and bitterness could be avoided in this life with a little grace followed by forgiveness. The apostle Paul exhorts us, "Get rid of all bitterness, rage and anger, brawling and slander, along with every form of malice. Be kind and compassionate to one another, forgiving each other, just as in Christ God forgave you" (Ephesians 4:31–32 NIV).

We have no idea as we encounter people what it is that they are going through at the time. Just ask yourself, "Can this be forgiven?" There is not a single one of us who doesn't need to be the recipient of grace each and every day.

Lord, make my life one that pours out grace on others.
Bitterness and anger are so easy, but as much as I
deserve wrath, You have bestowed grace on me. Amen.

See You at the Pole

Repent at the Pole

"Produce fruit in keeping with repentance."
MATTHEW 3:8 NIV

John Adams was the first vice president and second president of the United States. He set aside a national day of fasting and prayer in 1798, encouraging Americans to "call to mind our numerous offenses against the most high God, confess them before Him with the sincerest penitence, implore his pardoning mercy, and through the Great Mediator and Redeemer, for our past transgressions, and that through the grace of His Holy Spirit, we may be disposed and enabled to yield a more suitable obedience to his righteousness requisitions in time to come."

He went on to quote Proverbs 14:34 (NIV), "Righteousness exalts a nation, but sin condemns any people."

This year, as we gather around the flagpole for See You at the Pole, let our petitions of God's forgiveness and favor be turned from words into actions. Let our repentance go deeper, our excuses diminish, our love for our neighbors and enemies show. Let us find brokenness in the little sins that we pardon ourselves from, and let the passion for a deeper godliness manifest itself in how we spend our money, our time, and our joy.

May See You at the Pole be the day remembered as the day we began to live in righteousness as a nation.

God, may my prayers be turned into action. Let me be the first to repent and be an example for others. Amen.

Suffering Changes You. . .for the Better

After you have suffered a little while,
[God] will himself restore you.
1 PETER 5:10 NIV

Before the Civil War, women avoided "improper" environments, including hospitals and battlegrounds. But as men faced death, women stepped into a new role.

Susie Taylor King was a laundress, teacher, and nurse for the Union Army. She said, "It seems strange how our aversion to seeing suffering is overcome in war,—how we are able to see the most sickening sights, such as men with their limbs blown off and mangled by the deadly shells, without a shudder, and instead of turning away, how we hurry to assist in alleviating their pain, bind up their wounds, and press the cool water to their parched lips."

Susie went from a woman of self-protection to compassion. Her actions reflected the nature of Christ, the suffering servant, who brought us living water (see John 7:38) and who bound up our wounds (see Psalm 147:3).

Don't despair in the dark places of suffering, but rather consider the ways God has used it to enrich your character. As the apostle Paul explained, "We also glory in tribulations, knowing that tribulation produces perseverance; and perseverance, character; and character, hope. Now hope does not disappoint" (Romans 5:3–5 NKJV).

In times of travail, watch as the Lord conforms you to His image, and consider yourself blessed.

Jesus, show me the value of my suffering,
and make me more like You through it all. Amen.

In His Presence

*In Your presence is fullness of joy;
at Your right hand are pleasures forevermore.*
PSALM 16:11 NKJV

Joseph Fort Newton said, "In the secret place of my heart there is a little door which, if I open and enter, I am in the presence of God."

What a striking depiction of the simplicity of meeting with God! Christians struggle to know the will of God, understand His Word, and control sin. But we only need to stop and enter in.

Newton's quote is reminiscent of *The Secret Garden* where Mary and Colin enter their world of beauty and friendship away from the oppressive world. They can play together and enjoy the work of the forgotten garden that they nourished back to life.

Similarly, we should long to enter through the secret door of our souls and spend time with the ultimate Restorer. No wonder so many Christians have shallow roots and withering leaves—they spend no time with God!

Bible study and congregational worship may sustain you temporarily, but without the nutrients and connectedness to the vine, death is the ultimate destination—like cut flowers in a shop.

God is personal. He doesn't just want your work. He wants *you*, and that requires meeting with Him, talking with Him, gleaning from Him. In His presence, we are refreshed.

*Lord, I say that I love You, but it has been so long
since I have spent time in Your presence. Forgive me,
and let us come together right now. Amen.*

Thank You for My Legs!

*Let the one who is wise. . .
ponder the loving deeds of the LORD.*
PSALM 107:43 NIV

Butch had to drive his jalopy car to school every day. The car gave Butch all kinds of trouble, so he kicked it and cursed it and the car finally broke down and couldn't be fixed.

So Butch had to ride his bike to school. Naturally, it was aggravating and embarrassing, so he kicked and cursed his bike until soon it also broke down, and Butch was forced to walk.

On the way to school that first morning, Butch considered what had happened to his car and his bike, so when he was tempted to curse and kick out of frustration, he reconsidered and cried out, "Lord, thank You for my legs!"

First Thessalonians 5:18 (KJV) says, "In every thing give thanks: for this is the will of God in Christ Jesus concerning you." If you want to know the will of God—here is a good indicator—be thankful for what you have.

And how much we all have to be grateful for! As evangelist Billy Bray said, "The Lord has given me both vinegar and honey, but He has given me the vinegar with a teaspoon and the honey with a ladle." Let us in return give God our petitions with a teaspoon and lavish our thanksgiving with a ladle.

Jesus, You have been so generous to me. Thank You for all the blessings, and forgive me for taking them for granted. Amen.

God's Gift

*"I tell you, you can pray for anything, and if you
believe that you've received it, it will be yours."*
MARK 11:24 NLT

Notice the words in this verse. It says we're to believe we have received what we pray for. That's past tense. It doesn't take faith to believe our prayers will be answered after what we asked for is in plain sight. Trusting Him for answers before we see them is what the Lord wants.

The Bible tells us that without faith it is impossible to please God (see Hebrews 11:6). That may sound harsh, but scripture also promises that He gives each of us a measure of faith (see Romans 12:3).

If you gave your daughter a present and she left it on a shelf, unopened, you'd be disappointed. It may have been something she really wanted, so you found the perfect gift and wrapped it beautifully, but it is useless just sitting there. It's the same with God's gift of faith. We don't have to struggle with positive thinking or work up enough faith. All we have to do is accept what He has already provided and exercise the faith He gives.

Some people misuse this scripture and pray for foolish things that aren't according to His will. But when we stay close to Him, our desires will line up with His, and we can have complete confidence that we will receive our request.

*Dear Father, thank You for the faith You generously give me. I want
my desires to perfectly align with Your desires for me so I can ask
with true faith, knowing You have already provided the answer. Amen.*

Heavenly Home

For we know that if the earthly tent we live in is destroyed,
we have a building from God, an eternal house in heaven,
not built by human hands.
2 CORINTHIANS 5:1 NIV

Can you picture the house you'll have in heaven? Neither can I, but it is fun to imagine what the Lord is building for those who love Him. Whatever He plans is sure to be more magnificent than anything my limited mind can come up with.

Today's verse mentions our earthly tent—the body we dwell in now. Tents are temporary; certainly not designed for eternity. We spend a lot of time caring for these tents. We keep them strong, decorate them with nice coverings, paint them, and sometimes patch or repair broken parts. But they won't last forever.

I love European castles that have weathered storms for hundreds of years. I'd like to wander through each one, to learn about the people who lived there and know what life was like for all the generations within those walls. In the United States, where two-hundred-year-old buildings are considered ancient, the idea of fortresses from the 1300s or before is mind-boggling. Yet even those will eventually crumble.

The house God is preparing for us isn't a do-it-yourself project. He's building us a mansion that will be more exquisite than any castle. It is crafted with His indescribable love. And no storm or fire or other disaster can destroy our heavenly home. It will endure for eternity.

Thank You, Lord Jesus, for the home You're building for me
with Your power and love, a home that will last forever. Amen.

Created for His Pleasure

For everything, absolutely everything, above and below, visible and invisible, rank after rank after rank of angels—everything got started in him and finds its purpose in him. He was there before any of it came into existence and holds it all together right up to this moment.
COLOSSIANS 1:15–18 MSG

An incredible trip to Australia included sailing to the Great Barrier Reef. From there we plunged beneath the ocean's surface in a small glass-sided submarine. I've never wanted to dive, but that experience made me think it might be worth the effort.

We've all seen underwater photos, but nothing compares to actually being close to such incredible creations. Fish are marvelous shapes and colors—God used every combination imaginable. And ever-changing coral provides camouflage for creatures that blend in perfectly.

What amazed me most was the thought that God created that vast wonderland simply for His enjoyment. Men wouldn't be able to explore those depths for a long time, but God was in the midst of the seas from the beginning.

The same Creator formed us for His pleasure. Can you believe that? We are beautiful in His eyes, each a unique masterpiece. He made everything and rules the entire universe, including our hearts if we allow Him to. He longs for each of us to delight in knowing Him and to find our purpose as we follow His lordship.

Heavenly Father, thank You for creating each of us, making us remarkable works of art, just because You like being with us. You hold everything together, even when we feel like our world is falling apart. Amen.

God's System of Justice

*Yet the LORD longs to be gracious to you; therefore he
will rise up to show you compassion. For the LORD is
a God of justice. Blessed are all who wait for him!*
ISAIAH 30:18 NIV

Do you yearn for more of God? This scripture tells us He longs to be gracious to us. If we believe that, our response should be a longing for more of Him, more of His grace, unless pride makes us pull away and try to earn His favor.

That famous line, quoted as though it is scripture, says "God helps those who help themselves." The truth is, when we can't do anything for ourselves, we're in the perfect place for God to pour out His grace.

The world's justice tells us we don't deserve God's graciousness—we've made too many mistakes—but God's justice is wrapped in love and mercy. Instead of pointing to our failures and telling us we're worthless, He forgives our sins and totally forgets them. They're as far from His thoughts as the east is from the west (see Psalm 103:12).

When we run into His arms of love and let His grace overwhelm us, we will long for more of Him. He's too magnificent to ignore. It's impossible to turn our backs on all He does for us. The natural response is to accept His compassion. He longs to give it and waits patiently until we're ready to receive.

*Dear Lord, I long to receive Your gracious compassion. I yearn
for more of You! Help me set aside my own desires and fall
down before You, amazed by Your astonishing justice. Amen.*

Pride versus Humility

Get serious, really serious. Get down on your knees
before the Master; it's the only way you'll get on your feet.
JAMES 4:7–10 MSG

A friend said to me, "I thought I had finally learned to be humble. Then I realized I was *proud* of it!"

I could relate. How do we balance humility with allowing the Lord to work through us to do something significant? Think of Moses, one of the notable men in the Bible. We're told he was meek, yet he led that huge nation of unruly Israelites for forty years in the wilderness.

How about Isaiah, a godly prophet? When God invaded his space, Isaiah realized he was unclean. Humility opened the door for the Lord to use him powerfully.

In more recent history, Abraham Lincoln and George Washington were humble men who honored God, and He used them to deal with enormous issues in a growing nation.

Most of us never reach such lofty positions, but whether we're raising children, working on an assembly line, or teaching college classes, everyone can become proud—or stay humble.

Picture yourself hand in hand with Jesus as you go about your daily life. Next to Him, there is absolutely no room for pride. Kneel before Him. Listen to His instructions and encouragement. The closer we stay to the Master, the more clearly we see ourselves and realize we are totally dependent on Him. In His presence, pride melts away and leaves us humble.

Father God, I fall to my knees before You in humble
adoration, and thank You for providing everything I need
to accomplish the work You have planned for me. Amen.

To Know His Ways

He made known His ways to Moses,
His acts to the children of Israel.
PSALM 103:7 NKJV

When the Israelites were slaves in Egypt, and while they wandered through the wilderness, God performed countless astonishing miracles. He separated them from the plagues that decimated the Egyptians. He brought them through the Red Sea on dry land, then provided food and water and even kept their clothes from wearing out on their forty-year journey. He revealed Himself to them continually in a pillar of cloud to lead them by day and a pillar of fire for a night-light. It's hard to comprehend how they could turn away and grumble. But they did.

They saw the things God did, His *acts*, but they didn't understand His *ways*—His loving heart. They complained each time life didn't turn out the way they wanted.

We read the story and wonder about their hard hearts. But wait. If I put myself in their place, how would I behave? In their place, I'm afraid I would have groused just like them.

But Moses saw beyond the visible into the infinite goodness of his Lord. Revelation 15:3 (NKJV) says: "They sing the song of Moses. . . 'Great and marvelous are Your works, Lord God Almighty! Just and true are Your ways, O King of the saints!' "

Everything God did was designed to reveal His heart of love. He hasn't changed.

Heavenly Father, I long to know You. Your works
are marvelous; but more than that, I want to
grasp the truth and integrity of Your ways. Amen.

Cord of Hope

By faith the harlot Rahab did not perish with those who did
not believe, when she had received the spies with peace.
HEBREWS 11:31 NKJV

The life of Rahab is beautiful. She was a harlot. Hardly worth noticing. Yet the writer of Hebrews pointed to her as a woman of faith. And even more astonishing, she is highlighted in Jesus' family tree.

You may know the story. Joshua sent spies to Jericho to scope out the land. They went to Rahab's house, which was probably an inn situated on the city wall. She, along with everyone in the town, knew about the strength of Israel and realized their victories came from "the Lord your God."

Rahab hid the spies on her roof when soldiers came searching for them and sent the soldiers off on a wild goose chase. Later, she asked the spies to spare her family when they attacked Jericho. She proved her faith by helping them escape; she lowered them on a scarlet cord from her window. Because of her assistance, they told her to mark her home with the scarlet cord in her window when they came to conquer the town.

The word translated in Joshua 2:18 as *cord* can also mean *hope*. So, Rahab tied a cord in the window as a sign of hope that she and her family would be saved. Her life may have been marked by a scarlet cord, but her heart was golden to the Lord.

Heavenly Father, show me that You don't keep track
of my past mistakes. Let my life reflect Your mercy.
You are my hope for the future. Amen.

The King's Temple

You realize, don't you, that you are the temple of God,
and God himself is present in you?
1 CORINTHIANS 3:16–17 MSG

The first thing that pops into my head when I think of a temple is an ancient cathedral, but God's temples are people—those of us who love Him. The living stones that make up His temple include tender hearts, willing hands and feet, and submissive minds. When we do the things He wants us to, we reflect His divine light from within, and that draws others into His kingdom.

Jesus says He wants to abide in us. Imagine. . .the King of kings, our Creator, chooses to make His home within us. That thought humbles me until I can barely lift my head. Yet at the same time, because He is in me, I know I have strength to conquer any evil that comes against me. If He dwells in us, and we are His temple, the idea of doing anything He wouldn't do should be unthinkable.

We take Him with us all the time. Wherever we are, He is there. We may feel His presence more some times and places than others, but we have the assurance that He will never leave us. Whether we're climbing majestic mountains, working at a desk in an office, or standing in the check-out line at a grocery store, He is there. We can depend on Him to provide everything we need to thrive.

Heavenly Father, I'm absolutely in awe, knowing
You want to dwell in me. Nothing can separate us,
and nothing is impossible when You are within me. Amen.

Columbus Day

Covenant People

"This is the covenant I will make with the people of Israel after that time," declares the LORD. "I will put my law in their minds and write it on their hearts. I will be their God, and they will be my people."

Most people know who Christopher Columbus was—at least, we know his name and realize that he discovered America. Columbus Day is on our calendars but doesn't get much attention except from schoolchildren.

Supposedly, Columbus wasn't searching for a new continent. He believed the earth was a sphere, rather than the flat surface many thought, and wanted to establish trade routes to Asia. He wasn't expecting a large, uncharted landmass to get in his way.

Columbus was interested in the Bible and often quoted from it in his logs and letters. Because of his explorations, others eventually settled this land, bringing godly principles with them when our nation was born.

Those early Americans came seeking religious freedom. The hardships they faced on the voyages stopped all but the most hardy. The ships were not luxury liners with well-equipped accommodations. The trip was rugged at best, and many didn't survive the months at sea.

After people arrived, conditions were beyond challenging, but God's Word burned in their hearts and minds—they were His people and He was their God. The motto our forefathers adopted, "In God we trust," still stirs our hearts.

Thank You, Lord, for those early settlers. In covenant with You, they established a new nation dedicated to their God. Help me treasure my own covenant with You, always. Amen.

Harvesttime

*"You know the saying, 'Four months between planting
and harvest.' But I say, wake up and look around.
The fields are already ripe for harvest."*
JOHN 4:35 NLT

When we notice a task that needs to be done, could it be a nudge from God? It's easy to think someone else will take care of it—whatever *it* is. We may believe we're not qualified or our schedule is too full, or we might even think it's beneath us. Whether it is a job at church or in the community or within our families, finding excuses is simple.

Sometimes when we wonder how we can work in the spiritual harvest Jesus mentions, we get grandiose ideas, beyond what God intends. He may ask us to serve in a food pantry when we thought we should preach the Gospel in some remote country and lead hundreds to faith in Christ. Or He might want us to go to another nation, but what we're to do there is play with children or carry concrete blocks to help build a one-room school.

The only way our work will matter eternally is to allow God to direct our plans, every day, and ask Him to show us exactly what will touch someone's life. Most often, He will tell us simply to show His love in some uncomplicated way that comes naturally. Obeying in those effortless situations prepares us for the times when the Lord directs us to do something that requires total dependence on Him to accomplish.

*Lord God, I choose to be available to work however
You want me to, as You harvest the ripe fields. Amen.*

Our Stronghold

The Lord is good, a strong hold in the day of trouble;
and he knoweth them that trust in him.
NAHUM 1:7 KJV

Out of curiosity, I checked the thesaurus on my computer for the word *stronghold*, and I chuckled over what came up: stranglehold, vicelike grip, and iron grip. I'm certain that isn't what this scripture means.

In the Bible, a stronghold is a place of security and survival, fortified for protection. When I think of a natural stronghold, I picture the ancient city of Petra, carved into sheer sandstone cliffs centuries ago in Jordan. People who lived there were protected by the towering canyon walls that enclose the city. They built cisterns and an aqueduct to preserve floodwater and carry it through an arid desert area. I was able to visit Petra, and I marveled at the craftsmanship and labor necessary to construct buildings in vertical rock surfaces. I thought of the people who lived there. They felt secure, depending on the almost impenetrable gorge for defense against their enemies.

Our enemy, Satan, comes against us with doubts and fears and disasters. He wants to destroy everyone, especially those who put their trust in Jesus for salvation.

But God is our supernatural stronghold, mightier than any fortress built by men. The Lord will protect us in times of trouble; He knows those who depend on Him for shelter and refuge. Nothing can destroy us when He wraps us in His loving strength. What a comfort in the face of adversity.

Father, thank You for providing a safe place, reserved for those who put our trust in You. Let me stay there forever. Amen.

Healing the Brokenhearted

"The Spirit of the LORD is upon Me, because He has anointed Me to preach the gospel to the poor; He has sent Me to heal the brokenhearted, to proclaim liberty to the captives and recovery of sight to the blind, to set at liberty those who are oppressed."
LUKE 4:18 NKJV

When our hearts break, we have assurance from these words of Jesus, knowing He is there for us. Even in the midst of deep sadness, He gives us strength.

My mom was a vibrant woman, but she needed surgery to replace a heart valve. The twelve-hour procedure was successful, and she was recovering in the hospital. But a nurse called one morning saying, "Your mother has taken a turn for the worse. You need to come to the hospital."

I had been with Mom at bedtime the night before and she seemed to be doing well, though she was still too weak to get up or walk by herself. What happened? It turned out a nurse took her to the bathroom and left her. Eventually a secretary found her on the bathroom floor. The nurse denied any responsibility. We'll never know how long Mom was alone. She died within a few hours.

The Lord healed my broken heart and set me free from the outrage I felt toward the nurse who left Mom alone. Blinding unforgiveness tried to hold me captive, but God liberated me from its grip and opened my eyes to see His goodness and sovereign power.

Praise You, Lord Jesus, for healing broken hearts and setting us free from whatever oppression holds us captive. Amen.

My Good Shepherd

"You are my flock, the sheep of my pasture. You are my people, and I am your God. I, the Sovereign LORD, have spoken!"
EZEKIEL 34:31 NLT

I don't think it's much of a compliment to be compared to sheep. Yes, we like to watch cute, fluffy lambs frolic in a pasture, but sheep aren't very smart. They go wherever the grass looks tastier, they follow a leader that may be heading in a wrong direction, and they can easily get cantankerous. On their own, they are dirty and smelly. Sound familiar?

But throughout scripture, we read about the good Shepherd who cares for us—His sheep. My Bible notes that a shepherd does more than just herd the sheep. He cherishes, feeds, and protects them.

Jesus told a parable about the lost sheep. Though ninety-nine were safe, the shepherd searched until he found the one that was missing. Our good Shepherd rejoices when He finds one sheep that strayed from the flock. He reminds us of the joy in heaven each time a sinner repents—when the Shepherd brings him safely from the wilderness to the sheepfold.

How desperately we need a Shepherd to care for us. God sets pastors over us to carry out His plans, but above them, the perfect Shepherd leads each of us into our eternal home. Even though sometimes we act like willful sheep, He cherishes and protects us, with every step we take.

Heavenly Shepherd, no matter how far I stray, I know You will find me and carry me home. Thank You that You never give up, no matter how obnoxious I behave. Amen.

His Abiding Presence

Whoever confesses that Jesus is the Son of God,
God abides in him, and he in God.
1 JOHN 4:15 NKJV

When we invite Jesus to abide in us, we can depend on His presence. He is always aware of us, even though we often get distracted by day-to-day life and don't keep Him at the front of our minds. Then He surprises us by doing something unexpected that leaves us in awe when He allows us to participate in His work.

My husband and I were on a mission trip in Slovakia not long after the collapse of Communism. Tiny groups of Christians were finally able to openly worship together, but darkness still tried to stifle their faith. One morning we met with a few believers to pray. They didn't speak English and we were clueless about their language, but little details like that don't bother God.

I prayed aloud for the Lord to reveal Himself in amazing ways to people in their town who didn't know Him. I asked for boldness in the believers—that they would know whom to speak to and how to share God's Word.

As soon as I finished, one of the Slovakians prayed. Our interpreter leaned close to me and whispered, "She is praying exactly what you just said, word for word." I was stunned. I wept for joy. The Lord was leading our prayers and assured me that He already had an answer on the way. He was abiding in both of us!

Holy Jesus, You are magnificent! Thank You for revealing Your heart to everyone who will pause long enough to listen. Amen.

Best Friends Forever

"You are my friends when you do the things I command you. I'm no longer calling you servants because servants don't understand what their master is thinking and planning. No, I've named you friends because I've let you in on everything I've heard from the Father."
JOHN 15:11–15 MSG

Imagine what it must have been like to be among Jesus' friends while He lived on earth? Wouldn't you have loved to go wherever He went, to hear Him speak, and to see the miracles? The Gospels give us a glimpse of some of His companions, who were ordinary people like us. They weren't perfect. The twelve disciples squabbled among themselves sometimes. Mary and Martha, too. And yet Jesus counted those select few among His closest friends. They understood more than anyone what Jesus thought and planned.

I'm so glad the Bible never gives the impression that people have to be superspiritual to be His followers. Look at Peter, the disciple many of us can identify with because he seemed to speak before he thought. It was important to include some of Peter's failures in scripture, and he wasn't alone. When we read about the disappointing acts of Jesus' friends, we don't have to despair when our own lives don't measure up.

Yes, they failed sometimes, but they repented and never gave up. Because they kept trying, Jesus called them friends. He is the same now as He was then, so we can be assured we are His friends, too.

Precious Friend, You don't give up on me because I sometimes crash. I long to be close to You forever—You're my Best Friend. Amen.

Holy Boldness

*"I tell you, whoever publicly acknowledges me before others,
the Son of Man will also acknowledge before the angels of God."*
LUKE 12:8 NIV

What if Jesus acts as though He doesn't recognize you when you stand before God? "Wait, Jesus! I accepted You when I was a kid—don't You remember?" The thought is terrifying.

But have there been times when someone needed to hear the good news about Jesus, and we kept quiet? I have, and the memory hurts. For anyone like me, we may feel embarrassed when we talk about the Lord—we wonder if people will think we're weird. Maybe we feel inadequate. What if someone asks us to show them in the Bible what we claim as truth and we can't remember the verses? So, we don't acknowledge knowing Him.

We can identify with Peter when he denied he knew Jesus. Imagine how miserable he felt after that. The wonderful assurance is that Jesus forgives us and doesn't hold those moments against us. Like He did for Peter, He will give us more opportunities. Jesus knows we will fail sometimes, but those mistakes can make us stronger in the future because we never want to be that wretched again.

I know better than to think I could never deny Jesus again. But when the Holy Spirit prompts me to be bold, I want to trust Him to give me the perfect words to share the good news.

Dear Lord, help me always be ready to speak up for You, regardless of what others think. I never want to deny knowing You. Amen.

Forever the Same

*"I am the Lord, and I do not change. That is why you
descendants of Jacob are not already destroyed."*
MALACHI 3:6 NLT

Most things change constantly. People grow from babies to adults, our minds gather information, and our emotions mature. . .hopefully. Even strong, stable things change, mostly deteriorating through the ages.

I love to wander through old buildings and see how they have changed. A house in Germany has belonged to my husband's family for over four hundred years. It still provides shelter, but through the generations the residents changed the layout to make space for things like bathrooms and garages that weren't needed in the 1600s.

When I think of all the things that change, I'm comforted to know that God doesn't. He won't throw us away because of the dumb things humans do. He hasn't resorted to stripping us of our free will, even though that would make things easier for Him. He didn't decide we aren't worth saving. He still invites us to work with Him.

And because He doesn't change, He will never destroy His people.

Jesus promised, "I am with you always, even to the end of the age" (Matthew 28:20 NKJV). And the writer of Hebrews said, "Jesus Christ is the same yesterday, today, and forever" (13:8 NKJV).

Because He doesn't change, we can look forward to eternity with Him. Just because of who He is.

*Dear Lord, I praise You for being changeless. As things
around me change, I can enjoy constant assurance,
knowing You are forever the same. Amen.*

Glorious Freedom

So Christ has truly set us free. Now make sure that you stay free,
and don't get tied up again in slavery to the law.
GALATIANS 5:1 NLT

The freedom we seek escapes those who haven't allowed Jesus to set them free. His freedom includes the cleansing power of forgiveness—both knowing God has forgiven us and freely forgiving others. Refusing either of those options imprisons us.

I grew up thinking I had to be good enough for God to love me, without even understanding what that meant. I was trapped, trying to achieve the impossible, while at the same time part of me wanted to ignore all the rules. I finally learned there is no such thing as good enough. Anyone who strives to be perfected by obeying the law can never experience the blessed freedom Jesus offers.

Our Lord endured undeserved torture, brutal beatings, and the agony of crucifixion. Yet as He died, He asked God to forgive the very people who did unspeakable things to Him. If anyone ever had a reason to pray, "Father, they aren't worthy of forgiveness," it would have been Jesus. Instead, He forgave.

He knew from the beginning the path He was to follow. He realized He would have to endure excruciating pain and humiliation, but He willingly faced it to free us from the bondage of the Law. He liberated us to live lives of forgiveness.

Praise You, Lord Jesus, for the wondrous miracle of salvation. Give
me grace to understand that as I receive forgiveness I'm free to offer
it to others, even if they don't deserve it. Neither did I. Amen.

We Are Children of God

"Blessed are the peacemakers,
for they will be called children of God."
MATTHEW 5:9 NIV

One day in a fabric store, a woman came to me and said, "I need a hug and you look like you'd be willing to give me one."

I was a little startled, but she seemed genuine, so I grinned and reached out to her. She held me close for a sweet moment.

As we separated, she said, "You seem so peaceful—I need some of that."

The incident made me aware of a few things. First, any peace people sense in me comes from my heavenly Father, the source of peace. Second, we only receive that peace when we spend time with Him. And finally, many yearn for peace but don't know where to find it.

That woman sensed something tranquil—fortunately, I'm not a serial killer—and thought a little of what I had might rub off on her. Others turn to drugs, alcohol, or relationships that merely mask their angst. This encounter provided an opportunity to talk to her about where to find true peace, the kind that doesn't depend on circumstances.

I know there are times when no one sees peace in me, when worries gnaw at my mind and I allow them to eat away the calm. But that's not what God wants. When I give Him my cares and concerns, He takes me beyond the doubts and restores my peace. He reminds me I'm His child.

Holy Father, fill me till I overflow with peace that comes from
time spent with You. Let others sense Your peace in me. Amen.

He Will Lift Us Up

The LORD upholds all who fall,
and raises up all who are bowed down.
PSALM 145:14 NKJV

Once we grow beyond the toddler stage, most people don't fall very often. Unless we go skiing. The first time on skis I learned several things, including how hard it is to get up after a fall with those ungainly things attached to my feet.

Day one on the slopes I probably set a world record for being the slowest person to come down the mountain. After countless tumbles and struggling to right myself, I just sat for a while, soaking up the beauty of snow-covered mountains. I figured it was a gorgeous place to die, or at least wait for the ski patrol to rescue me.

But I was with a friend who wouldn't let me give up. Each time I fell, she pulled me up again and encouraged me to keep trying. One of the incredible things about the experience was that I was eager to go out again the next morning, and I finally learned to ski without falling.

In our daily lives, the Lord is the one who picks us up when we fall. Our falls may not be the kind that lead to broken bones, but we plunge into sin or slip on some stupid temptation or collapse into a pit of depression. Through everything that comes our way, He teaches us to depend on Him to lift us up and encourage us to go on. Always.

Precious Lord, I cannot fall so low You won't rescue me.
I rejoice in Your faithfulness, my Redeemer. You rescue me. Amen.

God's Command

You made me; you created me.
Now give me the sense to follow your commands.
PSALM 119:73 NLT

It's a good thing I'm not God! (Aren't you glad?) I definitely would not have put up with all the disobedience humans have dished out through the ages. Some people think God is a cruel judge, waiting for us to mess up so He can punish us. That is so far from the truth, it has to break God's heart to know anyone believes it.

Everything God does is designed to show His children who He is. In the book of Ezekiel, nearly every chapter has sentences that say something like, "Then they will know that I am the Lord." He allowed some terrible things to happen to the people, but it was all intended to cause them to follow Him.

Many scriptures tell us He is slow to anger. He abounds in loving-kindness. He doesn't punish us as we deserve. Yet we tend to whine and feel abused when anything bad happens.

All God expects is obedience, and His rules are simple. He knows we will break His commandments, so He only asks that we love and trust Jesus. We can't just go through the motions or follow rituals, trying to get what we want. Our deep, genuine love and an intimate relationship are what He yearns for. The more we know Him, the easier it is to worship Him, to adore Him—to give back to Him the love He freely gives to us.

Heavenly Father, following Your commands is so simple.
You loved me first. Now I love You. Amen.

The Light of Jesus

For you were once darkness, but now you are
light in the Lord. Live as children of light.
EPHESIANS 5:8 NIV

Like many children, I was afraid of the dark when I was little. We lived in an old house with a stone basement that always felt sort of dank and creepy. Our furnace was a huge coal-burning monstrosity that roared and rumbled. Who knew what scary creatures lived in the coal bin or other dark corners, waiting to jump out at me?

When my parents asked me to go down to get something, like a jar of canned vegetables or preserves, I made the trip in lightning-quick time. Mom and Dad probably knew how frightened I was and figured sending me on errands would help me get over it. I didn't admit my fear, so I never talked to them about it. Of course, my brother teased me and made the whole thing worse.

Even as adults, darkness can envelope us, leaving us with unreasonable fears. But Jesus doesn't let us fumble and stumble through the dark places on our own. He became one of us and brought light into our lives. He wants to shine divine light into every dark situation.

Colossians 1:13 (NIV) assures us, "For he has rescued us from the dominion of darkness and brought us into the kingdom of the Son he loves." When we belong to Jesus, we're part of His kingdom. We become children of light, and the darkness dissipates.

Thank You, Lord, that darkness can't overshadow Your light. And
because I belong to You, I can shine light into other dark lives. Amen.

A Firm Foundation

When the whirlwind passes by, the wicked is no more,
but the righteous has an everlasting foundation.
PROVERBS 10:25 NKJV

A whirlwind, what we call a tornado, can ravage a wide swath of land and destroy everything in its path. I'm amazed that wind, something we can't even see, can cause so much devastation. Houses are reduced to rubble—bricks, rocks, wood splinters, and broken glass. Roofs, even cars, are sometimes tossed like dandelion fluff. Nothing remains except strong foundations.

God wants us to build our lives on a strong foundation that will withstand storms—sickness, broken relationships, financial losses, or actual destruction from a natural disaster. Jesus said, "Therefore whoever hears these sayings of Mine, and does them, I will liken him to a wise man who built his house on the rock" (Matthew 7:24 NKJV). Is your life built on a solid foundation that can endure the storms of life? Do you listen and obey the Lord?

Jesus is our everlasting foundation, our Rock when troubles come. He is eager for us to run to Him. But we can't wait until we see the storm coming—that wouldn't make sense. We don't build a storm shelter when the tornado looms on the horizon.

When we cling to Him, we have assurance that He will hold us safely in His tender care. That doesn't mean no storms will come, but when they do, we know that nothing can separate us from His love.

Dear Lord, when the storms of life approach, keep me
safe in the strong foundation of Your love. I want to
listen to You and do whatever You say. Amen.

Speak to Me, Lord

"I will pour out my Spirit on every kind of people:
Your sons will prophesy, also your daughters. Your
old men will dream, your young men will see visions."
JOEL 2:28-32 MSG

Has God ever given you a dream or vision? Peter quoted this verse from Joel on the day of Pentecost, when God poured out the Holy Spirit on new believers. The prophecy was fulfilled then, and continues today.

We need to ask God for wisdom and discernment about supernatural occurrences, but that doesn't mean we should dismiss dreams, visions, and prophecies as poppycock. God speaks to His children in many creative ways. It's thrilling to know He does—tragic if we don't listen.

Maybe we have trouble thinking the Lord would give us a significant dream because we feel unworthy. But after all, today's scripture mentions "every kind of people." That sounds pretty all-inclusive. If we don't expect to hear from Him, we won't even pay attention. If we belong to Him, we should have our spiritual ears tuned to hear Him whenever and however He chooses to communicate.

God does what it takes for us to notice—regardless of whether it seems logical. He even spoke through a donkey one time in the Bible (see Numbers 22:28). Hopefully, we won't be that hard of hearing. We should welcome His voice, whether it's through the scriptures, nature, dreams, a pastor, or any other creative means. Listen.

Precious Lord, I long to have my spirit tuned to receive Your
dreams or visions or whatever You use to get through to me.
Let me never ignore Your Spirit. Amen.

He's Coming

The Lord isn't really being slow about his promise, as some people think. No, he is being patient for your sake. He does not want anyone to be destroyed, but wants everyone to repent.

2 PETER 3:9 NLT

Are you eager for the Lord to return? Every generation, since Jesus ascended into heaven after His crucifixion and resurrection, has looked forward to His second coming, wondering if it would happen soon. Through the ages many so-called prophets have set dates, sure they had it all figured out, even though Jesus said no one knows except the Father.

What might we do differently if we knew for sure this would be the month or week or day of His return? Would we tell everyone we know about the love of Jesus, His sacrificial death, and resurrection? Would we pray for people we love, that they understand the importance of the moment? God might just be waiting, giving that person ample time to repent and turn to Him.

What about cleaning up our own lives? The Lord knows exactly what we do and think each day. No use trying to fool Him.

Or would we just look up? Expectant. Waiting.

Some people think it's never going to happen. But God promised, and He is never slow about fulfilling His promises. Our timetable may not match His, but we should have an urgency to share the good news about Jesus, because today could be that glorious day. Tomorrow might be too late.

Lord Jesus, I eagerly anticipate Your return, and I long for everyone I love to be ready. Touch their hearts to welcome You, right now. Amen.

He's My Everything

Not that we are sufficient of ourselves to think of anything as being from ourselves, but our sufficiency is from God.
2 CORINTHIANS 3:5 NKJV

Most of us try to show the world we can manage on our own. We spend a lifetime building an image we want people to see. But things can happen that strip us of our abilities. We hate the feelings of inadequacy, yet those times can be opportunities for God to reveal His love, His power, His presence.

For me, a horrible auto accident sent our whole family to the hospital with critical injuries. Every shred of dignity was erased as we lay on gurneys in ambulances and the emergency room. But the Lord took care of us with incredible miracles.

The first was a police officer who carried our four-year-old daughter in his arms while a bystander drove the police car to the hospital, because the ambulance was delayed. Why would anyone take such a risk? He knew it could cost his job, but he also knew she might not live if he waited for that ambulance. The doctors were stunned, and all agreed that his selfless act saved her life. A few more moments and she would have been a statistic. The Lord saved her. She became an amazing Christian woman with her own family and career.

When we could do nothing for ourselves, God saw our lack and provided everything we needed.

Dear Lord, thank You for being my sufficiency. When I have nothing, You freely give from Your abundance. My feeble words are never enough to praise You for all You are. Amen.

Lead Me

*Trust in the LORD with all your heart; do not depend
on your own understanding. Seek his will in all you
do, and he will show you which path to take.*
PROVERBS 3:5–6 NLT

I've always been directionally challenged. I can get lost in a revolving door. My husband says I have to drop bread crumbs when I go to the backyard, in order to find my way home. And when I'm confused, panic takes over so I can't think rationally.

I am extremely thankful for my GPS and the clever minds that developed those small wonders. Sometimes the voice says, "Lost satellite connection." So I have to wait for her to figure out where we are and what direction to go. But as long as I don't try to depend on my own understanding, I arrive at my destination.

God promises when we seek His will in all we do that He will show us the way we're to go—the path to take on our life's journey. He is our supernatural GPS, with no danger of losing the satellite connection. The Holy Spirit knows exactly where we are and where our next step should take us.

If we make a wrong turn and get off His course for a while, He will "recalculate" without making us feel like stooges. And U-turns are always legal on His eternal highway. He will bring us safely to our eternal destination.

*Thank You, Lord, that You never lose me. I cannot wander
too far off the path You've charted for me. You will always
turn me around and lead me back into Your presence. Amen.*

Live in Holy Light

*"If you are generous with the hungry and start giving yourselves
to the down-and-out, your lives will begin to glow in the
darkness, your shadowed lives will be bathed in sunlight."*
ISAIAH 58:9–12 MSG

I like the way the Amplified version of the Bible says this verse: "And if you offer yourself to [assist] the hungry and satisfy the need of the afflicted, then your light will rise in darkness and your gloom will become like midday." (Isaiah 58:10).

We can't pour anything out for others unless we are full to overflowing ourselves. That means, it doesn't work to try to encourage friends if we barely scrape by. We can't feed the needy when we're starving.

Jesus wants us to live an abundant life, and when we do—when we are full of His Spirit—we have plenty to share with the people He puts in our lives. That abundant overflow comes from spending time with God. When we pray, listen, read the Bible, meditate on His magnificence, and enjoy fellowship with other believers, we get filled to the brim. Whether we have material wealth or not, we will have spiritual riches to share with others.

We will "glow in the darkness" of the world. People will be drawn to the light they see in us. Our lives will be bathed in the Son's light, like noon on a clear, bright day.

*Father, may I feed Your Word to those who are hungry
and satisfy their need to know You. I long to shine
Your light and joy in dark places. Amen.*

No Condemnation

Who is he who condemns? It is Christ who died,
and furthermore is also risen, who is even at the
right hand of God, who also makes intercession for us.
ROMANS 8:34 NKJV

We know someone condemns us. Satan whispers lies continually into our minds: "You're worthless." "You've gone too far; God doesn't love you anymore." "No one could forgive someone like you." The accusations go on and on, but we don't have to believe them.

No matter what the devil says, his lies don't change God's mind, and we shouldn't pay any attention to him. The enemy is very convincing when he reminds us of our mistakes. We know he's right—we've blown it. He pollutes our minds and muddles our thoughts.

But Jesus is in heaven, at God's right hand. They are side by side, one mind, one heart. Jesus says to the Father, *"Satan is telling our kids lies again, making them think we won't forgive them. But all they have to do is repent, ask for forgiveness, and ignore his voice."*

God the Father sees us through His Son. Jesus is eager to forgive the worst sinner. When we turn to Him, all our sins are washed away in His blood; we're spotless. And there's a glorious celebration in heaven whenever a sinner turns to Jesus.

No matter how filthy we feel, we're never more than a prayer away from being clean, as pure as if we never sinned.

Thank You, Lord, for setting me free from the sin and
guilt that try to trap me. I praise You, that though I
don't deserve it, You intercede for me continually. Amen.

Lead My Heart

*May the Lord lead your hearts into a full understanding
and expression of the love of God and the patient
endurance that comes from Christ.*
2 Thessalonians 3:5 nlt

We can't begin to comprehend all God does for us. Even before we allow Him to lead us, He is part of our universe. Without Him, the world would be devoid of love, kindness, joy, patience, or anything positive that people take for granted and expect. His love directs the events of the entire cosmos—heaven and earth—with or without the consent of individuals or governments.

The Lord yearns to direct each of our hearts so we understand the patient, enduring love of Christ. Why would anyone resist? It makes no sense, yet we're all guilty of going our own way sometimes, not allowing the one who created us to complete His masterpiece the way He wants.

If we try to control our own destiny, we flounder and our lives are full of confusion. We search for love in the things of this world and find broken hearts. We seek joy, only to face emptiness. We convince ourselves there is no truth, because we ignore reality. We waste time searching for things that bring no satisfaction.

When we bow our hearts and minds to the Creator and follow Him, we can bask in the calm of His unwavering peace. He leads us into a full understanding of true love and abundant life.

*Dear Father, I ask You to continually fill me with Your love.
Please lead me into a full understanding of Your love,
and keep me from choosing the wrong path. Amen.*

Halloween

Behind the Mask

*God's loyal love couldn't have run out, his merciful love
couldn't have dried up. They're created new every morning.
How great your faithfulness! I'm sticking with God
(I say it over and over). He's all I've got left.*
LAMENTATIONS 3:22–24 MSG

So many things try to snatch our attention away from the Lord. They could be worthwhile or necessary or just fun, but if they aren't what God wants us to focus on, we need to ignore them and concentrate on Him. Sometimes even ministry can drain our energy so we are too exhausted to spend time with Jesus. We may not even realize we're slipping away.

Then we find ourselves just going through the motions of worship. Our friends still see us as faithful followers of the Lord, but it's as though we're wearing a disguise. We put on a mask to look like something we're not. Inside, our love has dried up. And what's worse, we may not even realize what has happened. The joy seeps away. There's no enthusiasm or satisfaction in the work, but we fight to maintain our image.

Or, the opposite extreme could be that we are so full of energy to accomplish our goals, we don't even miss the former sweet fellowship we had with Jesus. Distractions can blind us to what we've abandoned.

Whatever it is, if anything has taken the place of an intimate relationship with our Creator, it puts our spiritual lives in jeopardy. Don't masquerade. Be real. The Lord isn't fooled.

*Holy Jesus, I praise You for the loyal, merciful love You
faithfully pour into Your children to keep us close. Amen.*

A Month of Thanks

Rejoice always, pray continually, give thanks in all circumstances; for this is God's will for you in Christ Jesus.
1 THESSALONIANS 5:16–18 NIV

Welcome to November! This month is always full of many things for all of us. Together, we will focus throughout the month on being full of thanks! Whether you are in a season of peace in life or experiencing pain and stress, a spirit of thankfulness is always possible through the power of Christ. Let's explore what God's Word has to say about being thankful and how doing so can literally change your life.

Have you ever wondered what God's will is for your life? Here is the answer! First Thessalonians tells us exactly what God's will is for each of us: rejoice and pray always, and give thanks no matter the circumstances. Simple? Yes! Easy? No way!

How is it possible to pray and give thanks always? It is not possible on our own. But the great news is that we have the Spirit of God living inside of us, reminding us of God's truth and leading us each step of the way.

Are you walking in the Spirit of God?

God, we ask that Your Holy Spirit fill us with Your presence, Your guidance, Your wisdom, and Your peace. We can thank You in each moment because of Your great presence in our lives. We trust our lives and our decisions to You. We are thankful for Your great and abiding love for us. Amen.

A Thankful Mind

*Let the peace of Christ rule in your hearts, since as members
of one body you were called to peace. And be thankful.*
COLOSSIANS 3:15 NIV

How do we let the peace of Christ rule in our hearts? One way is to take every thought captive and make it obedient to Christ (see 2 Corinthians 10:5). That means when an unkind or impure thought comes into our minds, we take it straight to the cross of Christ.

Instead of obsessing over conversations and what other people might be thinking of you, you focus on Jesus. Sometimes just saying the name of Jesus out loud when you have a negative thought can stop the thought in its tracks and refocus your mind.

After allowing Jesus into your thought process, thank God for your blessings. Thank Him for His great love for you and others. Ask Him to give you something else to think about instead of going back to that original thought.

If you're having a convicting thought, take that to God as well. Ask Him to reveal what is true and right and what your response should be.

Surrendering our thoughts to Christ naturally leads to surrendering our actions to Him, too. When our hearts and minds are surrendered to Christ, the peace of Christ is free to rule in our lives.

*Thank You, God, for meeting me in each moment. Let my heart
be set on You. Allow my heart and mind to be full of thankfulness
for who You are and all that You've done in my life. Amen.*

No Worries

Do not be anxious about anything, but in every situation, by prayer
and petition, with thanksgiving, present your requests to God.
And the peace of God, which transcends all understanding,
will guard your hearts and your minds in Christ Jesus.
PHILIPPIANS 4:6–7 NIV

Do you find yourself being overly anxious at times? The enemy wants to fill you with fear and anxiety. His plan is to steal, kill, and destroy (see John 10:10), and that includes destroying your peace and thankfulness. But God's plan is that you have life and have it abundantly! So how can you shut of the anxiety and worry to make room for the abundant life God has for you right here and now? Our gracious God has given us a game plan:

- Whenever you find yourself worried or anxious, stop to pray.
- Give thanks! Tell God your worries and ask Him to fill you with joy in His presence (see Psalm 16:11).
- When you do those things, the very peace of God. . .which doesn't make any sense to our human minds. . .will guard your heart and mind through Christ.

Through the ages, men and women of God have relied on this game plan to get them through unimaginable circumstances: Mothers losing a child to cancer have been given peace through the power of Christ. Soldiers held captive by the enemy have been filled with the presence of God. If you are struggling with an uncertain future, find rest and peace in Christ alone.

God, I'm worried and afraid. Please fill me with Your peace
in this situation. Thank You for Your unfailing love! Amen.

A Good Dad

Give thanks to the LORD, for he is good;
his love endures forever.
PSALM 107:1 NIV

Our pastor often reminds us that God is a good Dad. He is the only perfect parent. Whenever you're tempted to believe the lie that God is just a grumpy old man keeping track of rights and wrongs from heaven, remind yourself that He is good. He loves you with an everlasting love. His Word tells us that it is His kindness that leads us to repentance (see Romans 2:4), not shame and false guilt over our past mistakes.

Did you grow up with loving parents? Or do you consider yourself a loving parent? If you've experienced what it's like to feel secure in that kind of love and give that kind of love. . .how much more does the Author and Creator of that love care for you!

In Luke 11:13 (NIV), Jesus says, "If you then, though you are evil, know how to give good gifts to your children, how much more will your Father in heaven give the Holy Spirit to those who ask him!"

God is a good Dad who gives us His Spirit to live in us and teach us in each moment. We are never alone. We have a constant, perfect, loving parent and friend with us at all times and in every situation.

What an amazing gift to be thankful for this month and always!

God, You are a good and loving Dad. The love I feel
for my children and others doesn't even come close to the
love and graciousness You have for me. Thank You! Amen.

Gratitude

Pray diligently. Stay alert, with your eyes wide open in gratitude.
COLOSSIANS 4:2-4 MSG

Gratitude is defined as the *feeling* of being grateful or thankful. Many times in our human bodies, our feelings don't match up with the truth. We may have all our needs met and a loving family, and still we struggle with a depression we don't understand. We may be married to an attentive and thoughtful husband, but we've lost that "in love" feeling.

When you have trouble with your feelings, immediately run to the truth of God's Word and recount what you know to be true. Write down truths from God and keep them in your regular line of vision:

- I am free and clean in the blood of Christ.
- He has rescued me from darkness and has brought me into His kingdom.
- God sings over me.
- He delights in me.
- I am a friend of Christ.
- Nothing can separate me from God's love (certainly not my feelings!).
- God knows me intimately.
- God sees me as beautiful and I am wonderfully made.
- God is for me, not against me.

This is truth from His Word! And when you focus on truth, your confusing thoughts start to become clear. . .and amazingly enough, your feelings begin to turn back on!

God, please remind me of what is true. I want to feel a sense of gratitude for You, for others, and for all the blessings in my life. Amen.

A Friend of God

Instead, be filled with the Holy Spirit, singing psalms and hymns and spiritual songs among yourselves, and making music to the Lord in your hearts. And give thanks for everything to God the Father in the name of our Lord Jesus Christ.

EPHESIANS 5:18–20 NLT

In John 15:15, Jesus says that we are His friends. He has given us His Spirit so that we can know His heart and His ways. A great woman of God said that when she spends time with God, He always makes her feel like His favorite daughter. It's so true. You're His favorite daughter, too. . .and He wants to be your best friend.

This same woman of God has a very special relationship with her heavenly Father. She sings songs of praise to God throughout the day. If you were to have a conversation with her in the hallway at church, she would likely break into song as God prompted her. Her heart is so full of thanks to God for His faithfulness to her. You wouldn't know by the joy oozing from her that she had many heartbreaking moments, including her husband being taken from her by a freak strike of lightning as he was standing beside her on vacation. She pressed into God during that time instead of pushing Him away. She has allowed God to guide her every step and heal her brokenness. She is always pointing others to the one true God.

Will you be God's friend in joy and sorrow?

God, please strengthen my faith in You. Show me Your love and faithfulness in a personal and powerful way. Amen.

Praying for Wisdom

If any of you lacks wisdom, you should ask God, who gives
generously to all without finding fault, and it will be given to you.
JAMES 1:5 NIV

The prayers of the righteous are powerful and effective (see James 5:16). When we pray, we become a part of the solution and a part of the blessing. Prayer is a great mystery, but Jesus tells us to pray always. Our prayers are heard and somehow, in a powerful way, they make a difference.

As you pray today, ask God to help you make wise decisions. Be thankful for the key leaders in your life: your pastor, your mentors, your spouse and family members. Pray for your children and young relatives to grow up as strong leaders. Pray for your local and national leaders. Pray for wisdom as you help select those leaders who will make decisions for you. God will give you His wisdom if you ask for it.

God's Word also tells us that we "do not have because [we] do not ask God" (James 4:2 NIV). You've probably heard that said this way: You have not because you ask not. If you are lacking wisdom, it may be because you've never really asked for it. You can change that today. Spend time with God asking Him to fill you with truth and wisdom.

God, I know this is an important day. I ask for Your
great wisdom as I make decisions concerning
leadership in my life and family. Amen.

Without Excuse

Yes, they knew God, but they wouldn't worship him as God or even give him thanks. And they began to think up foolish ideas of what God was like. As a result, their minds became dark and confused.
ROMANS 1:21 NLT

In Romans 1, Paul is reminding us all that we are without excuse (see Romans 1:20). We have a supernaturally created world around us each day, a sun to warm and light our earth and a moon to light our nights. Only our Creator is to thank for those blessings.

But mankind, though they knew God, chose not to worship Him or give Him thanks. This resulted in dark and confused minds. This can be true of our world today. When we choose ourselves over God, life becomes confusing and dark.

If we believe the truth of God and His Word that we are made clean and new in the blood of Christ, then we are without excuse when it comes to thanking Him for all He is and all He has done. We either believe it and it means absolutely everything—changing our entire lives—or we are lukewarm in our faith and the Christian life is really just a supper club. There is great danger in the latter (see Revelation 3:16).

Will you give your thanks and worship to the true God?

God, I do not want to be lukewarm in my faith. I want to live for You and give all my thanks and worship to You alone. Please rid me of selfishness and fill me with Your Spirit. Amen.

His Love Never Quits

Give thanks to GOD—he is good and his love never quits. Say, "Save us,
Savior God, round us up and get us out of these godless places, so we
can give thanks to your holy Name, and bask in your life of praise."
1 CHRONICLES 16:34–36 MSG

God's Word tells us in Psalm 139 that we can never escape the presence of God. He is with us always, no matter where we go or what we do. His love never quits on us. First John 4:10 (NIV) says, "This is love: not that we loved God, but that he loved us and sent his Son as an atoning sacrifice for our sins." God doesn't love us because we did a lot of good things for Him. He doesn't love us because of our last names or because of the jobs we do. He can't love us any more or any less than He already does. He loves us simply because He is our Father and our Creator. In fact, He gave up His very life to show you how much.

You may have had a parent, friend, or spouse abandon you at some point in your life. God won't do that. You may feel alone and fearful. God won't leave you. You may feel sad and crushed. God says He is close to the brokenhearted and saves those who are crushed in Spirit (see Psalm 34:18).

God, please remove me from godless places of darkness
and loneliness and fear. I trust that You love me
and that You will be with me always. Amen.

Voices Raised

The trumpeters and singers performed together in unison to praise and give thanks to the Lord. Accompanied by trumpets, cymbals, and other instruments, they raised their voices and praised the Lord with these words: "He is good! His faithful love endures forever!"
2 CHRONICLES 5:13 NLT

Do you enjoy singing praises to God? Maybe you have a lovely voice and sing for an audience, or maybe you are solely a shower singer and would rather die than sing in front of others. Either way, God loves to hear you praise Him with your voice! He created you and thinks you are beautiful. . .that includes your voice!

Zephaniah 3:17 (NLT) tells us some very encouraging words: "For the Lord your God is living among you. He is a mighty savior. He will take delight in you with gladness. With his love, he will calm all your fears. He will rejoice over you with joyful songs." Amazing that God sings over us, right?

Take a moment and think of your favorite worship song. Find your journal or some paper and write down a chorus or two. Hum along with the words and then lift your voice loud and clear to your Maker. He loves to hear from you! Remember, it doesn't matter what you sound like. You don't have to be a contestant on *The Voice* to make God smile with your song.

God, here is my praise song to You! Thank You for loving me just the way I am. I will sing and make music to You because I'm so thankful for all You've blessed me with. Amen.

Thank You, Veterans!

We put our hope in the LORD. He is our help and our shield.
In him our hearts rejoice, for we trust in his holy name. Let your
unfailing love surround us, LORD, for our hope is in you alone.
PSALM 33:20-22 NLT

On November 11, 1919, President Wilson said: "To us in America, the reflections of Armistice Day will be filled with solemn pride in the heroism of those who died in the country's service and with gratitude for the victory, both because of the thing from which it has freed us and because of the opportunity it has given America to show her sympathy with peace and justice in the councils of the nations." This was the beginning of what is now known as Veterans Day.

If you are a veteran or have a loved one who is serving or has served, we thank and honor those faithful men and women who are willing to give up their lives for another. Here are some encouraging words to pray over and share with the veterans in your life:

Second Timothy 1:7 (NLT): "For God has not given us a spirit of fear and timidity, but of power, love, and self-discipline."

Deuteronomy 31:6 (NIV): "Be strong and courageous. Do not be afraid or terrified because of them, for the LORD your God goes with you; he will never leave you nor forsake you."

God, I am incredibly thankful for the veterans in
my life and my community. Please bless them
and give them Your Spirit and courage. Amen.

Common Days

And so, dear brothers and sisters, I plead with you to give your bodies to God because of all he has done for you. Let them be a living and holy sacrifice—the kind he will find acceptable. This is truly the way to worship him. Don't copy the behavior and customs of this world, but let God transform you into a new person by changing the way you think. Then you will learn to know God's will for you, which is good and pleasing and perfect.

ROMANS 12:1-2 NLT

Author William Arthur Ward said, "Gratitude can transform common days into Thanksgiving, turn routine jobs into joy, and change ordinary opportunities into blessings." When we live a life of worship, every day can be Thanksgiving! Each task that God gives you to do—even the mundane acts of mopping the floor—can be done as an act of worship to God.

God tells us that He wants us to live a life of everyday worship. He wants to transform us from the inside out. This isn't about trying harder to please God or going to church more and giving more money . . .it's about letting the Spirit of God lead you in every moment and thanking Him along the way. It's about listening for His still, small voice and following Him no matter what everyone else is doing.

If we let gratitude do its work in our hearts, the common days become holidays! Is every day Thanksgiving in your heart?

*God, I want to worship You in all that I do.
Show me how to live a life of everyday worship. Amen.*

Let the Whole World Know

Give thanks to the LORD and proclaim his greatness.
Let the whole world know what he has done.
PSALM 105:1 NLT

With social media influencing our world in countless ways, believers truly do have the opportunity to tell the whole world what God has done in our lives! It's easy to get caught up in drama and politics when you go online to connect with friends, but God wants us to be lights in those dark places. Instead of getting involved in heated discussions, encourage. Instead of adding to negative comments or getting frustrated with someone who won't change her mind, show love.

Give thanks to the Lord and tell others of the great things He's done in your life. Telling people what they should or shouldn't do is not our job. Shaming people is never helpful. Only God can change hearts and minds. Our job is to tell what God has done in *our* lives.

If you don't have much to tell, ask God to fill your heart to overflowing with His joy and goodness. Get to the bottom of your faith and find out what is true and right based on God's great love for you. Then out of the overflow of your heart you can speak truth into other people's lives (see Luke 6:45).

God, help me to be a light in the darkness. Give me
the words to say when interacting with others online.
Help me love with my words and actions. Amen.

Thank God

Hallelujah! Thank GOD! And why? Because he's good, because his love lasts. But who on earth can do it—declaim GOD's mighty acts, broadcast all his praises? You're one happy man when you do what's right, one happy woman when you form the habit of justice.

PSALM 106:1-3 MSG

Are you in the habit of thanking God? Taking one minute each morning to turn your thoughts toward thanks to God can change the outlook of your entire day. Maybe you woke up to the reminder of all the extra work on your plate this week. Maybe your children didn't sleep well last night but you have a nonstop day today. Maybe you just don't feel like being in a good mood!

Stop. Just stop what you're thinking for a moment and focus your mind on God. Allow His Spirit inside you to remind you of His goodness. His love lasts. Always. Now thank Him for at least one great blessing in your life right now.

You are the only one in charge of your attitude. Many things will happen today. Some good, some maybe not so good, but all are outside of your control. You can control how you respond to everything that happens this day. Why not thank God no matter what? Think that might change how well your day goes? Why not give it a try and see what happens!

God, please remind me in this moment of Your goodness and Your great love for me! Please help me choose YOU in each moment. Help me thank You in every circumstance. Amen.

Battle Prayers

I urge you, first of all, to pray for all people. Ask God to help them;
intercede on their behalf, and give thanks for them.
1 TIMOTHY 2:1 NLT

Does God ever bring someone to mind and you feel the immediate need to contact or pray for that person? Maybe it's someone you haven't seen or thought of in years. When this happens, it's important to pray for that person. We know that prayer is a great mystery, but God tells us that our prayers are powerful and effective. Our prayers really do make a difference!

We are told many times throughout God's Word that there is a spiritual realm we cannot see (check out Ephesians 6). There is a battle going on all around us that we often forget. Good versus Evil is playing out in our lives and the lives of those we love in every moment. C. S. Lewis said that "There is no neutral ground in the universe. Every square inch, every split second is claimed by God, and counterclaimed by Satan."

It's time to claim the ground around our friends and loved ones. When God brings someone to mind, pray! You have no idea what battle they are facing, but you can be sure they are facing one whether they know it or not. Your job is to battle against the enemy in the name of Jesus. Take up the full armor of God (see Ephesians 6:10–18) and pray that same protection over your loved one. Ask God to help them and then give thanks for them!

Thank You God for bringing _____ to mind.
Surround him/her with Your love and protection. Amen.

A Life of Thanks

My counsel for you is simple and straightforward: Just go ahead with what you've been given. You received Christ Jesus, the Master; now live him. You're deeply rooted in him. You're well constructed upon him. You know your way around the faith. Now do what you've been taught. School's out; quit studying the subject and start living it! And let your living spill over into thanksgiving.

COLOSSIANS 2:6–7 MSG

You can know everything there is to know about the Bible and church and still miss having a powerful and close relationship with Christ. First Corinthians 13:1–2 (NLT) tells us this: "If I could speak all the languages of earth and of angels, but didn't love others, I would only be a noisy gong or a clanging cymbal. If I had the gift of prophecy, and if I understood all of God's secret plans and possessed all knowledge, and if I had such faith that I could move mountains, but didn't love others, I would be nothing."

Jesus tells us that the greatest commands are to love God and love others (see Matthew 22:36–40). Period. Nothing else matters if we aren't doing those two things! God's Word tells us that we are nothing without love. Ask God to transfer your head knowledge into heart knowledge so that you can start living in a moment-by-moment relationship with Christ.

When we live a life of love, it spills over into a life of thanksgiving.

God, please fill my heart with Your truths so that I can live a life of love. Move in me so that I can start living out what I believe with thanksgiving. Amen.

With All My Heart

I will give thanks to you, LORD, with all my heart;
I will tell of all your wonderful deeds.
PSALM 9:1 NIV

God, your Creator, is the only one capable of healing your heart and making you whole again. He heals broken hearts and binds up wounds (see Psalm 147:3). It's also been said that God can heal your broken heart but first you must give Him all the pieces.

Have you given God all the pieces? Have you given Him your whole heart? Maybe your heart has been torn in two and you've been betrayed more times than you can count. God won't betray you. He will never leave or forsake you. Maybe you've been hurt so badly you're not sure if God is even there anymore. Ask Him to reveal Himself to you. Psalm 73:26 (NIV) says, "My flesh and my heart may fail, but God is the strength of my heart and my portion forever."

When you build walls to protect your heart, you end up keeping out the bad. . .but you also keep out the good. Allow God to break down the walls of your heart so He can start putting the pieces back together. Then you'll be able to give thanks with all your heart.

God, I want You to have my whole heart. . .all the pieces!
I admit I'm afraid to open myself up to love.
Please break down my walls and reveal Yourself to me. Amen.

Brimming with Worship

Do you see what we've got? An unshakable kingdom!
And do you see how thankful we must be? Not only thankful,
but brimming with worship, deeply reverent before God.
HEBREWS 12:28–29 MSG

Author and pastor Louie Giglio said that all of us have the same testimony. We were dead. . .and now we're not! The rest of our story is details.

Do you see what we've got? New life! Does that bring a sense of wonder and thankfulness to your heart? If not, ask God to fill you with His wonder and thankfulness. For those of us who have grown up in the church and have heard the Gospel twice a week for our entire lives, it can become just more words instead of the life-giving truth of who God is and who we are.

If you aren't brimming with worship, ask God to wake you up and change you from the inside out! Remember, God's Word tells us that we have not because we ask not (see James 4:2). . .so why not ask? If our prayers are in line with God's will, He longs to give us the desires of our hearts (see Psalm 37:4).

The presence and power of God in your daily life will change you. Even if you're in the middle of a dark time, God wants to give you His peace that goes beyond your understanding. He will. . .if only you will let Him!

God, I want to be brimming with worship for You,
but my heart feels numb sometimes. Please wake me
up so that I can know and love You more! Amen.

A Sacrifice of Praise

"Spread for me a banquet of praise, serve High God a feast of kept promises, and call for help when you're in trouble—I'll help you, and you'll honor me."

PSALM 50:7-15 MSG

There are times in life when our faith wavers and we're not sure what we believe anymore. It's easy to trust God when everything in life is going well or when you've experienced a miracle. Maybe a loved one has been healed of a disease. Or maybe you've just witnessed the miracle of birth. Or had a mountain top experience with God in His creation. It's easier to trust God when you can see the tangible evidence that He is working in your life.

But what about when life is dark? What about when a loved one isn't healed or financial burdens are wreaking havoc in your life? Is God still there?

In Hebrews 13:15 (NIV), God's Word tells us, "Through Jesus, therefore, let us continually offer to God a sacrifice of praise—the fruit of lips that openly profess his name." To sacrifice in worship means to have faith in God even when you don't feel like it. Even when you can't see Him anymore. The only way we can do that is through the power of Christ working in our lives in each moment. Because of the cross, we can rise above our circumstances and trust that the God of heaven has purpose for everything that comes our way. We are able to look at situations from God's perspective and trust Him no matter what.

God, please increase my faith so that I can trust You and worship You despite my circumstances. Amen.

This Is My God

"The LORD is my strength and my song; he has given me victory. This is my God, and I will praise him—my father's God, and I will exalt him!"

EXODUS 15:2 NLT

In Acts 17, Paul was preaching to the people of Athens who were worshipping a host of gods. He even found an idol they had built to an "unknown god." Paul called out their ignorance and told them the truth about the Living God:

The God who made the world and everything in it is the Lord of heaven and earth and does not live in temples built by human hands. And he is not served by human hands, as if he needed anything. Rather, he himself gives everyone life and breath and everything else. From one man he made all the nations, that they should inhabit the whole earth; and he marked out their appointed times in history and the boundaries of their lands. God did this so that they would seek him and perhaps reach out for him and find him, though he is not far from any one of us. "For in him we live and move and have our being." (v. 24–28 NIV)

This is our God, and He is worthy of all our praise! He is our strength and our song. He gives us victory through Christ. We are exactly where He has placed us, and He has a great purpose for doing so.

Lord of heaven and earth, I know that You are the only true and living God! I praise You that You are not far from me. You are my life and my very breath. Amen.

My Eyes Have Seen

"He alone is your God, the only one who is worthy
of your praise, the one who has done these mighty
miracles that you have seen with your own eyes."
DEUTERONOMY 10:21 NLT

Do you remember the moment that God first spoke to your heart?
Close your eyes and think back to the first time you felt the Spirit
whispering to your heart. You had heard of God and what He can do,
but you finally let it sink into your heart! Job 42:5 (NIV) says, "My ears
had heard of you but now my eyes have seen you."

God is not only the great Creator of all things; He is a personal
God actively alive in every moment of your life. He knows your words
before you even speak them. He wants you to know Him intimately
(see Psalm 139). When that miraculous moment occurs—the head
knowledge turning into heart knowledge—God begins to open your
eyes to see Him in everything.

Suddenly, hard times begin to make sense. God is working them
all out for good in your life (see Romans 8:28). You start to notice
God's hand at work in all areas of your life. He knows everything about
you, and He promises that you will find Him when you look for Him
(see Jeremiah 29:13).

God, please open my eyes to see You at work in my life.
Move in my heart to see things from Your perspective
and great purpose. You are worthy of all my praise! Amen.

Safe and Saved

I sing to GOD, the Praise-Lofty, and find myself safe and saved.
PSALM 18:3 MSG

In Christ we are safe and saved. How do we know? The truth in God's Word tells us this:

We are hidden with Christ in God (see Colossians 3:3).

"He will cover you with his feathers, and under his wings you will find refuge; his faithfulness will be your shield" (Psalm 91:4 NIV).

"God is our refuge and strength, always ready to help in times of trouble" (Psalm 46:1 NLT).

"God is a dwelling place, and underneath are the everlasting arms" (Deuteronomy 33:27 NASB).

"For in the day of trouble He will conceal me in His tabernacle; in the secret place of His tent He will hide me; He will lift me up on a rock" (Psalm 27:5 NASB).

"The name of the LORD is a fortified tower; the righteous run to it and are safe" (Proverbs 18:10 NIV).

God gives us His Word so that we won't be afraid. He is closer to us than we think. Whenever you feel afraid or lonely, call on His name. Ask Him to make Himself known to you. Copy these scripture verses on note cards and read them again and again. God's Word is living and active, and the Spirit of God will remind you of these truths when you need them most. Don't be ashamed when you feel afraid . . .just take your fears straight to the only one who can free you from them. He will comfort you and cover you with His loving-kindness.

God, please hide me in Your shelter and cover me with Your truth and love. When I'm afraid, help me put my trust in You. Amen.

Overflowing Grace

*And they will pray for you with deep affection
because of the overflowing grace God has given to you.
Thank God for this gift too wonderful for words!*
2 CORINTHIANS 9:14–15 NLT

Happy Thanksgiving! As you gather with friends and family today, consider the words of Ralph Waldo Emerson: "Cultivate the habit of being grateful for every good thing that comes to you, and to give thanks continuously. And because all things have contributed to your advancement, you should include all things in your gratitude."

Today as you give thanks, remember to thank God for working all things together for your good and for His glory. Even the most stressful and hurtful times in your life have contributed to who you are. Nothing is wasted in the kingdom of God. He will use all things—the good and bad—and make them into something beautiful. He can turn ashes into beauty and despair into praise (see Isaiah 61:3).

Because of Christ's work on the cross, God is overflowing with grace toward us. When He looks at us, He sees Jesus! Now we can go "boldly to the throne of our gracious God. There we will receive his mercy, and we will find grace to help us when we need it most" (Hebrews 4:16 NLT).

*God, we come before You in thanksgiving today.
Thank You for Your great love and mercy toward us.
Your gift is too wonderful for words! Amen.*

God-Things and God-Songs

*I waited and waited and waited for GOD. At last he looked; finally he
listened. He lifted me out of the ditch, pulled me from deep mud.
He stood me up on a solid rock to make sure I wouldn't slip. He taught
me how to sing the latest God-song, a praise-song to our God.*

PSALM 40:1–3 MSG

When God alone teaches us how to worship, it is true and from the
heart. Isaiah 30:20–21 (NLT) tells us that "Though the Lord gave you
adversity for food and suffering for drink, he will still be with you to
teach you. You will see your teacher with your own eyes. Your own
ears will hear him. Right behind you a voice will say, 'This is the way
you should go,' whether to the right or to the left."

God Himself wants to rescue you and to teach you. He alone is
your Savior. No other human—as much as that person might try or
intend to help you—can save you. If you allow Him, the God of heaven
and earth will lift you up out of your despair and striving and set
you free. He will teach you how to praise Him, even in the midst of
suffering and trials. Quiet yourself before God and He will teach you.

*God, I want to hear from You. Forgive me for
wanting others to rescue me. That is only Yours to do.
Please quiet my heart so that I can learn from You. Amen.*

I Will Praise Him Again

Why am I discouraged? Why is my heart so sad? I will put my
hope in God! I will praise him again—my Savior and my God!
PSALM 42:5–6 NLT

When we allow the worries of this world to consume us, it's easy to fall into sadness and depression. Psalm 13:3 (NLT) is a very honest prayer: "Turn and answer me, O LORD my God! Restore the sparkle to my eyes, or I will die." Do you feel like the sparkle has left your eyes? Can others see the light of Christ in you, or are you known for being weighed down with sadness?

A life of faith isn't one where you walk around with a smile pasted on your face telling everyone that Jesus loves them even if you're not sure that's really true. A life of faith is marked by an authentic, loving relationship with God. You tell Him your burdens and He carries them for you. You're weighed down by sadness and stress and God gives you rest. You take your suffering and depression to God and He gives you a new heart!

What God wants from you is this: instead of telling every person but God your troubles, go to Him first. He will lovingly restore you and meet your every need. He will bring resources to you and show you the way! If you let go of trying to manipulate your circumstances and allow God to come to your rescue, He will!

God, forgive me for going to everyone but You for help. I give
You my needs and desires. Please fill my heart with hope. Amen.

My One Defense

I will give thanks to the LORD because of his righteousness;
I will sing the praises of the name of the LORD Most High.
PSALM 7:17 NIV

Take a moment and hum through the old hymn "The Solid Rock." Do you remember the words? The songwriter is clear that our hope is built on nothing but the blood of Jesus and His righteousness. And when we stand before the throne, we are dressed in the righteousness of Christ. He is our only defense and the reason we stand before God without fault or stain.

Think about that for a moment. What images come to mind? Do you see yourself hidden in Christ before God? Do you see God looking upon you with love? Can you see that nothing we could possibly do will make God love us any more or less? Do you know for sure that you cannot earn your way to a right relationship with God?

Christ is our one defense. We stand before God without stain or blemish because of Christ. We are made perfect in God's sight because of Christ. We are wholly and dearly loved children of God—completely acceptable in His sight.

All because of Christ.

God, I give thanks to You because of Christ. You made a way
for me to come to You boldly, without fear. Christ is my one defense,
and I stand before Your throne knowing that. I give You my life,
Father. I love You with my whole heart. Amen.

Confidence in God

My heart is confident in you, O God; my heart is confident.
No wonder I can sing your praises!
PSALM 57:7 NLT

We can gain confidence in God in many ways. We read His Word and hear true stories of men and women who have followed God through the ages. We encourage each other by meeting with other believers in churches and Bible studies. We share how God has moved in our lives and we increase the faith of friends and family.

Another way to be confident in God is to start a blessings journal. Look back on your life and write down the dates and details of how you've seen God's hand in your life. You've probably experienced more miracles and blessings than you can remember! When you write down these faith-building testimonies, you have something concrete to look at when you feel like giving up. You can read the truth of how God has showed up in your life. You can pass along this journal to loved ones who are feeling similarly. You have your own faith journey to share with anyone you meet.

God, my heart is confident in You, and I will give You praise.
I have seen You work in my life in countless and untold ways!
I commit to write down the blessings and miracles You have shown
me. Use these journal entries to increase the faith of those who hear
them and to remind me of Your intimate loving ways. Amen.

All Glory to God

Now all glory to God, who is able to keep you from
falling away and will bring you with great joy into
his glorious presence without a single fault.
JUDE 24 NLT

Jude is one of the shortest books of the Bible, consisting of only one chapter. Written by Jude himself (who was a half brother to Jesus), this little book contains great truths that should not be overlooked.

Jude warns all believers to reject false teachings and stay close to Christ in prayer. Believers today face many of the same challenges as the people in Jude's time. We have false teachers who claim to trust God yet teach rules contrary to what Christ taught. We have wolves in sheep's clothing who want nothing more than to cause drama and dissension in our groups and churches. False teachers can be very convincing, and sometimes it's difficult to know whom to follow. They often mix a lot of truth with just a tiny bit of lies.

That's where Jude's words come in. The book of Jude ends with great hope and is well known as one of the greatest doxologies (verses of praise) in the New Testament. He reminds us that God is completely able to keep us from falling away as we stay close to Him and remain in His Word.

When we stay close to God, His Spirit gives us discernment to know the truth.

God, I thank You and praise You for Your Spirit that
lives in me, guiding me and reminding me of all truth.
I give You all my worship and praise. Amen.

Fill Your Minds with Good

*Summing it all up, friends, I'd say you'll do best by filling
your minds and meditating on things true, noble, reputable,
authentic, compelling, gracious—the best, not the worst;
the beautiful, not the ugly; things to praise, not things to curse.*
PHILIPPIANS 4:8–9 MSG

Do you categorize yourself as an optimist or a pessimist? Do you look on the bright side of things, or can you always find something negative in every situation?

If you are more of a Debbie Downer, don't lose hope! Even if your mind goes directly to the negative, God can change you. He does this by transforming you and renewing your mind. Ask Him to daily fill your mind with good things: thinking the best about people and circumstances, not the worst. Seek the power of God to take every thought captive and you'll begin to see a change in you! Make a list of scriptures that will renew your mind. Start with these:

"Do not conform to the pattern of this world, but be transformed by the renewing of your mind. Then you will be able to test and approve what God's will is—his good, pleasing and perfect will" (Romans 12:2 NIV).

"We demolish arguments and every pretension that sets itself up against the knowledge of God, and we take captive every thought to make it obedient to Christ" (2 Corinthians 10:5 NIV).

If you are perpetually optimistic, stay the course and pray for the people in your life who have a tendency to bring others down.

*God, please fill my mind with good things. Renew my
thoughts and make them obedient to Your will. Amen.*

Great Expectation

All praise to God, the Father of our Lord Jesus Christ. It is by his great mercy that we have been born again, because God raised Jesus Christ from the dead. Now we live with great expectation, and we have a priceless inheritance—an inheritance that is kept in heaven for you, pure and undefiled, beyond the reach of change and decay.

1 PETER 1:3–4 NLT

As we head into the Christmas season, we do so with great expectation. Not just because of holiday joy, but for the joy set before us in Christ. Second Corinthians 5:17 (NLT) tells us that "anyone who belongs to Christ has become a new person. The old life is gone; a new life has begun!" Not only do we have an inheritance in heaven, but we have a new life here on earth, too. God doesn't want us to live a joyless life here, trudging through mud like a weary soldier on our way to heaven. He wants us to live a life of joy in His presence—no matter the circumstances.

If heartache and trials have marked your life, it's time for a new beginning. Take heart from Isaiah 43:19 (NLT): "For I am about to do something new. See, I have already begun! Do you not see it? I will make a pathway through the wilderness. I will create rivers in the dry wasteland."

If you are weary and burdened, take those burdens straight to the cross of Christ and allow Him to give you new life. Then be on the lookout—with great expectation—for the amazing ways that God shows up in your everyday life.

God, I give You praise today. I will watch with great expectation as You make Yourself known in my life. Amen.

Spiritual Medicine

*"The virgin will conceive and give birth to a son, and they
will call him Immanuel" (which means "God with us").*
MATTHEW 1:23 NIV

Not everyone looks forward to having a "merry little Christmas." The holidays can be difficult for those who live alone, those who have lost loved ones, and those who feel depressed about their lives. One of the names of Jesus is "God *with* us." God Himself in a human body lived on earth from His underprivileged birth to His torturous death. He knows what we go through, how weak and emotional and lonely we can be. He felt tempted in every area yet did not sin. "Let us then approach God's throne of grace with confidence, so that we may receive mercy and find grace to help us in our time of need" (Hebrews 4:16 NIV).

Neediness has a solution. The One who will never leave us or forsake us gives mercy and grace when we enter His throne room. He can redeem our losses, compensate our loneliness, understand our emotions, and satisfy our longings. How? By filling us with Himself. We have the fruit of the Holy Spirit when we focus on God. Colossians 3 gives practical steps for focusing our minds: put on love, let peace rule our hearts, fill our lives with the Word of Christ, sing to the Lord, and give thanks in all things. That is God's Rx for what ails us.

*God of mercy and grace, as You have ministered to me
when I am broken, give me sensitivity to others who are
hurting this month so I can point them to You. Amen.*

How God Meets Needs

*And my God shall supply all your need according
to His riches in glory by Christ Jesus.*
PHILIPPIANS 4:19 NKJV

Does God meet all your needs, or do you sometimes wonder if this verse is true? While our needs may be financial as they were for Paul and the Philippians, God's "riches in glory" are not limited to food, clothing, and shelter. We also need security, love, endurance, worthwhile goals, satisfying accomplishments, etc. Would God's promise extend to emotional cravings as well?

God knows that our deepest soul need is to know and love Him and to learn to be satisfied with Him. He has to be *enough*! To get us to that place, He may deprive us of things. He cares about our character more than our comfort. When we lack or long for things we consider vital, it can drive us to Him. A wife may pray for marriage harmony and start fighting more with her spouse. God centers on her *need* to deal with her selfish desire to dominate her husband. When she lets God prune out *her* faults, her *husband* will improve!

We may ask for healing, but our health worsens—weakness and disabilities highlight our need to depend on God. Personal failure can wean us from pride; sorrow and loss open us to God's comfort and increase our intimacy with Him. In other words, what God knows we need may not be what we want! God wisely supplies our needs, not our greeds.

*Loving Father, help me accept that what You provide, and what
You deprive, will ultimately meet my soul's deepest need. Amen.*

Who Is Jesus to You?

"Today in the town of David a Savior has been born to you;
he is the Messiah, the Lord."
LUKE 2:11 NIV

This first Sunday of Advent turns our attention to Jesus' entrance (advent) on earth. Churches or families may have an Advent wreath with four candles surrounding a center white candle called the Christ Candle. That candle, symbolizing Jesus' birth, is lit on Christmas Eve. The other four candles can be symbolic of Prophecy, Bethlehem, Shepherds, and Angels or of values such as Hope, Peace, Joy, and Love. Traditions like the Advent wreath help us keep our focus on Christmas as a celebration of Christ's birth more than on shopping and consumerism, decorating, and getting "everything done." Christmas is a birthday first of all.

The angel told shepherds about a baby born "to you," the Jewish people. Israelites had looked for the Messiah all their lives. He had finally come. The angel called him Savior, Messiah (Hebrew for *Christ*), and Lord. The shepherds spread the good news about Jesus (see Luke 2:17–18). That news blesses us as well. He is our *Savior* from sin. That was the main reason for His first advent—to die in our place. *Messiah* means "Anointed One." Anointed as Priest and King, He fulfilled over four hundred prophecies during His first coming to earth; the rest will be fulfilled when He comes the second time. And He is our *Lord* when we surrender all areas of our lives to Him and accept His assignments.

Lord, I celebrate You with all my heart. Help me to serve
You by spreading the Good News to others. Amen.

Walking and Talking with Jesus

Mary Magdalene came and told the disciples that she had seen the LORD, and that he had spoken these things unto her.
JOHN 20:18 KJV

"In the Garden" is a well-loved hymn used at many funerals. The author, C. Austin Miles, wrote numerous scripture-based hymns. This one focused on Jesus being "the voice I hear falling on my ear," as Jesus "walks with me and He talks with me." Such wording implies that we can hear Jesus' voice today. Respected authors and speakers even write books about how to listen to God, as if the Bible is not complete and God gives us individual present-day revelations. However, that is not what inspired Miles in 1912. Whom was he writing about?

Miles meditated on the story of Jesus talking with Mary Magdalene in the garden of His tomb on resurrection morning. Imagining the intimate exchange between Mary and her Lord, Miles wondered how Mary must have felt. If she had a poetic nature like Miles did, what would she have written about Jesus revealing Himself to her? Those thoughts inspired him to write "I come to the garden alone" and to give it the beautiful melody that has become a well-known favorite of many.

To have an experience like Mary's, we need to let Jesus *talk* to us through God's Word, and to *walk* in prayerful fellowship with Him daily, whether in our kitchens, offices, cars, or gardens.

Lord God, thank You for the Bible, which draws me near to You and draws You near to me. Your promises are real. They confirm Your will to me and Your loving presence with me. Amen.

Understanding the Bible

*So Philip ran to him, and heard him reading the prophet Isaiah,
and said, "Do you understand what you are reading?"
And he said, "How can I, unless someone guides me?"*
ACTS 8:30-31 NKJV

Ravi Zacharias said that people today hear with their eyes and think with their feelings. We all tend to believe pictures more than words and accept truth based on our feelings more than facts. Philip did not ask, "How do you feel about that scripture?"

To know what God has communicated, we study the Bible like literature, seeking the central truth of a passage and never divorcing a verse from its context. For example, many Christians take Philippians 4:13—doing all things through Christ who strengthens us—as a promise that God will give us power to accomplish anything we desire. However, the context involves Paul learning to be content with little or much because he has Christ. By application, we can be content in our relationship with Christ, despite our circumstances. A misapplication would be having this verse as a T-shirt slogan for running a marathon!

We often distort God's truth by adding our own ideas to a verse and ignoring its context. We should first discern God's meaning to the original readers, then we can understand what He is saying to us. Interpreting scripture correctly allows the Holy Spirit to customize the application of God's truth to our needs at the time.

*Father, thank You that I will grow in grace and knowledge as
I study Your Word. Help me understand what You said and
why You said it so Your truths can speak to my heart. Amen.*

God Speaks for Himself

The eunuch asked Philip, "Tell me, please, who is the
prophet talking about, himself or someone else?"
Then Philip. . .told him the good news about Jesus.
ACTS 8:34-35 NIV

Someone has said, "Wonderful things in the Bible I see—things that were put there by you and by me." We sometimes make scripture mean what God never meant. Philip did not answer: "What does the verse say to you?" Instead, Philip explained that in Isaiah 53, God spoke about the death of Jesus.

The Bible was written for us but not necessarily to us. To understand scripture, we must consider the original hearers. What did God say to them? For example, in Jeremiah 29:11 God promised the Jewish captives in Babylon that His plans for them were for prosperity, not harm, and that they would go home after seventy years. Yes, God is loving and generous, but this passage does not promise *to us* a prosperous, harmless future in this life.

Likewise, Psalm 46:10—"Be still, and know. . ."—is not a command to us regarding worship or hearing God speak. In context, God told the nations to stop striving and know Him as the true God who will judge the earth and be exalted.

We learn truths about God from such verses, but they may not be promises *for* us or commands *to* us. Let us not be guilty of making the Bible say whatever we want it to, no matter how meaningful that might seem to be.

Dear God, help me understand Your Word correctly so I will know You
better and respond with loving trust and joyful obedience. Amen.

Does God Speak Today?

By his divine power, God has given us everything we need for living a godly life.... He has given us great and precious promises.
2 PETER 1:3-4 NLT

The biblical accounts of Jesus' birth include supernatural ways God communicated to His people. Angels spoke to Zacharias, Mary, and the shepherds. The Magi learned from a star that the King of the Jews had been born. God gave dreams to the Magi in Bethlehem, as well as to Joseph four times.

In Bible times, God spoke through various means, including a talking donkey (see Numbers 22:28-34), but His written revelation is now complete. The Bible contains everything necessary for godliness, yet we like the idea of personal revelations. A devout Christian said, "We can easily deceive ourselves about spiritual experiences. Receiving special revelations tempts us to sinful pride. We should not desire for God to manifest Himself to us, because selfishness is hidden in that desire; rather we should manifest ourselves to God in prayer and focus on loving Him with all our mind, heart, strength, and being."

Probably every Christian experiences God's "interventions," especially during times of duress. But even atheists know what it's like to feel inspired or be prompted by something beyond themselves, yet some Christians claim that is God's voice! God commands us to love Him with all our mind and heart. The heart involves emotions, which are not a way to determine what God wants—they are our response to Him. Don't confuse the two.

Because I desire intimacy with You, Lord, I want to tell You everything, get to know You through Your Word, and respond with trust and obedience. Amen.

A Cloud of Witnesses

Since we are surrounded by such a huge crowd of witnesses to the life of faith. . . . let us run with endurance the race God has set before us.
HEBREWS 12:1 NLT

Does it seem like the Bible gets less respect today than twenty years ago? Religious leaders point to humanistic thought and increased secularization as causes for this trend. How have viewpoints that marginalize God become popular? Perhaps they grew from the contagious desire to do what is right in our own eyes. We resent being told what to do, even by God's Word. The Bible is like an instruction manual for life, and although its principles show how life works best, we prefer running our own lives, thank you very much. So when God's Word calls us to holiness and to pleasing Him rather than ourselves, we desire an easier way.

Following Christ involves discipline. It can be hard to deny ourselves something like sexual gratification outside of marriage when media and culture say "Go for it!" "You deserve this," or "It's no big deal." Sometimes we wonder if following Christ is worth it: The Hebrews 11 believers testify that it is.

Take this challenge—read Hebrews 11 and list every mention of reward, inheritance, and what the saints looked forward to. You will discover their motivation, which enabled them to bear life's grueling challenges with steadfast faith. They witness to us that living for eternity is worth every sacrifice and struggle we endure on earth.

Lord, living for You is often like rowing upstream while others just go with the flow. Help me be faithful to You despite the cost. Amen.

Bewilderment

"Behold the maidservant of the Lord!
Let it be to me according to your word."
LUKE 1:38 NKJV

We cannot figure God out. If we had all our questions answered, we could trust in ourselves, and God would not be glorified. Therefore, circumstances often make us feel perplexed, like they did for an old man and a young woman in Luke 1.

Both Zacharias and Mary were bewildered by the sudden appearance of an angel. Gabriel told them not to be afraid. When he said they would each have a son, they asked, "How can this be?" Zacharias asked how God *could* do this—he wanted proof—while Mary questioned how God *would* do it. There's a big difference between questioning God and asking God questions.

Zacharias said in essence, "Why is this happening to me? I don't know what You're doing, and I'm not sure You know either!" (see Luke 1:18). Mary's response was: "Why is this happening to me? As a virgin, how can I possibly do what You say?"(see Luke 1:34). The next time you are bewildered, will you be a Zacharias or a Mary?

God accomplishes His plan, sometimes through great expense and suffering of His servants. But when we accept His yoke and learn from Him, He promises that we can rest in Him, making our burdens easy and light (see Matthew 11:29–30). When we are troubled or afraid, let's choose Mary's response: "I am Your willing maidservant. Do whatever You say."

Lord and Master I am Your humble and willing servant. Amen.

God as Paradox

"Surely I spoke of things I did not understand,
things too wonderful for me to know."
JOB 42:3 NIV

Satan challenged God to a kind of duel, with Job as the test case. God let Satan destroy Job's wealth, children, health, and reputation. No wonder Job complained about paradoxes with God (see Job 7:20–21; 9:22–24; 10:3; 30:20–24), so God showed Job paradoxes in nature.

The first was that God spoke out of a storm (Job 38:1; 40:6), yet lightning and wind had caused most of Job's losses. God also presented paradoxes in the animal kingdom. Wild animals cannot be tamed and seem to have no purpose, yet God made them (Job 39:5–12). Likewise, there is no sensible explanation to undeserved suffering except that God wills it, even allowing Satan to cause it in Job's case. The ostrich cannot fly, yet it runs faster than a horse (Job 39:13–18). No one controls Behemoth (Job 40:15–24) or Leviathan (Job 41). If Job cannot explain the natural world that God created, how could he understand the spiritual world or try to "tame" the Creator Himself?

Job realized he should not question God, demand answers, or think he can advise God (Job 42:2–4). God is a paradox—we can know Him, and yet He remains inscrutable and incomprehensible. He is just, because that is His nature, but we cannot prove it. We simply believe it.

Satan's challenge was to see if Job would keep believing God for who He is, apart from the blessings He gives. Job did. Do you?

You know what You're doing in my life, Lord, and that means
I don't have to. I trust You and Your ways, no matter what. Amen.

Enigmas

Then Simeon blessed them and said to Mary, his mother....
"A sword will pierce your own soul too."
LUKE 2:34-35 NIV

Parenting can be arduous. We mothers would rather die than see our children suffer, especially undeservedly. If they get into trouble with the law, we grieve for them. We may not understand their choices and pursuits. Some mothers even have to bury a child. Although Mary raised a son who never sinned, His life and death caused her to suffer all these hurts. She, along with the disciples, could not understand how the Messiah could be rejected or that God could die.

The two Emmaus disciples said, "We had hoped that he was the one who was going to redeem Israel" (Luke 24:21 NIV). He still was. But before He could rule the world as King, He had to atone for the world's sins. The cross before the crown. Grief preceded glory. We may understand this about Jesus, yet we stumble over other enigmas: how God seems to ignore worldwide suffering. That violence and unjust killings abound. What about our sincere prayers that go unanswered?

We must accept that God is inscrutable. Our minds cannot comprehend His ways. Mary was "blessed above all women" and yet pierced in her soul. Remember that the sword-pierced wounds we experience on earth will one day be completely cured. In God's methodology, what we suffer on earth yields glory in eternity (see 2 Corinthians 4:17–18; Romans 8:17–18; 1 Peter 1:6–8). God compensates our losses by giving us more of Himself.

Lord, You are all-wise, all-loving, all-knowing. When I cannot understand You with my mind, I still trust You with my heart. Amen.

Hanukkah beings at sundown

Hanukkah

. . .that you may proclaim the praises of Him who
called you out of darkness into His marvelous light.
1 PETER 2:9 NKJV

When Antiochus IV captured the Temple Mount in Jerusalem, he put out the menorah lights in the temple and desecrated it by sacrificing a pig on the altar and setting up an idol. His troops killed all Jews who would not eat the pig because doing so violated their religious laws.

In 165 BC, a small group of faithful Jews, the Maccabees, defeated a large army and reclaimed the temple. They purified and rededicated it three years to the day (December 25) after the temple was defiled. They relit the menorah with a one-day supply of oil, which miraculously burned for eight days. To commemorate this miracle and their triumph, they instituted the Feast of Dedication, later called the Festival of Lights or Hanukkah. Practicing Jews celebrate Hanukkah for eight days, beginning today, by lighting menorahs and spending time with loved ones.

Did Jesus observe Hanukkah? John 10:22–23 puts Him in Jerusalem during the Feast of Dedication. He used the occasion to call Himself the "Light of the World." Those who followed Him would not walk in darkness but have the light of life (see John 8:12). He demonstrated this in chapter 9 by giving sight to a blind man.

We who have accepted the Light of the World as our Savior are called to walk in the Light (see 1 John 1) and shine it to others (see Matthew 5:16).

Lord, thank You for miraculously shining in my heart
to give me the light of the Gospel. Amen.

Expect the Unexpected

*While they were there, the time
came for the baby to be born.*
LUKE 2:6 NIV

Was Jesus born the night Mary and Joseph arrived in Bethlehem? We sometimes assume Mary was in labor while Joseph was knocking on doors and being told, "No room." While speculating about scripture can be inspiring, we should not add details that skew the text. Does it surprise you that the Bible does not say Mary rode a donkey? Nor does it mention an innkeeper, stable, or little drummer boy. All we know is that Mary and Joseph had access to an animal feeding trough (manger). They must have found shelter close to where domestic animals were kept—perhaps a stable, but it could have been a courtyard, cave, or first-century barn. Also note, He was *laid* in a manger, not *born* in one!

Now for a speculation alert! Mary and Joseph may not have anticipated that God's promised Messiah would arrive "while they were there." They had to improvise for their baby's care. (Perhaps Joseph's handcrafted cradle was back in Nazareth.) Yet their adverse circumstances fulfilled God's prophecy about Bethlehem in Micah 5:2. He may have given Mary and Joseph what they least expected, as He often does with us. We cannot predict God. But we can trust Him to meet our needs, especially during times of deprivation. We trust Him by giving up our expectations and accepting a meager manger if that is what God gives.

I'm sorry I usually try to figure You out, Lord, or tell You what I think You should do. How arrogant of me. I rest in Your sovereignty. Amen.

The Bread of Life in a Feeding Trough

"I am the bread of life."
JOHN 6:48 NIV

Jesus taught people they must believe in Him for eternal life. He illustrated His messages with object lessons, references to the Hebrew scriptures, and analogies. In John 6, He called Himself the true bread of life which came down from heaven, and referred to bread three ways: (1) the loaves of bread He had miraculously multiplied the previous day (John 6:26), (2) the manna that God sent from heaven in Israel's history (John 6:32, 49, 58), and (3) His body which would be broken for sin (John 6:50–51). Jesus spoke in spiritual terms (John 6:63), but many did not understand. They interpreted His words as cannibalism and stopped following "Rabbi Jesus" (John 6:66).

When Jesus said those who "eat His flesh and drink His blood" will have eternal life (John 6:53–58), He was giving an analogy for believing in Him. Jesus' other analogies for believing included receiving, being born a second time, looking, coming, entering, etc. Jesus said, "Very truly I tell you, the one who believes has eternal life" (John 6:47 NIV).

Believing what Jesus said is like "ingesting" Jesus into your whole being. In Ghana, Africa, the word for *believe* means "take God's words and eat them." How significant that God's Son had a manger—an animal feed box—for His cradle.

Lord, thank You for being the bread of (eternal) life, which You gave me when I believed. I want to faithfully nourish my relationship with You by richly enjoying You every day and obeying the spiritual manna of Your Word. Amen.

The Shepherd's Sign

"This will be a sign to you: You will find a baby
wrapped in cloths and lying in a manger."
LUKE 2:12 NIV

No special star shone over Jesus' manger. The star shone to Magi in a country east of Israel (see Matthew 2:2). Nor did the star appear to shepherds. They saw dazzling lights, but that came from the glory of the Lord shining around them. God's spectacular audio-visual display declared His good news to them (see Luke 2:9). In that culture, wealthy people would hire musicians to play instruments and sing or shout announcements as they paraded through the town. Could it be that God the Father heralded His Son's birth in the grandest way possible?

But why to shepherds? Perhaps because the next time Jesus was announced, John the Baptist called him "the Lamb of God, who takes away the sin of the world" (John 1:29 NIV). Shepherds would be interested in a lamb's birth, especially when the angel said it was Messiah (Christ) the Lord. Scholars believe the fields near Bethlehem were for temple sheep to graze—sheep raised for sacrifice. Newborn lambs would be wrapped in cloths to protect them from blemishes. The angel told the shepherds they would find the Savior wrapped in cloths. In those days, a person was swaddled in cloths on two occasions—birth and death.

Jesus willingly died as an unblemished sacrifice for our sins. He is our Savior, Christ the Lord. The shepherds rejoiced, and so do we.

Thank You, Jesus, for coming into the world to pay the penalty
for my sins and giving me the free gift of eternal life. Amen.

Don't Ruin Your Gift

God gives the gift of the single life to some,
the gift of the married life to others.
1 CORINTHIANS 7:7 MSG

As a child, do you recall how long it took for Christmas to arrive? *When will Santa come? Will I get that special gift or not?*

One year I made a terrible mistake and decided I could not wait until Christmas. I knew where Mother hid the gifts before wrapping and placing them under the tree. When she drove off to run errands, leaving me in charge of my preschool-aged sister, I beelined to the closet and carefully peeked into shopping bags. I found it! My first watch that I desperately wanted. I felt happy and smug. Then as Christmas approached, I started to regret finding my gift too soon. On Christmas morning, I acted surprised and enthusiastic when I opened my beautiful watch, but inside I hated what I had done.

Not waiting until marriage for sexual fulfillment is disastrous and regretful as well. No matter how difficult self-control can be, pleasing God means only two options: sex in marriage between a man and a woman, or celibacy. God commands restraint for everyone who is single, widowed, divorced, or LGBT. Sex is a gift we must not open too soon, but celibacy is also a God-given gift and responsibility. Offer your sexuality back to Him, rely on His all-sufficiency, and wait for His timing. Find satisfaction in Him.

Lord, I accept my status as the way You desire for me to
glorify You. Thank You for giving me strength for my
weakness and grace equal to my burdens. Amen.

The Life of Christ in Me

Shall we continue in sin that grace may abound? Certainly not!
How shall we who died to sin live any longer in it?
ROMANS 6:1-2 NKJV

God is the perfect parent. He cannot ignore His children's bad behavior because: (1) sins not dealt with will worsen; (2) pursuing sinful pleasure never satisfies—it leaves us craving more; and (3) sin has consequences, which can be permanent. Thus God disciplines us, not because He is mad or condemning, but for our good (see Hebrews 12:4-11).

God told King Solomon if the nation sinned and God punished them, they should do three things—humble themselves, pray and seek God, and turn from wickedness. Then God would do three things— hear, forgive, and heal the land (see 2 Chronicles 7:14). If our country seems to be suffering from effects of God's wrath (anger over sin), it is not unbelievers but the "people called by His name" who must turn from wicked ways and humbly seek God.

However, many Christians live as if God imposes no standards: we have freedom in Christ, and God is all about grace. Yes, but we must not treat God's grace lightly. Can a child of God attend church and hear the Bible taught but also sleep with her boyfriend, dress provocatively to attract men, not report all taxable income, abuse harmful substances, hold a grudge? If she does, she can expect dissatisfaction, sin's consequences, and God's discipline. Paradoxically, pursuing God's pleasure, not our own, actually satisfies our deep longings.

Lord God, I'm sorry I sometimes think sin is no big deal. Help me to
be so alive to Christ that my behavior matches my beliefs. Amen.

For Such a Time as This

"Do not fear their threats".... Always be prepared to give an answer to everyone who asks you to give the reason for the hope that you have.
1 PETER 3:14-15 NIV

At the time of Jesus' birth, a ruthless king ruled Judea. Not only did Herod the Great slaughter the baby boys in Bethlehem, but he had his own wife and sons put to death during his rule. Yet his reign is the exact "fullness of time" God chose for His Son's incarnation to earth (see Galatians 4:4). Jesus' life would be threatened before He turned two. Innocent babies would be killed, and His parents would make a hasty nighttime departure to Egypt, living in exile until Herod died.

What conditions has God chosen for your birth or that of your children? While our national leaders may not be tyrannical and cruel, many are corrupt. Their own self-interests determine their political decisions. What does America stand for today? Immorality, abortion, homosexual marriage, consumerism, and avoiding public mention of God. But God has us here for such a time as this.

God always preserves a remnant and tasks them with the responsibility to make Him known. When the evening news is bad, it becomes more urgent to share the Good News and shine the light of God's love to a dark world (see Philippians 2:15-16). We should also prepare our children to face opposition graciously and learn to present Christ to their generation.

Lord, I want to faithfully tell others about You,
not to win them to my side but to invite them to
respond to what You are doing in their lives. Amen.

Living in Nazareth

*And when they had come into the house, they saw the young
Child with Mary His mother, and fell down and worshiped Him.*
MATTHEW 2:11 NKJV

We don't know Jesus' age when the wise men visited Him. The Bible calls Him a young child, not a *baby* (different Greek word), who was in a house, not a manger. Since jealous King Herod had all male infants two and under killed, Jesus must have been less than two. One wonders why Mary and Joseph were still in Bethlehem a year or so after Jesus' birth. Why hadn't they gone home to Nazareth?

One theory involves Nazareth's bad reputation (see John 1:46). Like good parents, Mary and Joseph would want the best environment for their child. How could that be Nazareth, where Jesus would have the stigma of being an illegitimate child? Perhaps they stayed in Bethlehem where Mary could escape her reputation of getting pregnant while engaged (through no guilt on her part), and Jesus could grow up where His birth had been validated by angels and shepherds and also by Simeon and Anna in Jerusalem. However, God had a different plan. He eventually sent the young family back to Nazareth (see Matthew 2:21–23).

Perhaps we feel stuck in undesirable surroundings—a rundown neighborhood, public schools teaching antibiblical views, sinful lifestyles on display, a job with no potential for advancement. These Nazareths may be the exact training ground our character needs and the place where God will use us best.

*In a culture that shows increasing disregard for Christian values,
help me to shine where You have placed me, Father. Amen.*

Is Jesus King?

"Where is He who has been born King of the Jews? For we have seen His star in the East and have come to worship Him."
MATTHEW 2:2 NKJV

At His birth and death, Jesus was called the King of the Jews. A supernatural star had revealed to Magi that the Jewish Messiah-King had arrived. They journeyed to Israel to worship Him and give gifts. They did not follow the star, or it would have led them right to Bethlehem. Instead, they went to Jerusalem and inquired at Herod's palace. Herod's scholars found Micah 5:2 and directed the Magi to Bethlehem, a six-mile journey. As they headed there, the star miraculously appeared again, causing them great joy (see Matthew 2:10). Yes, they followed the star, but only for the last six miles of their trip.

The "King of the Jews" is not mentioned again until Jesus' final days. Pilate said it to test, not worship Him, and soldiers mocked Him with that title. Ironically, the legal charge against Him, posted on the cross, was "King of the Jews." But the Jews had declared, "We have no king but Caesar." Never again has Israel been ruled by a king. Not yet. But scripture promises a future day when "every knee will bow and every tongue will confess" Jesus as the Lord of all.

Like the Magi, wise women seek and worship Jesus at every stage of life, from birth to death. We decide what becomes king of our priorities, preferences, and perspectives.

*I bow to You, King Jesus, and give You the gifts
of my life, my loves, and my longings. Amen.*

Looking Forward

What kind of people ought you to be? You ought to live holy and godly lives as you look forward to the day of God and speed its coming.
2 PETER 3:11-12 NIV

Two Josephs ministered to Jesus. His earthly father, Joseph, took care of Him from His birth. The other Joseph in Jesus' life ministered after His death. Joseph of Arimathea, a rich man and follower of Jesus, owned a new tomb that had been carved out of rock (see Matthew 27:57-60). He courageously asked Pilate for the body of Jesus and wrapped it in fine linen, much like the first Joseph and Mary had swaddled Jesus in as a newborn.

Then Jesus conquered death by rising again. After His resurrection, for forty days, Jesus appeared to His followers many times and then ascended to heaven, passing into the clouds. Two angels told the believers Jesus would come again in the same way—that is, descending from heaven through the clouds (see Acts 1:11). The believers had great joy and were continually praising God (see Luke 24:52–53).

But Jesus did not return in their lifetimes. In fact, Christians still look forward to His appearing—His second coming to earth (see 2 Timothy 4:8). Until then, we ought to make every effort to live holy and godly lives so that when He appears we can be confident and unashamed before Him at His coming (see 1 John 2:28).

Jesus, thank You for Your first advent, which provided the gift of salvation. As I await Your second advent, I gratefully give You myself. I want my choices and activities to reflect my love and longing for You. Amen.

Bible Bookends

"Look, I am coming soon.... I am the Alpha and the Omega, the First and the Last, the Beginning and the End."
REVELATION 22:12-13 NLT

God often used literary structure in His Word to call attention to something important. For example, the Bible has "bookends," showing that history (His-story) will go full circle and accomplish His purposes. These bookends are the first two and last two chapters of the Bible.

In Genesis 1–2 the world had perfect environment, no sin or death, and God conversing with His people. Revelation 21–22 portrays a new heaven and earth, again without sin or death and with unhindered fellowship between God and His people. The 1,185 chapters in between contain rebellion against God, people in conflict, evil and violence, tears, pain, and death. However, those chapters also display God's redemptive plan through Jesus, who atoned for our sins, conquered death, and will destroy the works of the devil. He lived a sinless life, experienced the death we deserve, and rose again.

At this time in history, we are in the "between" chapters. Corruption and evil abound. Society grows increasingly godless and amoral. Families are fragmented; relationships are disposable. But Revelation 21–22 will come. Everyone who has accepted the redemption Jesus provided will live with Him forever, because He said, "Let anyone who is thirsty come. Let anyone who desires drink freely from the water of life" (Revelation 22:17 NLT).

Until You come again or I go to You, Lord, help me to abide in You and depend on Your Word so I will not live in depression or fear, despite conditions in the world. Amen.

Christmas Music? Maybe Not

Shout for joy to the LORD, all the earth,
burst into jubilant song with music.
PSALM 98:4 NIV

Nothing gives me Christmas spirit better than listening to Handel's *Messiah*. In 1742, George Frideric Handel wrote this unparalleled oratorio in only twenty-four days. It comprised 259 handwritten pages! Since the common people at that time could not read (and English Bibles were rare), Handel set scripture portions to music to teach the life of Christ. He used a text his friend Charles Jennens had given him, taken mostly from the King James Bible. So powerful was the chorus, "Hallelujah," that the king stood when he heard it. That meant everyone present in the audience and orchestra had to stand also!

Most people associate "The Hallelujah Chorus" with Christmas, and yet it has more to do with Easter, since Handel placed it after Jesus' resurrection and ascension. Likewise, the hymn "Joy to the World" actually speaks about Jesus' still-future second coming to earth, not about His birth. Isaac Watts, a prolific hymn writer, wrote it in 1719, based on Psalm 98. The music was composed one hundred and twenty years later by Lowell Mason, who used a melody from Handel.

Whether these are Christmas songs or not, they glorify our Lord Jesus Christ with their jubilant melodies, exquisite harmonies, and biblical wording. At the end of the *Messiah* manuscript, Handel wrote "SDG," which meant, "To God alone the glory."

Someday You will rule the world with truth and grace, and all nations
will know Your righteousness and wonders of Your love. Until then,
I glorify You, my King of kings and Lord of lords. Hallelujah!

Christmas Eve

The Perfect Gift

Every good gift and every perfect gift is from above,
and comes down from the Father of lights.
JAMES 1:17 NKJV

At this time of year, we look for a perfect gift for loved ones on our shopping lists. We hope to surprise them and give them joy. But our best choices may not fit or be appreciated. The gift ends up returned with the reason given as: "didn't want."

I've felt that way about some of God's surprises to me. *A house fire doesn't fit my agenda. . . . I don't appreciate this cancer. . . . We didn't really need that car accident. . . . I'd like to return this [fill in the blank] that I don't want.* But these things were for my good.

God led His Hebrew children "through that great and terrible wilderness, in which were fiery serpents and scorpions and thirsty land where there was no water" in order to humble them, test them, and do them "good in the end" (Deuteronomy 8:15–16 NKJV). The "good" that God intends involves our character, our intimacy with Him, and our usefulness to others. Despite the fact that our wish list to God includes fulfillment and ease. We seek material advantages, but God gives spiritual advances, often through adversity.

Therefore, we must learn to receive all circumstances as wise gifts from God's loving hand. Viewing our troubles as tools to enhance our relationship with the Giver results in the joy He knew would be the "perfect gift" for our needs.

Father, You have blessed me with many good and
perfect gifts, including adversity. May I be thankful
for all You give me because it glorifies You. Amen.

God Honors Our Choices

The Word became flesh and made his dwelling among us. We have seen. . .the glory of the one and only Son. . .full of grace and truth.
JOHN 1:14 NIV

How did people initially respond to God taking on flesh and living on earth? Mary's response was submission (see Luke 1:38). She treasured in her heart all the events regarding Jesus' birth (Luke 2:19). In today's culture, she would have journaled!

Joseph responded with obedience and self-restraint. Possibly, Mary did not tell Joseph her pregnancy was supernatural—she let God handle the consequences. That may be why Joseph pursued a divorce. God had to tell him the details through a dream. He willingly obeyed and married Mary. Then, to protect her from uncleanness according to the law, he refrained from intercourse until Jesus was over forty days old (Luke 2:22–24).

How did the shepherds respond? They spread abroad the good news (Luke 2:17–18). Simeon recognized the baby Messiah in the temple. He praised God and blessed Mary and Joseph (Luke 2:25–34). An old woman, Anna the prophetess, also gave thanks to God and spoke about Jesus, the Messiah-Redeemer, to those who came to the temple (Luke 2:36–38).

Wise men embarked on a long journey to worship Him and give Him valuable gifts (Matthew 2:11). However, Herod, the ruler of the Jews, responded with jealousy, fear, anger, and murder (Matthew 2:14–18).

Because God gave us intelligence, minds, and wills, He does not violate our freedom to choose. Let us respond by submitting, meditating, obeying, restraining our lusts, praising, and telling others about Him.

Following You is a privilege I have chosen, Lord.
May You find me faithful. Amen.

Genealogy of Christ

Forgetting those things which are behind. . .I press toward the goal for the prize of the upward call of God in Christ Jesus.
PHILIPPIANS 3:13-14 NKJV

Everyone's heritage contains reasons for both pride and shame. The ancestry of Jesus in Matthew 1:1–17 included four surprising women. Three were not even Jewish. (1) Tamar prostituted herself to seduce Jacob. (2) Rahab, a Canaanite, was a prostitute before she trusted in the God of the Hebrews. (3) Ruth had integrity, but Israelites were not to associate with Moabites. (4) Uriah's wife (Bathsheba) may have been a Hittite; she committed adultery with King David. All had skeletons in the closet, but God redeemed their pasts and chose them to be ancestors of the Messiah.

By application, regardless of one's minority status or ethnicity, God does not marginalize those who look to Him. Even with a sexual history, if we confess our sins, God forgives and cleanses. His plan includes every child despite how inadequate or flawed we are, because His strength becomes paramount when we are weak (see 2 Corinthians 12:1–10).

In contrast to these four women stands Mary, known for virginity and submission. All five women played their roles to give Messiah a physical heritage, and by Him to bless the world. What was their part? Simply to raise a son. We sometimes think motherhood has little significance, but every day matters. In eternity we will discover the influence God allowed us to have.

Thank You for accepting me into Your family, Father. Despite my unworthiness, I celebrate my heritage as Your child. Amen.

Growing through Groaning

It is good for me that I have been afflicted,
that I may learn Your statutes.
PSALM 119:71 NKJV

Learning to ski as an adult is harder than expected. Fatigued muscles, bruises, cold toes, and lack of confidence do nothing to make that first day on the slopes enjoyable. If one keeps trying, however, the ski bug will bite. Sometimes a new skier will boast, "I skied all morning without falling." This is not the best goal a beginner should have. Ski instructors say, "If you're not falling, you're not learning." No one improves without trying new trails, pushing limits, and even wiping out. Eventually we master a skill if we don't give up.

Spiritually, we also learn most through adversity not prosperity. The process of growing in holiness often hurts. God allows things that trip us up because it increases our dependence on Him. A child in pain runs immediately to her parent. God's pruning does the same for us.

That may be why God tells us to rejoice when we fall into various trials, because when our faith is tested, we learn patience (endurance) and grow in maturity. He also invites us to ask Him for wisdom during trials, and He will generously provide (see James 1:2–5).

Therefore, when we feel bruised, fatigued, hurt, or exhausted, let's remember these can be the crucial things that develop our spiritual muscles, produce the most growth, and improve our ability to persevere.

When I can't take any more or fall any lower, God, may I
remember to rejoice in what I am learning through the
School of Trials. Your teaching methods are best. Amen.

A Joy Focus

For the joy set before him he endured the cross....
Consider him who endured such opposition from sinners,
so that you will not grow weary and lose heart.

HEBREWS 12:2-3 NIV

We cannot sustain emotional health without hope—something good to anticipate. Believers in Christ have a hopeful future even when our prognosis is death, because we will forever be with the Lord (see 2 Corinthians 5:8). Nonetheless, during trials, it takes determination and spiritual power to meditate on the joys set before us, like Jesus did.

One way to keep a joyful focus is found in Psalm 68:19–20 (NIV): "Praise be to the Lord, to God our Savior, who daily bears our burdens. Our God is a God who saves; from the Sovereign LORD comes escape from death." In the margin by these verses, I have listed the "escapes from death" God has mercifully granted our family—fifteen times so far we have been delivered from life-threatening accidents or potentially fatal illnesses. (What names and dates can you list in your Bible?)

What if God does not deliver *from* a trial? Then He will sustain us *through* the trial by bearing our burdens with us every day.

When we "grow weary" and find ourselves "losing heart" in 2018, let's focus on God our Savior, our sovereign Lord, our Burden-bearer. If the joy of the Lord is our focus, it will also be our strength (see Nehemiah 8:10).

God of my salvation, I look forward to spending eternity with You.
Until then, thank You for bearing my burdens and giving me escapes
from death. Help me stay joyful because I'm focused on You. Amen.

Eternal Life Now

I am come that they might have life,
and that they might have it more abundantly.
JOHN 10:10 KJV

Jesus invited people to receive Him as their Life. This means future eternal life, which is for real and forever, but also "abundant life" now. He wants to permeate a believer's present consciousness—all our decisions and goals, spending habits, opinions, and use of time. We must realize that our old self has died and Christ is our new life (see Colossians 3:3–4; Galatians 2:20).

Romans 5–8 tells us how to live as Christians, not how to become a Christian, which is the theme of chapters 3–4. The word *believe* occurs twenty-nine times in Romans 3:1–5:2 to show that God's righteousness comes through faith (the Greek word for *believing*). Then the words *live/life* show up twenty-five times in chapters 5–8, where Christians are to experience the resurrection-life (abundant, eternal life now) by resisting sin and pleasing God. Romans 8 does not contrast believers with unbelievers. It speaks of believers who either live according to the flesh (sinful nature) or according to the Spirit (vv. 4, 12–13). What makes the difference? Our minds (vv. 5–7).

Seeing Romans this way may be a new concept, but eternal life is not only our future destination; it should be our present mind-set of fellowshipping with Christ daily so we seek His pleasure, not our own. Pleasing Him is the best life.

Thank You for being my Savior so I will live with
You after I die. Be my Lord as well, so I will deny
sinful lusts and live for You until I die. Amen.

Deepen Your Prayer Life

*Jesus told his disciples a parable to show them
that they should always pray and not give up.*
LUKE 18:1 NIV

What is your prayer history? Most women find their prayer life jump-starts during affliction, darkness, and grief. Suffering can make God more real and intimate, or have the opposite effect—where we shake our fist instead of bend our knee. Therefore, we must fight despair with prayer. This spiritual battle requires disciplines, like talking to God instead of listening to our self-talk, which can be deceptively untrue. When our minds do not have to concentrate on something, we can form the habit of turning our self-talk into "meditation moments" to nurture our relationship with God.

What if prayer is boring? We will minimize our need to pray if we forget to whom we are talking—our Personal Loving Father *and* the Awesome Almighty God. A practical suggestion is to use a 3x5 spiral card pack and write a scripture verse on each card. Select verses about God's character or names, about a temptation or struggle you face, or encouragement to trust Him. Deliberately find times to pray these "battle verses"—God's words—back to Him. Try it while exercising or walking your dog, while waiting in line or riding as a passenger. You may think you could have battle verses on your phone instead, but that would tempt you to let your device steal your prayer time. Instead of texting a friend, take out your card pack and talk to your Best Friend Forever.

*My mind is a spiritual battlefield, Lord.
Help me make it the place for victories in 2018. Amen.*

Epiphany

And when he had gathered all the chief priests and scribes of the people together, he demanded of them where Christ should be born.
MATTHEW 2:4 KJV

Epiphany is observed as the day the Magi visited Christ Jesus in Bethlehem, traditionally on January 6. His birth was celebrated by these important foreign scholars as well as by humble local shepherds. Why didn't Jewish religious leaders get excited about the Messiah's arrival? They knew Hebrew scriptures enough to inform Herod that Israel's "Ruler-Shepherd" would come out of Bethlehem (see Micah 5:2–5). But this contradicted their expectations that the Messiah would be a glorious conqueror, not a baby. (Herod put more credence in the scriptures than they did, because he secretly ordered the Magi to find the baby and report back to him.) Sadly, each reference to chief priests and scribes in Matthew finds them opposing Jesus and eventually insisting on His execution.

Although the Magi deemed Jesus' birth important enough to make a long trip, although they spoke of a supernatural star revelation, although Herod took them seriously and murdered babies, the local religious leaders didn't accept the Messiah. Sometimes the most religious people miss God's truth. Entrenched in man-made doctrines, they will not investigate opposing options.

We can blindly follow what self-proclaimed prophets teach, or we can study God's Word for ourselves. That's what wise men and women do. Try this New Year's resolution: read the Gospel of John and note two things—why Jesus came, and what Jesus said about Himself. Like the Magi, your spiritual journey can result in your personal epiphany.

Savior and King, may I never stop seeking
to know and love You more. Amen.

Contributors

Marcia Hornok, managing editor of *CHERA Fellowship* magazine for widows/ers, is the wife of a retired pastor and the mother of six. She has authored nine books and contributed to a dozen more, and has credits in periodicals and a theological journal. (christiangals.blogspot.com) Her readings can be found in the month of December.

Ardythe Kolb is a wife, mother, and freelance writer with three books and devotions or stories in over a dozen compilations. She serves on the board of Heart of America Christian Writer's Network as editor of its monthly newsletter. Besides writing, she volunteers as a CASA for abused children. Her readings can be found in the month of October.

Donna K. Maltese is a freelance writer, editor, and writing coach. Mother of two grown children, she resides in Bucks County, Pennsylvania, with her husband. Donna is active in her local church and is the publicist for a local Mennonite project that works to feed the hungry here and abroad. Learn more about Donna at writefullyconfident.com. Her readings can be found in the month of January.

Sabrina McDonald is the author of *Open the Windows of Heaven* and *The Blessings of Loneliness*, and she is a featured writer for FamilyLife.com. You can follow her blog at www.sabrinamcdonald.com. Her readings can be found in the month of September.

Lydia Mindling is inspired by three things: God's love, Christ's sacrifice, and creation. When not writing, Lydia enjoys horseback riding, hikes, and attempts at baking the world's best brownies. Her readings can be found in the month of April.

MariLee Parrish lives in Ohio with her husband, Eric, and young children. She's a freelance musician and writer who desires to paint a picture of God with her life, talents, and ministries. Her readings can be found in the month of November.

Vickie Phelps lives in East Texas with her husband, Sonny, and their schnauzer, Dobber. She divides her time between family, writing, and church activities. Her readings can be found in the month of May.

Iemima Ploscariu is a history researcher who spends most of her time in Sacramento, California. She holds an MLitt in Central and Eastern European history and is pursuing further studies. Along with her freelance writing, she also serves in the children's and women's ministries of her local Romanian church. Her readings can be found in the month of March.

Valorie Quesenberry is a pastor's wife, mother, musician, editor of a Christian women's magazine, and writer. She periodically contributes devotionals to a Christian literature provider. Her first book released with Wesleyan Publishing House in April 2010. Her readings can be found in the month of August.

Shana Schutte is an author and speaker. She is the author of several books including *30 Days of Hope*. You can learn more about Shana by visiting shanaschutte.com. Her readings can be found in the month of July.

Janice Thompson, a full-time author living in the Houston, Texas, area, is the mother of four married daughters. Her readings can be found in the month of February.

A California native transplanted to the Midwest, **Jennifer Vander Klipp** navigates the tweens and teens with stepchildren and high-needs kids. She has fifteen years experience in publishing, most recently as a managing editor at Zondervan. Her readings can be found in the month of June.

Scripture Index

OLD TESTAMENT

Genesis

1:1-2 . . . . 1/1
1:11 . . . . 8/3
13:3-4 . . . . 1/21
16:7, 9, 13 . . . . 1/22
18:13-14 . . . . 1/27
19:17, 26 . . . . 1/29
25:32-33 . . . . 5/19
33:4 . . . . 5/24
39:2-3 . . . . 5/27

Exodus

14:13-14 . . . . 5/22
14:14 . . . . 4/4
15:2 . . . . 11/20
17:11-13 . . . . 4/12
20:3 . . . . 7/23

Numbers

27:4 . . . . 6/18

Deuteronomy

4:19 . . . . 3/28
10:21 . . . . 11/21
20:4 . . . . 2/28

Joshua

1:8 . . . . 6/1
1:9 . . . . 1/11
1:16-18 . . . . 6/2
2:3 . . . . 6/3
3:17 . . . . 6/4

4:20-22 . . . . 5/29
5:13 . . . . 6/5
7:1 . . . . 6/6
7:12 . . . . 6/7
8:1 . . . . 6/8
9:14 . . . . 6/9
9:20 . . . . 6/10
10:8 . . . . 6/11, 6/12
11:23 . . . . 6/13
13:14 . . . . 6/14
14:9 . . . . 6/15
23:11 . . . . 5/2
23:14 . . . . 1/7
24:15 . . . . 2/23

1 Samuel

16:7 . . . . 5/17

2 Samuel

6:14 . . . . 9/21
20:16, 19 . . . . 4/24
22:30 . . . . 5/20
23:3-4 . . . . 4/9
24:10 . . . . 4/5

1 Kings

19:11-13 . . . . 4/20

1 Chronicles

16:9-12 . . . . 4/2
16:34-36 . . . . 11/9
22:19 . . . . 4/11

2 Chronicles

5:13 . . . . 3/29, 11/10
15:7 . . . . .2/13
17:20 . . . . 8/2
20:15, 17 . . . . .1/19

Nehemiah

6:9 . . . . .1/23

Job

12:10 . . . . 8/9
42:1-2 . . . . 4/6
42:3 . . . . .12/10

Psalms

4:8 . . . . 8/27
7:17 . . . . .11/26
9:1 . . . . 11/17
9:9-10 . . . . .3/13
13:1, 5-6 . . . . 4/17
16:6 . . . . 7/9
16:11 . . . . 9/29
17:5 . . . . 5/6
17:8 . . . . 8/10
18:3 . . . . .11/22
19:14 . . . . 5/26
23:1-2 . . . . 4/29
23:4 . . . . .5/18
24:8-9 . . . . .1/25
25:4-5, 15 . . . . .1/3
27:13-14 . . . . .1/8
32:11 . . . . 8/28
33:20-22 . . . . .11/11
34:4-5 . . . . .3/1

36:5 . . . . 7/6
37:3-5 . . . . .1/15
37:5-6 . . . . 2/27
40:1-3 . . . . .11/24
42:5-6 . . . . .11/25
46:1-2, 10 . . . . 1/20
50:7-15 . . . . 11/19
51:10 . . . . .2/1
56:11 . . . . .1/23
57:7 . . . . 11/27
63:3-7 . . . . 3/10
63:7 . . . . .1/23
72:18 . . . . .9/13
84:11 . . . . .7/19
86:4-5 . . . . .1/2
90:12 . . . . 2/4
98:4 . . . . .12/23
100:1-2, 4 . . . . 5/28
103:7 . . . . 10/6
105:1 . . . . 11/13
106:1-3 . . . . 11/14
107:1 . . . . 11/4
107:43 . . . . 9/30
108:2-4 . . . . .3/12
111:9 . . . . 4/8
118:24 . . . . .8/1
119:30-32 . . . . 3/19
119:46 . . . . 9/5
119:71 . . . . .12/27
119:73 . . . . .10/21
119:105 . . . . .7/15
120:7 . . . . .1/23
121:2 . . . . .1/23
127:4 . . . . 9/18

135:3 . . . . .8/8, 8/30
139:9-10 . . . . 8/19
139:14 . . . . .8/12
145:14 . . . . 10/20
145:18-21 . . . . 4/26
146:1 . . . . 9/8

Proverbs
1:20, 22-23 . . . . 3/14
3:5 . . . . 9/25
3:5-6 . . . . . . .1/6, 2/2, 10/27
4:23 . . . . .1/17
8:33 . . . . 5/3
10:25 . . . . 10/23
11:22 . . . . 8/23
13:15 . . . . .3/15
12:26 . . . . 7/30
14:15 . . . . 9/6
14:29 . . . . 2/10
15:1 . . . . 5/7
15:15 . . . . .1/26
16:31 . . . . .8/21
18:10 . . . . .5/15
18:14 . . . . 3/16
18:24 . . . . 2/24
25:11-12 . . . . 3/9
28:13 . . . . 9/11
29:25 . . . . .7/21, 9/22
31:10-12 . . . . .5/31
31:30 . . . . 2/20

Ecclesiastes
2:24 . . . . 8/4
3:11 . . . . .8/13
9:10 . . . . 9/16

Song of Solomon
2:10-12 . . . . 3/20

Isaiah
1:18 . . . . 3/8
25:7 . . . . 3/11
25:8-9 . . . . 4/18
26:3 . . . . 7/1, 7/12, 8/18
26:3-4 . . . . .1/14
30:18 . . . . 10/4
30:21 . . . . 7/28
33:2 . . . . .1/4
35:1-2 . . . . 4/23
40:10-11 . . . . 4/27
43:1 . . . . 3/2
43:16-21 . . . . .1/5
58:9-12 . . . . 10/28
58:13-14 . . . . .8/20
62:2 . . . . 9/9

Jeremiah
17:7-8 . . . . 2/6
29:13 . . . . 7/26
31:33 . . . . 10/9
33:3, 6 . . . . 3/23

Lamentations
3:22-24 . . . . .10/31

Ezekiel

17:24 . . . . 3/22
34:31 . . . . 10/13

Daniel

9:23 . . . . 3/3

Hosea

6:3 . . . . 3/27
12:6 . . . . .4/1
13:4-5 . . . . 4/7

Joel

2:28-32 . . . . 10/24

Micah

3:8 . . . . .1/23
5:4 . . . . 4/28

Nahum

1:7 . . . . 10/11

Habakkuk

2:2-3 . . . . .1/16
3:17-18 . . . . 7/11
3:17-19 . . . . 1/12

Zephaniah

3:16-17 . . . . .1/13

Zechariah

2:12-13 . . . . 4/13
3:9-10 . . . . 3/25
7:5-6 . . . . 4/22
14:20-21 . . . . 4/3

Malachi

3:6 . . . . .10/17

NEW TESTAMENT

Matthew

1:23 . . . . 12/1
2:2 . . . . 12/20
2:4 . . . . 12/31
2:11 . . . . 12/19
3:8 . . . . 9/3, 9/27
4:1 . . . . 4/25
5:3-6 . . . . 4/30
5:9 . . . . .10/19
6:6 . . . . 2/8
6:15 . . . . .7/14
9:20-22 . . . . .1/18
15:28 . . . . 6/19
18:19 . . . . 8/6
18:21-22 . . . . .2/22, 7/31
25:1-2 . . . . 3/4

Mark

5:27-28 . . . . .5/21
9:23 . . . . 7/29
11:24 . . . . .10/1

Luke

1:38 . . . . .12/9
2:6 . . . . .12/13
2:11 . . . . .12/3
2:12 . . . . .12/15
2:34-35 . . . . 12/11
4:18 . . . . .10/12

6:20	9/15
6:35	2/9
9:26	8/22
11:1	5/4
11:2-4	3/30
11:33	9/23
12:8	10/16
16:10	8/14
18:1	12/30
19:10	8/26

John

1:4-5	4/14
1:14	12/25
3:5-7	1/28
4:28-29	6/21
4:35	10/10
4:49	6/22
5:6	6/23
6:9	6/24
6:18-19	6/25
6:35	6/26
6:48	12/14
8:32	7/22
8:44	8/29
10:10	12/29
12:3	6/27
13:9	6/28
13:12-14	2/5
13:18	6/29
15:11-15	10/15
16:33	2/26
20:18	12/4

Acts

2:17	2/21
8:29-30	3/5
8:30-31	12/5
8:34-35	12/6
16:9	3/17
20:35	2/18
21:13	3/18

Romans

1:21	11/8
3:10	7/3
5:3-4	7/4
5:8	7/20
6:1-2	12/17
8:11	1/31
8:14-15	3/24
8:28	8/7
8:34	10/29
8:35-39	7/7
8:37	7/25, 9/19
11:33-36	4/15
12:1-2	11/12
12:2	1/9
12:6-8	2/16
12:16-18	2/19
12:20-21	5/8
15:13	3/7, 5/9

1 Corinthians

1:8	9/7
2:5	3/6
3:3	2/11
3:6	5/10

3:16-17 . . . . 10/8
7:7 . . . . .12/16
7:17. . . . . .6/30
10:31. . . . . .7/2
12:18 . . . . 5/11
15:58. . . . . 9/24

2 Corinthians
1:5. . . . . 7/8
3:5 . . . . 10/26
5:1. . . . . 10/2
5:7 . . . . 7/27
5:18. . . . . 9/10
9:14-15 . . . . .11/23

Galatians
4:6 . . . . 1/31
5:1. . . . . 5/12, 10/18

Ephesians
2:4-5 . . . . 2/14
2:10. . . . . 4/10
4:2 . . . . 8/16
5:8 . . . . 10/22
5:18-20. . . . . .11/6

Philippians
1:6. . . . . .5/13
2:5 . . . . .5/1
2:5-7. . . . . 4/19
2:12-13 . . . . 1/30
2:15. . . . . .8/11
3:13-14 . . . . 12/26

4:4 . . . . .2/15
4:6-7 . . . . 11/3
4:8 . . . . 2/25
4:8-9 . . . . .11/29
4:13. . . . . .5/30
4:19. . . . . 7/16, 12/2

Colossians
1:15-18. . . . . 10/3
2:6-7. . . . . 11/16
3:15. . . . . 11/2
4:2-4 . . . . 11/5
4:6 . . . . .9/12

1 Thessalonians
4:4 . . . . .5/16
4:11-12. . . . . 5/23
5:15. . . . . .9/17
5:16-18 . . . . 11/1
5:19. . . . . 9/20

2 Thessalonians
3:5 . . . . 10/30

1 Timothy
2:1. . . . . 11/15
4:4-5 . . . . 8/5

2 Timothy
1:5. . . . . 5/14
1:7 . . . . 5/5
2:1 . . . . 9/26
2:14. . . . . .7/17

Hebrews

4:9-11 . . . . .2/17
4:12-13 . . . . .7/10
6:19-20 . . . . 4/16
11:1, 6 . . . . .6/17
11:16 . . . . .8/17
11:31. . . . . 10/7
12:1 . . . . .12/8
12:1-3 . . . . 3/26
12:2. . . . . .6/20
12:2-3 . . . . 12/28
12:14-15 . . . . .3/21
12:28-29. . . . . 11/18
13:8. . . . . .1/10
13:20-21 . . . . .1/24

James

1:2. . . . . .9/1
1:5. . . . . 11/7
1:17 . . . . 12/24
1:19-20 . . . . .4/21
3:8-10. . . . . 8/25
3:13. . . . . .7/13
4:7-10. . . . . 10/5
5:13. . . . . 5/25
5:16. . . . . 9/14

1 Peter

1:3-4 . . . . .11/30
1:22. . . . . .7/5
2:9 . . . . 12/12
3:14-15 . . . . .12/18
5:4 . . . . 8/4

5:5 . . . . .8/31
5:7 . . . . .8/15
5:10. . . . . 9/28

2 Peter

1:3-4 . . . . .12/7
1:20-21 . . . . 8/24
3:9 . . . . 10/25
3:11-12. . . . . 12/21

1 John

1:9. . . . . 2/3
2:6 . . . . 7/24
2:15. . . . . .7/18
4:4 . . . . 9/2
4:15. . . . . .10/14

3 John

1:2 . . . . 2/7

Jude

1:24. . . . . .11/28

Revelation

3:22 . . . . .3/31
21:4. . . . . .2/12, 6/16
22:12-13 . . . . .12/22

DISCOVER THE POWER OF PRAYER

Power Prayers Devotional
Scripture encourages us to "come boldly unto the throne of grace" (Hebrews 4:16)—and this Power Prayers Devotional will help with 180 inspiring prayer starters. These powerful meditations encourage women of all ages and backgrounds to approach God in intimate, joyful, confident prayer. Whenever you say, "Here I am, Lord," He is thrilled to listen to your deepest hopes and fears. Start on your journey of truer, deeper, more effective communion with the Lord who loves you with an everlasting love.
DiCarta / 978-1-61626-608-0/$14.99

Power Prayers to Start Your Day Devotional Journal
This delightful journal from Barbour Publishing fits perfectly into a woman's prayer life. Journalers will find themselves encouraged and inspired to record all of the ways they are blessed and loved by their heavenly Father. Fabulous as a gift—or for personal use—this journal will be cherished for years to come.
DiCarta / 978-1-63409-636-2 / $17.99

Power Prayers Coloring Book
Color your way to a more powerful prayer life with the brand-new *Power Prayers* coloring book. Forty-five unique images on quality stock will comfort and inspire through beautiful design and refreshing prayers. The backs of each generous 8x10 coloring page are left blank—perfect for coloring with crayons, colored pencils, and markers.
Paperback / 978-1-63409-968-4 / $9.99